Music Stones

*Peter Crosthwaite's Music Stones. Photograph © John Dobson. Courtesy of the Wordsworth Trust and Keswick Museum and Art Gallery.*

# Music Stones

## THE REDISCOVERY OF RINGING ROCK

Mike Adcock

ARCHAEOPRESS

Archaeopress Publishing Ltd
13-14 Market Square
Bicester
Oxfordshire
OX26 6AD
www.archaeopress.com

ISBN 978-1-80583-014-6
ISBN 978-1-80583-015-3 (e-Pdf)

© Mike Adcock and Archaeopress 2025

Front cover photo: © Matthias Brodbeck, rear photo of Mike Adcock: © Alexander Caminada and rear photo of the Till Family Rock Band: Courtesy of Dr Michael Till

All rights reserved. No part of this book may be reproduced, or transmitted, in any form or by any means, electronic, mechanical, photocopying or otherwise, without the prior written permission of the copyright owners.

This book is available direct from Archaeopress or from our website www.archaeopress.com

# Contents

List of Figures .................................................................................................... iv
Acknowledgements and thanks ............................................................................ x
Foreword - *by Dame Evelyn Glennie* ................................................................ xi
Preface ............................................................................................................... xii
Introduction ...................................................................................................... xiv

## Chapter One: Peter Crosthwaite - The man and his Music Stones ............ 1
India .................................................................................................................. 2
Blyth, Northumberland ..................................................................................... 6
Keswick ............................................................................................................. 7

## Chapter Two: The new contenders - Limestone, lithophones and a rock harmonicon ............ 17
William Todhunter ......................................................................................... 17
Joseph Richardson ......................................................................................... 20
Messrs Richardson and Sons' Original Rock Band ..................................... 26

## Chapter Three: A stonemason, a boatman and a fiddler - Two cousins, William Irwin and the sound of slate ............ 34
William Bowe ................................................................................................. 34
The other William Bowe ................................................................................ 35
The Harrison Brothers ................................................................................... 36
Sonorous slate ................................................................................................ 37
William Irwin .................................................................................................. 39

## Chapter Four: Richardson's Original Rock Band - London and beyond ............ 42
Music in London ............................................................................................ 42
The first concerts .......................................................................................... 44
On the road .................................................................................................... 48
Ireland ............................................................................................................. 50
England and Wales ........................................................................................ 51

## Chapter Five: Playing by Royal Command - Richardson's Rock, Bell and Steel Band at Buckingham Palace ............ 56
Julia Gould ..................................................................................................... 58
The final years ............................................................................................... 61

## Chapter Six: The Till Family Rock Band - Following in the footsteps ............ 68
The Skiddaw Rock Band ............................................................................... 71
Crystal Palace ................................................................................................ 72
On tour ........................................................................................................... 74
John Ruskin .................................................................................................... 76
A new opportunity ......................................................................................... 78

## Chapter Seven: The Tills in the USA - The rise of the rockophone ... 81
- The Chautauqua Institute ... 81
- The Till Family Concert Company ... 83
- Thomas Edison ... 84
- A return to England ... 86
- The next generation ... 87
- Postscript ... 93

## Chapter Eight: Honoré Baudre - Antediluvian music and a geological piano ... 96
- Paris ... 98
- England and Ireland ... 100
- Belgium ... 102
- A return to England ... 102
- The USA and Canada ... 103

## Chapter Nine: The Abrahams - Limelight in the Lakes ... 110
- An Evening of Pictorial and Musical Entertainment ... 113

## Chapter Ten: A Yorkshire Dalesman and a Menorcan Don - Neddy Dick and Don Antonio Roca y Várez ... 117
- Neddy Dick ... 117
- Antonio Roca y Várez ... 127

## Chapter Eleven: Circuses, music halls and musical pavements - Arthur Nelson, the Pavanellas and the Bozza Troupe ... 132
- Arthur Nelson and the circus ... 132
- Music hall stones ... 136
- The Pavanellas ... 138
- The Bozza Troupe ... 142

## Chapter Twelve: The Twentieth Century - A chronological miscellany of musical stone ... 144
- Albert Coates ... 144
- William Davey ... 145
- Helen Cumpson ... 148
- Edward Troxell ... 149
- The Great Stalacpipe Organ ... 152
- Carl Orff and Klaus Becker-Ehmck ... 158
- Tom Wasinger ... 162
- Lunar music ... 165

## Chapter Thirteen: Vietnam - The rediscovery of lithophones in South East Asia ... 166

## Chapter Fourteen: Experimental Music Stones - Investigations in geological indeterminacy ... 177
- Cornelius Cardew ... 177
- Christian Wolff ... 184
- Pauline Oliveros ... 185
- Frog Peak Music ... 187

## Chapter Fifteen: The gift of sound and vision - Sculptural music and musical sculpture ... 190
- Barbara Hepworth ... 193

Henry Moore.................................................................................................195
Paul and Limpe Fuchs...................................................................................196
Elmar Daucher..............................................................................................196
Klaus and Hannes Fessmann.........................................................................199
Pinuccio Sciola.............................................................................................202
Andrea Granitzio..........................................................................................207
Peter Randall-Page.......................................................................................209
Ann-Margreth Bohl.......................................................................................213

**Chapter Sixteen: The new stone age - Statements from contemporary practitioners .. 215**
Jim Doble - USA............................................................................................215
Jochen Fassbender - Germany......................................................................218
Páll Gudmundsson - Iceland.........................................................................221
Jay Harrison - UK..........................................................................................223
Terje Isungset - Norway ...............................................................................227
Will Menter - France.....................................................................................230
Bobbie Millar - UK.........................................................................................233
Nguyen Minh Ngiệp - Vietnam......................................................................237
Pietro Pirelli - Italy .......................................................................................239
Sound of Stone 1..........................................................................................242
Franci Krevh and Matevž Bajde - Slovenia ...................................................242
Sound of Stone 2..........................................................................................244
Alenka Vidrgar - Slovenia .............................................................................244
Gayle Young - Canada ..................................................................................254

**Bibliography** ................................................................................................... 256

**Index** ............................................................................................................. 259

# List of Figures

Frontispiece. Peter Crosthwaite's Music Stones. Photograph © John Dobson. Courtesy of the Wordsworth Trust and Keswick Museum and Art Gallery.

Figure 1.1. Peter Crosthwaite's Memorandum entry for 11th June 1785. Courtesy of Keswick Museum and Art Gallery ..................1

Figure 1.2. Close-up of Peter Crosthwaite's Music Stones showing incised lettering. Photograph: Mike Adcock, Courtesy of Keswick Museum and Art Gallery ..................2

Figure 1.3. A view of Surat ..................3

Figure 1.4. The Ensign of Peace, title page ..................6

Figure 1.5. One of Peter Crosthwaite's tourist maps showing Derwentwater and surrounding attractions. Courtesy of the Cumbria County History Trust ..................7

Figure 1.6. Derwentwater Regatta handbill 1789. Courtesy of Keswick Museum and Art Gallery ..................8

Figure 1.7. The Crosthwaite Museum, Keswick ..................9

Figure 1.8. Peter Crosthwaite's second Memorandum entry referring to the discovery of his Music Stones. Courtesy of Keswick Museum and Art Gallery ..................10

Figure 1.9. Peter Crosthwaite's Music Stones. Courtesy of Keswick Museum and Art Gallery ..11

Figure 1.10. Crosthwaite Museum poster 1845. Courtesy of Keswick Museum and Art Gallery ...15

Figure 2.1. Stricklandgate in the early 19th century, the location of the Todhunter Museum. Courtesy of Kendal Town Council ..................18

Figure 2.2. Announcement of auction of the contents of the Todhunter Museum, 1835. Carlisle Journal Saturday 11th July 1835 ..................19

Figure 2.3. Joseph Richardson's Rock Harmonicon in its final version, showing the added upper rows of steel bars and bells. Photograph Mike Adcock, Courtesy of Keswick Museum and Art Gallery ..................20

Figure 2.4. Early photograph of the Richardsons' cottage in Applethwaite, with the byre where the rock harmonicon was built at the near end. With thanks to Tony Gibbs who photographed the picture ..................23

Figure 2.5. Close-up showing the hornfels slabs in position. Photograph: Mike Adcock. Courtesy of Keswick Museum and Art Gallery ..................24

Figure 2.6. Announcement of Whitehaven residency. Courtesy of Andy Aliffe ..................27

Figure 2.7. Receipt for hire of room at Mechanics' Institute, Manchester for a six day stay. Courtesy of Andy Aliffe ..................27

Figure 2.8. Extract from James Nasmyth's letter to Joseph Richardson. Courtesy of Andy Aliffe ..................31

Figure 3.1. Newspaper announcement of William Bowe's appearance in Edinburgh. The Scotsman Saturday 24th 1842, p3 ..................36

Figure 3.2. The Elterwater Set. Photograph: Mike Adcock, Courtesy of Keswick Museum and Art Gallery ..................37

Figure 3.3. Lower end of slate lithophone in Kendal Museum. Reproduced with kind permission of Kendal Museum. Object accession number, KMS2016.6 ..................38

Figure 3.4. Three of William Irwin's fiddle tunes as transcribed by Anne Gilchrist. The titles of the lower two refer to the woman who was to become his wife, Dorothy Greenup. Courtesy of the Vaughan Williams Memorial Library ..................40

Figure 4.1. Louis Jullien ............................................................................................................43
Figure 4.2. Sheet music of a set of original pieces composed by the Richardsons, illustrated with a drawing of the three men playing. © John H. Phillips ........................47
Figure 4.3. Drawing from article on Richardson and his Rock Harmonicon in Illustrated London News, 28th May 1842. © John H. Phillips ...............................................50
Figure 4.4. Egyptian Hall, Piccadilly, London. Courtesy of Andy Aliffe .............................52
Figure 4.5. Poster for Egyptian Hall summer residency, 1845. Courtesy of Andy Aliffe ....53
Figure 4.6. Poster for concert in Banbury on Saturday 23rd May by Richardson's Original Monstre Rock Band. Courtesy of Andy Aliffe ....................................................54
Figure 4.7. Showing additions to the Rock Harmonicon: steel bars, Swiss bells and one of the drums. Courtesy of Keswick Museum and Art Gallery ........................................55
Figure 5.1. Lithograph of the Richardsons at Buckingham Palace by Charles Baugniet. © John H. Phillips ................................................................................................57
Figure 5.2. Julia Gould. Courtesy of Andy Aliffe ................................................................59
Figure 5.3. Poster for concert in Banbury featuring Julia Gould as vocalist. Courtesy of Andy Aliffe ...........................................................................................................61
Figure 5.4. Poster for concert in Chard, Tuesday 4th February. Courtesy of Andy Aliffe ...63
Figure 5.5. Richardson Henderson (centre), William Tangye (left) and Tangye's son (right) in their revival of the Rock, Bell and Steel Band. © John H. Phillips ..................66
Figure 6.1. Daniel Till and sons Daniel and William with their rock harmonicon. Courtesy of Dr. Michael Till .................................................................................................68
Figure 6.2. The Skiddaw Rock Band as they appeared at the Crystal Palace in 1881. Courtesy of Dr. Michael Till ................................................................................72
Figure 6.3. Publicity for the Skiddaw Rock Band performances at the Crystal Palace in 1881. Courtesy of Dr. Michael Till .....................................................................73
Figure 6.4. The Till Family Rock Band. Courtesy of Dr. Michael Till ................................74
Figures 6.5 and 6.6. Concert tickets. Courtesy of Dr. Michael Till .....................................76
Figure 6.7. Facsimile copy of letter from John Ruskin to William Till. Courtesy of Dr. Michael Till ......................................................................................................77
Figure 6.8. Ruskin's lithophone as shown in a postcard from Ruskin Museum in the 1900s. Courtesy of Dr. Michael Till ................................................................................78
Figure 6.9. Ruskin's lithophone as it is today, with several stones missing. Photograph by Mike Adcock. Courtesy Ruskin Museum, Coniston .............................................79
Figure 6.10. Handbill for concert in Perth, Wednesday 18th February 1885. Courtesy of Dr. Michael Till ...........................................................................................................80
Figure 7.1. The Till Family Rock Band, probably taken soon after they arrived in the USA. Courtesy of Dr. Michael Till ................................................................................82
Figure 7.2. The Till Family Concert Band: William, Daniel jnr., Annie and Lizzie, their father no longer performing with the band. Other instruments, including a pair of ocarinas and the musical glasses visible in addition to the rock harmonicon. Courtesy of Dr. Michael Till ................................................................................83
Figure 7.3. Thomas Edison with an early version of his phonograph ..............................85
Figure 7.4. The Rock Band Concert Company. Courtesy of Dr. Michael Till ....................88
Figure 7.5. Till Concert Company Programme. Courtesy of Dr. Michael Till ....................89
Figure 7.6 and 7.7. Two-sided handbill. Front (Left), reverse (Top). Courtesy of Dr. Michael Till ......................................................................................................90
Figure 7.8. William Till's instructions for setting up the rockophone. Courtesy of Dr. Michael Till ......................................................................................................91

Figure 7.9. William Till, in later years, at home with his rockophone. Courtesy of Dr. Michael Till ..................................................................................................92
Figure 8.1. Honoré Baudre with his geological piano. Engraving used in article about Baudre in l'Illustration, Saturday 13th July 1901 ..........................................................96
Figure 8.2. Engraving of Honoré Baudre by Louis Poyet .............................................99
Figure 8.3. The Old South, Boston, Massachusetts.................................................104
Figure 8.4. Newspaper announcement. The Boston Globe, Thursday 20th April 1880 p2 .......105
Figure 8.5. Newspaper announcement. The New York Times Sunday 30th January 1881 p11 105
Figure 8.6. Sketch taken from lIustration engraving. Warder and Dublin Weekly Mail, Saturday 24th August 1901, p11 ............................................................107
Figure 8.7. St Louis Post-Dispatch, Friday 2nd August 1946, p36 .................................107
Figure 8.8. Possible photographic source for l'Illustration engraving. San Francisco Call and Post, Saturday 17th August 1901, p6 .....................................................108
Figure 9.1. George Perry Abraham's visiting card produced from his own photographic studio. Courtesy of Sue Steinberg.........................................................110
Figure 9.2. George Perry Abraham with his his three sons, Ashley, Sydney and George. Courtesy of Sue Steinberg...................................................................111
Figure 9.3. The Abrahams' rock harmonicon...........................................................112
Figure 9.4. An Abraham's hand-tinted postcard showing Keswick town centre ................113
Figure 9.5. Poster for the Limelight & Musical Entertainment. Courtesy of Andy Aliffe .........114
Figure 9.6. Ashley and George Abraham. Courtesy of Sue Steinberg ..............................115
Figure 9.7. Image from sleeve of "Wee" Jimmy Scott's Magical Memories LP. Courtesy of Dr. Michael Till..................................................................................116
Figure 10.1. Neddy Dick with his musical stones. Courtesy of Keld Resource Centre..............118
Figure 10.2. Keld today Photograph: Mike Adcock ....................................................118
Figure 10.3. Inside Neddy Dick's cottage, with his musical stones to the left of the harmonium. Courtesy of Keld Resource Centre .........................................119
Figure 10.4. Neddy Dick playing his stones. Courtesy of Keld Resource Centre ..................121
Figure 10.5. Neddy Dick. Courtesy of Keld Resource Centre .......................................123
Figure 10.6. The cottage in Keld where Neddy Dick lived, as it is today. Photograph: Mike Adcock ......................................................................................127
Figure 10.7. Antonio Roca playing his lithophone. Courtesy of Carles Garcia-Roca ................128
Figure 10.8. Gold medal inscribed "Antonio Roca y Várez, Mahon 1901". Courtesy of Carles Garcia-Roca....................................................................................129
Figure 10.9. Don Antonio Roca y Várez.. Courtesy of Carles Garcia-Roca.......................129
Figure 11.1. Poster for Arthur Nelson's stunt in Great Yarmouth. Courtesy of Andy Aliffe ....133
Figure 11.2. Pablo Fanque. Courtesy of Andy Aliffe..................................................134
Figure 11.3. Publicity for Pablo Fanque's Edinburgh show featuring Arthur Nelson. Courtesy of Andy Aliffe ..................................................................................134
Figure 11.4. Poster of the Jee Brothers ................................................................137
Figure 11.5. Poster for Canterbury Theatre of Varieties featuring the Pavanellas. Courtesy of Andy Aliffe ..................................................................................139
Figure 12.1. Conductor and composer Albert Coates .................................................145
Figure 12.2. William Davey, then curator of Keswick Museum playing the Richardson instrument in the 1930s. Courtesy of Keswick Museum and Art Gallery .................146

Figure 12.3. Norman Byers' set of musical stones. Courtesy of Andy Aliffe ...............................148
Figure 12.4. Newspaper photograph of Edward Troxell playing his petrophone. Hartford Courant, Saturday 29th March 1941, p3........................................................................150
Figure 12.5. Edward Troxell teaching at Trinity College, Hartford, Connecticut, 1950s ..........152
Figure 12.6. The Great Stalacpipe Organ in the Luray Caverns, Virginia. Courtesy of Luray Caverns, VA, USA ..................................................................................................153
Figure 12.7. One of the rubber mallets used to strike each stalactite, triggered by a solenoid connected by cable to the organ console. Courtesy of Luray Caverns, VA, USA .....154
Figure 12.8. Organ console, Luray Caverns. Courtesy of Luray Caverns, VA, USA ....................155
Figure 12.9. Advertisement for The Great Stalacpipe Organ. Richmond Times-Dispatch Sunday 13th April 1958................................................................................................156
Figure 12.10. Klaus Becker-Ehmck's Steinspiel Courtesy of Bernd Becker-Ehmck, Studio 49 .158
Figure 12.11. Carl Orff 1953. Photograph © Schott Promotion.................................................159
Figure 12.12. Gathering for 25th anniversary of foundation of Studio 49, 1974. Photograph shows Gunild Keetman, Klaus Becker-Ehmck, Carl Orff and behind him his wife, Liselotte Orff. Courtesy of Bernd Becker-Ehmck, Studio 49 ......................................161
Figure 12.13. Tom Wasinger's Stone Marimba. Courtesy of Tom Wasinger ..............................162
Figure 12.14. Tom Wasinger's Stone Slit-drums . Courtesy of Tom Wasinger............................163
Figure 12.15. The Lost Angel Stone Ensemble. Courtesy of Tom Wasinger ...............................164
Figure 13.1. Ancient musical stones in the Vietnamese Institute of Musicology, Hanoi. Photograph: Mike Adcock ..........................................................................................167
Figure 13.2. Lithophones in Raglai Centre, Khanh Son. Photograph: Mike Adcock .................168
Figure 13.3. Khánh Son stones being played in 1980 Courtesy of Khánh Hòa Museum, Nha Trang ..................................................................................................................169
Figure 13.4. Dinh Linh & Truy Mai, Ho Chi Minh City. Photograph: Ingrid Lund ......................171
Figure 13.5. Undated lithophone in Hanoi music shop, 2008. Photograph: Mike Adcock........172
Figure 13.6. Three ringing stones, until relatively recently played by the M'nong people in the Central Highlands of Vietnam. Photograph: Mike Adcock ..................................172
Figure 13.7. Phan Tri Dung playing his chromatic lithophone in his company office in Ho Chi Minh City, 2008. Photograph: Mike Adcock .......................................................173
Figure 13.8. Lithophone built by Nguyen Minh Ngiệp being played in Tuy Hòa Photograph: Mike Adcock ...............................................................................................................173
Figure 13.9. Stone instruments at the Ancient Soul Centre. Photograph: Mike Adcock ..........175
Figure 13.10. Playing of lithophones at the Ancient Soul Centre. Photograph: Mike Adcock.175
Figure 14.1. Cornelius Cardew 1970 Photograph © John Walmsley............................................178
Figure 14.2. Entry in programme for Cheltenham Music Festival 1968. Courtesy of Chris Cundy .................................................................................................................179
Figure 14.3. The Scratch Orchestra. Photograph by Raha Tavallali. Courtesy of Cornelius Cardew Concert Trust.................................................................................................183
Figure 14.4. Christian Wolff .........................................................................................................184
Figure 14.5. Pauline Oliveros. Picture taken at Deep Listening retreat in Norway, June 2015. Photograph © Will Dibrell................................................................................185
Figure 14.6. Title page of Frog Peak Rock Music Book. Courtesy of Frog Peak Music ...............187
Figure 14.7. Instructions for Jon Gibson's Rock Game Courtesy of Frog Peak Music ................188
Figure 14.8. Score for Rock Game. Courtesy of Frog Peak Music ................................................188

Figure 15.1. Lida Kindersley. Courtesy of Cardozo Kindersley Workshop .................. 190
Figure 15.2. Constantin Brancusi .................................................................................. 192
Figure 15.3. Barbara Hepworth carving Head, 1930. Photograph © Bowness ............ 193
Figure 15.4. Priaulx Rainier. Photograph © Schott Promotion ..................................... 194
Figure 15.5. Barbara Hepworth with The Cosdon Head 1949. Photograph by Hans Wild, © Bowness ..................................................................................... 194
Figure 15.6. Elmar Daucher's Klangstein, the replacment for the sculpture accidentally destroyed in Lahr .................................................................... 197
Figure 15.7. Stephan Micus playing one of Elmar Daucher's Klangsteine in Ulm Cathedral during the recording of his album The Music of Stones. Photograph © Jean Gallus ................ 198
Figure 15.8. Klangsteine by Hannes Fessmann .............................................................. 200
Figure 15.9. Hannes Fessmann playing one of his Dolphin series of Klangsteine .................... 201
Figure 15.10. Pinuccio Sciola in front of the installation created for Turandot, Teatro Lirico, Caligari. Courtesy of Sciola Foundation Archive. Photograph © Fabio Marras ....... 202
Figure 15.11. Pinuccio Sciola, Sound Harp Courtesy of Sciola Foundation Archive. Photograph © Ettore Cavalli ........................................................ 203
Figure 15.12. The Sound Garden of Pinuccio Sciola. Courtesy of Sciola Foundation Archive. Photograph © Ettore Cavalli ............................................. 204
Figure 15.13. Pinuccio Sciola playing a sounding stone. Courtesy of Sciola Foundation Archive. Photograph © Riccardo Rigo ........................................... 205
Figure 15.14. Pinuccio Sciola caressing one of his basalt sculptures. Courtesy of Sciola Foundation Archive. Photograph © Luca Pinna ........................................... 206
Figure 15.15. Andrea Granitzio conducting the final concert by Pinuccio Sciola in San Pietro, Vincoli, Rome. Courtesy of Andrea Granitzio .................................................. 208
Figure 15.16. Peter Randall-Page's sound sculpture Bell. Courtesy of the artist .................. 210
Figure 15.17. Peter Randall-Page's sculpture Dartmoor End. Courtesy of the artist .............. 211
Figure 15.18. Ann-Margreth Bohl, Sound in Stone 1. Courtesy of the artist ..................... 213
Figure 15.19. Ann-Margreth Bohl, Sound in Stone 2. Courtesy of the artist ..................... 213
Figure 15.20. Will Menter, Touchstone. Courtesy of the artist ................................. 214
Figure 16.1. Jim Doble lithophone .................................................................................. 215
Figure 16.2. Jim Doble .................................................................................................... 216
Figure 16.3. Jochen Fassbender lithophone .................................................................... 218
Figure 16.4. Jochen Fassbender ...................................................................................... 219
Figure 16.5. Páll Gudmundsson ...................................................................................... 221
Figure 16.6. Páll Gudmundsson ...................................................................................... 222
Figure 16.7. Jay Harrison's electromechanical lithophone ............................................. 223
Figure 16.8. Jay Harrison ................................................................................................ 224
Figure 16.9. Sylvain van Iniitu ........................................................................................ 225
Figure 16.10. Sylvain van Iniitu; Brunehaut megalith .................................................... 226
Figure 16.11. Terje Isungset's musical stones ................................................................. 227
Figure 16.12. Terje Isungset. Photograph © Knut Bry ................................................... 228
Figure 16.13. Will Menter. Lithovortex .......................................................................... 230
Figure 16.14. Will Menter. To hear the world in a grain of stone .................................. 231
Figure 16.15. Ruskin Rocks. Project led by Bobbie Miller ............................................ 233
Figure 16.16. Bobbie Miller. Photograph of Bobbie Millar by CS Millar ..................... 234

Figure 16.17. Tony di Napoli. Photograph: from the Fête de la préhistoire, Musée de l'Homme. © MNHN J.C.Domenech ................................................................................. 235
Figure 16.18. Nguyen Minh Ngiệp. Photograph Thuy Van Nguyen ............................................. 238
Figure 16.19. Pietro Pirelli ................................................................................................................. 239
Figure 16. 20 Pietro Pirelli ................................................................................................................. 240
Figure 16.21. Sound of Stone 1 Matevž Bajde and Franci Krevh ................................................. 242
Figure 16.22. Sound of Stone 2 Sound stone bench by Alenka Vidrgar ....................................... 244
Figure 16.23. Alenka Vidrgar ............................................................................................................ 246
Figure 16.24. Jesse Stewart Photograph © Nate Storring ............................................................. 247
Figure 16.25. Stone Alphabet. Photograph © Matthias Brodbeck ............................................... 249
Figure 16.26. The Stone Alphabet Matthias Brodbeck and Dominik Dolega ............................. 250
Figure 16.27. Christian Wolff Photograph © Kelly Burgess ......................................................... 252
Figure 16.28. Rockenspiel by Gayle Young ..................................................................................... 254
Figure 16.29. Gayle Young ................................................................................................................ 255

# Acknowledgements and thanks

For their invaluable help in sourcing the material used in the book, I'd like to thank particularly: John H. Phillips for the use of images relating to his ancestors in the Richardson family, Dr Michael Till for the loan and use of material from his family and to Andy Aliffe for sanctioning the use of images he collected for his own book on the subject.

I have compiled a list of just some of the others I'd like to thank for helping me in different ways in the years leading to the publication of this book. If your name doesn't appear and you think it should have done, I heartily apologise and will buy you a drink next time I see you. But my thanks do go to Alenka Vidrgar, Alexander Caminada, Angela Rackham, Ann-Margreth Bohl, Bernd Becker-Ehmck, Bill Huffman (Luray Caverns), Bobbie Millar, Carles Garcia-Roca, Chris Cundy, Christian Wolff, Christoph Wagner, Clive Bell, Dame Evelyn Glennie, Dominik Dolega, Elio Marcusciello, Franci Krevh, Gayle Young, Hanna Adcock, Helen Guy (Keld Resource Centre), Howard Hull (Brantwood), Howard Skempton, Ingrid Lund, Jamie Barnes, Jay Harrison, Jeff Cloves, Jesse Stewart, Jim Doble, Jochen Fassbender, Joseph Massey (Keswick Museum), Kate Buchanan (Orff Society), Keith Chandler, Kendal Museum (staff and volunteers), Keswick Museum (staff and volunteers), Lida Kindersley, Limpe Fuchs, Margaret Makepeace (British Library),  Matthias Brodbeck, Michael Chant, Michael Parsons, Mick Smith (The Dalesman), Mike Cooper, Nguyen Minh Ngiệp, Nicola Lawson (Keswick Museum), Páll Gudmundsson, Peter Randall-Page, Philip Blackburn, Pierre Favre, Pietro Pirelli, Professor Bruce Yardley, Simon Adcock, Steven Halliday,  Stuart Cresswell (Kendal Museum), Sue Steinberg, Sylvain van Iniitu, Terje Isungset, Thuy Van Nguyen, Tony di Napoli, Tracy Hodgson (Ruskin Museum) and Will Menter.

# Foreword
## *by Dame Evelyn Glennie*

There are moments - rare and reverberant - when we are made to feel how much we have forgotten. When a sound, ancient and unfamiliar, slips through the cracks of our modern noise and reminds us of something elemental: that before language, before architecture, even before organized rhythm, there was resonance.

Mike Adcock's *Music Stones – The rediscovery of ringing rock* is a work of excavation - not just of geological curiosity, but of forgotten soundscapes, buried intuitions, and the tactile intelligence of listening. This book doesn't merely chronicle the history or acoustics of ringing rocks. Crucially, it does not seek to trace a linear history or speculate on how stone may have been used musically in the distant past. Instead, it focuses on something more immediate and perhaps more surprising: the ways in which people in the modern era have stumbled upon, or intentionally sought out, the resonant properties of stone, and what that has meant for them.

As someone with a long-standing fascination for lithophones and stone percussion instruments, I have spent years exploring the strange and beautiful ways in which stones can produce sound. There is something both primal and transcendent in striking rock and experiencing it respond. In those moments, you feel time collapse. You are not just making sound - you are connecting with a sound that has waited, often for millennia, to be heard again.

This is where Mike Adcock's book resonates so deeply with me. His exploration is not only scholarly, but deeply intuitive - attuned to the subtle interplay between material, context, and human perception. *Music Stones* speaks to my own conviction that sound is not merely a product of culture, but a bridge to something older than culture - something geological and spiritual.

The idea that a stone might ring let alone sing runs counter to the metaphors we have built our world on. We think of stones as silent, still, and weighty - lacking in motion or voice. Mike Adcock's book identifies a truth long known by indigenous cultures and quietly passed over by empirical ones: that materials hold music, and that music can be found where we least expect it.

This book is as much about wonder as it is about sound. In an age increasingly dissonant with over-amplified opinion and under-attended attention, *Music Stones* is an act of listening. It reminds us that the earth still hums, still resonates with sounds not yet catalogued. It challenges our assumption that music is man-made. And it asks a question both subtle and seismic: What else have we stopped listening to?

I believe *Music Stones* will shift your listening; not only to stones, but to the ancient murmurings beneath our feet. When a rock rings, it's not just making sound – it is making memory.

And we would do well to remember.

June 2025, Cambridgeshire, England.

# Preface

In the final year of the last millennium I had two coincidentally close encounters, just a month apart, with the musical possibilities of stone. They were to trigger a fascination which has continued for a quarter of a century, and resulted in the writing and publication of this book. The first occasion was in May 2000, when I undertook a short tour in the south of England with a band we called Spill, a collaboration between three British and three Norwegian musicians. The percussionist Terje Isungset had travelled from Norway with a battery of instruments, many of his own making, utilising birchwood, willow and other natural materials. As he unpacked his equipment for the first of our rehearsals he produced what I initially took to be some kind of foam packing material. It was actually a lump of Norwegian granite and was to provide one of the particularly distinctive sounds coming from the stage in the days to come.

A month later, I was one of many who took part in a performance of three movements from Cornelius Cardew's epic composition *The Great Learning*, at the Union Chapel in North London. For the first movement, known as Paragraph 1, Michael Parsons, one of the three directors on the day, handed me two pebbles to strike together as indicated in the score. He showed me how, by flexing the cupped hand in which I held one of the pebbles, I could change the pitch of the note produced by striking it with the stone in the other hand. Later I acquired two fine shiny pebbles of my own which I now keep in a little tin and bring out to play from time to time.

Following on from these encounters I decided to investigate further ways in which stone, like other materials from the natural world, had been employed for its sound qualities and found that there was a long and widespread history of stone being used musically. I learned that instruments made from stone were known as lithophones, though this was a word so little used that it failed to appear in many dictionaries. I was surprised to discover that there were lithophones from the eighteenth and nineteenth centuries to be found in my own country, in Keswick Museum in England's Lake District. Seeing them for the first time I was astonished to be faced with Joseph Richardson's five-octave Rock, Bell and Steel Band, an instrument taking up the best part of a gallery wall in the museum and which visitors are permitted to play, using the beaters provided. Also to be seen there was Peter Crosthwaite's smaller lithophone which he'd assembled in 1785 and which, like the later Richardson instrument was constructed from the local hornfels stone.

Symptomatic of a predilection I've long had for the unconventional in music, the first written piece I had published, back in 1982, was an article on the subject of novelty music which appeared in the magazine *Collusion*, edited by musicians Steve Beresford and David Toop. In writing *Music Stones* I realise that I have, in some ways come full-circle. The word "novelty" has acquired a negative connotation, being used to describe something frivolous and lacking lasting value, but I was always convinced that there was more to it than that, the term sometimes indicating true innovation, musical ideas which were too easily dismissed because they didn't conform to mainstream practice and taste. In the early years of commercial recordings the word novelty was used by record companies to describe music which didn't fit into established categories, perhaps because it came from a different culture or used unorthodox instrumentation. I have a 78 rpm shellac record from as late as 1953 which couples two very different harmonica recordings. On one side is Sonny Terry playing *Hootin' Blues* and on the reverse is British harmonica-player Tommy Reilly's version of *Bop goes the weasel*. Each is described on the label, with a whiff of condescension, as a "novelty instrumental". Yet a century earlier, with the emergence of music halls in Britain, along with their equivalents elsewhere, there had been a growing appetite among audiences from an expanding urban population for something new. Novelty was promoted as a desirable aspect of entertainment and in that context the vogue for the playing of musical stones fitted the bill perfectly, with the term "novelty" being used unashamedly in the publicity.

My initial lines of enquiry soon enlightened me to the fact that sonorous stone had been far more ubiquitous than I'd imagined. There were the naturally formed rock gongs played in different parts of Africa, researched and documented in the early 1950s by archaeologist Bernard Fagg and others; in China, ceremonial chimes were made from marble and jade because in the Chinese philosophical concept of the harmony of the universe, seen as being perfectly expressed through music, stone was the most exalted of materials; on the island of Pohnpei in Micronesia the resonating rhythms produced during the pounding of the intoxicating kawa root in basalt bowls developed into a musical tradition; in the central African country Togo, the Kabiyé people continue to play upon groups of five stones laid on the ground, though only during a short period following the harvest. And I learned too that in Vietnam, in the second half of the twentieth century, there was a resurgence of interest in musical stone following the unearthing of eleven large slabs, each tuned to a different note and believed to have been played in ancient times.

I visited Vietnam in 2008 and again in 2023 and saw for myself how lithophones, while by no means among the most commonly played instruments, have a public presence unparalleled anywhere elsewhere in the world. In 2017 I travelled to Indonesia, going to the large archaeological site at Gunung Padang in West Java to see an ancient table of stone which can be played with the fingers and referred to there as a stone gamelan. In the west of Sumatra, in the remote small village of Nagari Talang Anau, I was able to play on an ancient set of six large stones, known as the *talempong batu*, or stone gong.

Some of this I have already written about in shorter articles and on my website dedicated to the subject, https://lithophones.com, but for this book I decided not to attempt an all-embracing survey of lithophones, globally and historically, but to consider a number of ways in which the musical potential of stone has been approached in the modern era, from the late eighteenth century onwards. In doing this I've approached the subject from an essentially musical perspective and while that touches on aspects of geology, archaeology, philosophy and a range of other disciplines, the focus is on documented examples of actual performances, rather than engaging in speculation about ancient musical practice. The history I have outlined has evolved not so much into an account of the stone instruments themselves but a story of a series of extraordinary people, whose exploration of the musical potential of stone played a significant part in them becoming extraordinary.

# Introduction

Music stones go back a long way. Nobody knows how long, but it could well be that stone, along with bone, wood, reeds and grass, was one of the first materials used by humans with the intention of making sound. It is of course in the nature of the medium, being transient, that it's not possible to know what sounds they were making in those far distant days. With visual images, whether they be petroglyphs carved into stone or cave paintings, the proof that they were produced is there to be seen with our eyes, but with sound the only evidence is circumstantial.

The oldest known musical instrument is thought to be a bone flute, possibly between fifty and sixty thousand years old and its identification is based on the existence of a hollow piece of bone with holes in it, which has survived. There may well have also been flutes made from wood and reed flutes, but they have long since perished. Stone endures and the evidence that it might have been used percussively is found in markings on its surface: if there seems to have been repeated striking with no other explanation as to why that should have taken place, it might be deduced that the purpose was to make sound. Sounds produced in this way may have had a functional application, being used as a form of communication over distances, possibly for sending warnings, or perhaps incorporated into rituals or ceremonial occasions. The point at which any of these activities can be defined as music remains open to debate.

The purpose of this book is not to trace, or speculate on the history of stone being used musically. Nor is it a survey of the way in which different cultures around the world have included the playing of resonant stone within their musical traditions. Rather, it is looking at how, in the modern era, a number of people have discovered the aural properties of stone, often unintentionally, and chosen to pursue the idea in a musical way. Some have done this quite independently, pursuing their own chosen path of travel, while others, having seen existing examples, chose to develop the idea in their own way. This is what happened in England in the nineteenth century with the formation of a series of so-called family rock bands. Those responsible, all residents of the town of Keswick in Cumbria's Lake District, built large instruments incorporating stone bars sourced from the local terrain and two of the resulting bands went on to have extraordinarily successful musical careers. The story being told here starts with those pioneers in Keswick and has continued to develop through to the present day in numerous locations. The question of why people should have chosen to make music from this unlikely material is one which lies at the heart of this investigation.

When struck together any two pieces of stone will make some kind of noise. In most cases it will be a dull thud, which according to most definitions would not be described as particularly musical. But some rocks will resonate with an attractive ring, reverberating in such a way that the sound continues, at least for a short time, before dying away and it is these resonating pieces of rock which have been utilised by certain cultures across the world and across time. Although there is no guarantee that a particular kind of rock will ring there are some types which are more likely to do so, with hard rock, for example, being generally more resonant than soft. It might be igneous, volcanic rock formed from lava, such as black granite or basalt, or one of the varieties of metamorphic rock, including slate and marble. Some kinds of sedimentary rock will ring, particularly limestone, whose hardness partly comes from being formed from fossils and shell fragments. Even among geologists there is a degree of uncertainty as to why it is that one piece of rock from a certain place will ring while a similar piece beside it will not. The reason seems to lie in the condition of its internal structure. Although very porous rock may well not be hard enough to ring, being porous itself is not an impediment. As long as the outer wall of each pore is intact the sound vibration can travel, but if it is fractured, it will not.

From the second half of the twentieth century onwards, there has been a good deal of research supporting the belief that stone was used for musical purposes in prehistoric times. The unearthing of eleven large slabs of stone in Vietnam in 1949 which, on examination were judged to have been tuned for musical use, possibly thousands of years ago, was followed by further similar discoveries in the same country. An increased awareness of the part played by stone instruments in the musical history of some of Vietnam's musical minority cultures has resulted in a revival of interest in the playing of stone instruments in the country, on a scale not found to such an extent anywhere else. The way in which this has happened is told in Chapter 13.

It goes without saying that musical instruments made from stone are not a common sight. They may date back to the neolithic period but what has happened to them since cannot rate as a great success story. There are good reasons for this, one self-evidently being one of weight, an instrument built from substantial pieces of rock highly being impractical to transport. Another factor is the limited feasibility of stone as a material to work with: other materials such as wood and later bronze proved to be far more malleable and thus suitable for making necessary refinements.

The general name given to a stone instrument, lithophone, is derived from the Greek words for stone and sound. There are those who insist that the word specifically applies to a set of tuned bars of stone, played with hand-held beaters and that to call any musical instrument made of stone a lithophone would be the equivalent of calling any wooden instrument a xylophone. Whilst there is a case to be made for this, the history of language shows that logic does not always prove to be an effective decider on such matters. The remit of this book, stretching as it does beyond such a tight definition, sidesteps the controversy by neatly excluding the word "lithophone" from its title.

The reason for the commonly experienced surprise and fascination upon seeing a lithophone for the first time seems to be more than just its novelty, but to lie in the nature of the material it's made from. The associations we have with stone and the way we use the word metaphorically doesn't tally with attributes generally associated with music: stone-cold; stone-dead; stone-deaf; heart of stone. Stone is inanimate, lifeless, probably not something we would wish our music to be. Yet in the visual sphere we have long been fully aware of the potential of stone to be turned into things of beauty and profundity: architecture, jewellery, sculpture being common examples. These things are part of our world. But in them stone is no longer rough, visibly hacked from the landscape, it has been transformed into something else. And we do like our musical instruments to be things of visual beauty too: the subtle curves of a violin or a Les Paul guitar, the magnificence of a concert grand, the brazen flamboyance of a trumpet or trombone or the sparkle of a drum-kit. So a row of roughly hewn stone slabs doesn't initially hold much promise, yet paradoxically that seems precisely why, when those low expectations are defied, the enjoyment is all the greater. It was the sheer amazement at the quality of music being produced, as these familiar dance tunes and popular classics were played on rustic-looking stone slabs in English towns in the early 1840s, which led to the success of the family rock bands.

When stone first began to be employed in the playing of music may be impossible to pinpoint and remains a matter of conjecture, but we can perhaps be more specific about the first documented use of the term "music stones". Peter Crosthwaite, while curator of the Crosthwaite Museum in Keswick, wrote in a memorandum: "On the 11th June 1785 Peter Crosthwaite found his first Music Stones".[1] Having collected enough stones from the foot of the nearby Skiddaw mountain, he went on to assemble them into a musical instrument. The story of Crosthwaite and his extraordinary background leading up to his creation of a lithophone is told here in Chapter 1. It was his Music Stones, which he displayed and played in his museum, which later inspired Joseph Richardson to build his much larger lithophone and form the first of the family rock bands. From our standpoint in time, the difficulty of having to contend with the idea of rock bands being around in the nineteenth century is rather confusingly compounded by the fact that this term was not only applied to the group of musicians but also at times to the instrument itself.

The different achievements of these bands, principally those of the Richardsons, the Tills and later the Abrahams, all from Keswick, is the subject of the early chapters in the book. Their popular success, coming at a time when connections between the arts and science were being actively encouraged, also produced a new-found interest in the musical use of stone amongst a number of engineers, scientists and eminent thinkers, including critic and geologist John Ruskin who was to acquire a stone instrument of his own.

While much of the prolonged burst of activity with stone instruments in the nineteenth century revolved around the town of Keswick, there were others following parallel paths. One such was a Frenchman called Honoré Baudre whose story is told in Chapter 8. He spent most of his adult life trying to perfect an instrument he had built from pieces of flint he had gathered in fields. Also attracting the attention of scientists, geologists and archaeologists, he was to deliver presentations of his findings in both Europe and North America.

The pursuits of other individuals who were less widely known in their lifetimes can now be discovered through the tools of modern technology. Details of the life of Yorkshire Dalesman Neddy Dick, who built his own lithophone which he played at home to passers-by, have come from searches of newspaper archives, sometimes in the form of reminiscences from some who knew him. The lithophone constructed by a Menorca don, Antonio Roca y Várez in 1893 would have been forgotten by the world were it not for his great-great grandson, Carles-Garcia Roca, who has written about it in his online blog. Further material relating to the instrument and its creator has been gratefully obtained through direct email contact with Carles-Garcia Roca and is presented in Chapter 10, along with an account of what is known about Neddy Dick and his music.

---

[1] Peter Crosthwaite's Memorandum, Keswick Museum.

As more people moved to towns and cities during the course of the nineteenth century, leading to a rise in the number of industrial workers as well an increasingly influential middle class, there were new expectations of entertainment. An appetite for something new was whetted by an increasing number of novelty acts. The family rock bands fitted the bill and audiences lapped up what they had to offer. Later, circus and music hall acts picked up on the idea of using musical stones but on a less grand scale, using a small set of tuned stones as just one element in their performance. Some of those to do so, including clown and musician Arthur Nelson and the Four Jees, plus the Pavanellas and the Bozza Troupe who produced music from paving slabs, are the subject of Chapter 11.

As the century drew to a close there was a steady decline in interest in rock harmonicons and musical stones and they were no longer so visible. The otherwise highly fertile and eclectic twentieth century proved to be decidedly restrained in its use of sonorous stone compared with its predecessor. Nevertheless, that period, continuing until the present day, was punctuated by a series of generally discrete but occasionally connected examples of stone being specially chosen for the sound it produces. Chapter 12 is therefore devoted to the twentieth century, presenting a miscellany of fascinating but mainly unrelated examples of musical stone, ranging from German composer Carl Orff commissioning the construction of a lithophone to be included in the score for a choral stage production, to the construction of the Great Stalacpipe Organ in the Luray Caverns in Virginia, using the in-house sound of stalactites.

Chapter 14 is given over to what has become referred to as "experimental music", a term which gained usage in the early 1950s and represented a different approach to modern composed music than that of European avant garde composers such as Karlheinz Stockhausen and Pierre Boulez. Following an exploratory, questioning approach to music and spearheaded by the ideas and music of John Cage, its protagonists looked beyond conventional instrumentation, with some, including Americans Christian Wolff and Pauline Oliveros and British composer Cornelius Cardew, choosing to specify the use of stone in some of their pieces.

Some of those who have chosen to explore the sound potential of stone came to do so having already been working with stone. As well as the sound of stone being an intrinsic part of the process of stone-carving, that process also depends on another musical quality, rhythm. Sculptor Barbara Hepworth, who had always had an interest in music and dance, was particularly aware of these connections and later sculptors such as Pinuccio Sciola extended the visual and haptic qualities of their work to include the aural. Having already achieved international recognition as a sculptor, Sciola in later life became especially known for his sound sculptures. The connections between music, stone-carving and sculpture are explored in Chapter 15.

The concluding chapter of the book brings things up to date, presenting a series of first-hand insights into recent and contemporary practice involving the aural properties of rock. This takes the form of a series of statements from instrument-builders, sculptors and musicians, most of whom would probably identify themselves as being a combination of all three, who were invited to write about their own practice. They live in different parts of the world - Belgium, Canada, France, Germany, Iceland, Italy, Norway, Slovenia, Switzerland, the UK, the USA and Vietnam - and underlying all their similarities and differences they have shown, to a greater or lesser extent, a fascination with the sound of stone.

# Chapter One

# Peter Crosthwaite

## The man and his Music Stones

Peter Crosthwaite had known since childhood that the slopes of the Skiddaw mountain contained rocks which rang with a pleasing sound when struck. But it was not until he was in his fiftieth year that he began gathering them from the bed of the River Greta with the express purpose of making a musical instrument. Later he was to record the occasion in his diary:

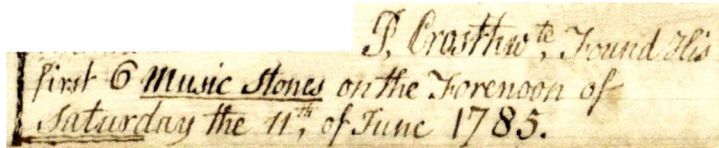

Figure 1.1. Peter Crosthwaite's Memorandum entry for 11th June 1785. Courtesy of Keswick Museum and Art Gallery.

Five years earlier Crosthwaite had founded a museum in the town of Keswick, which lies at the foot of Skiddaw in England's Lake District. The area had become a major attraction for visitors and the Crosthwaite Museum was one of the first provincial museums of its kind. But it was important that tourists were aware of its existence, so Crosthwaite had taken to using musical sounds to catch their attention, enlisting members of his family to play a variety of instruments. When he found that the six stones he had gathered each emitted a different note he began to think he could perhaps construct a small instrument which would be good enough to playing simple tunes on. The type of stone he collected, which made such an attractive sound when struck, was called hornfels, a fine-grained metamorphic rock which has been further hardened through contact with cooling igneous rock.

Each of the first six stones which Peter Crosthwaite gathered were, according to him, already in perfect tune but when, over a six-month period, he collected a further ten he found that some adjustment was required. This he achieved by carefully chipping away and honing the stones, working twelve hours a day, until they matched the notes of a major scale. In undertaking this task he would have learned the principles underlying such an instrument, the note pitch of each bar being principally determined by its length (the shorter it was the higher the note) and its thickness (a thinner bar producing a lower note). Once the stones had been tooled to their required pitch he incised into each one its note name, though these don't correspond with modern concert tuning (Figure 1.2). He then arranged them in ascending note order from left to right and laid them across two lengths of rope attached to a piece of wood. For the stone bars to ring properly the points at which each one rested on the rope would also have been critical. When finished the set of sixteen stones measured between approximately half a metre and two metres in length.

*Figure 1.2. Close-up of Peter Crosthwaite's Music Stones showing incised lettering. Photograph: Mike Adcock, Courtesy of Keswick Museum and Art Gallery.*

Anyone seeing Crosthwaite's Music Stones today, where they are on display in the current Keswick Museum, would immediately recognize the set of stones as a musical instrument akin to a xylophone, but in eighteenth century England such instruments, whether made from wood, metal or anything else, were not widely known, if they were to be found at all. A more obvious way of producing an instrument from ringing stones at that time would have probably been to suspend them like bells or chimes, but by choosing to lay the stone bars horizontally Peter Crosthwaite had produced possibly the first such tuned percussion instrument in Britain. So the question arises as to how a man with no musical training and limited musical knowledge should independently arrive at a design solution which resembles so closely tuned percussion instruments to be found in different parts of the world, from the west of Africa to South East Asia. Were Peter Crosthwaite's Music Stones purely the product of his undoubtedly inventive mind or had he come across something similar before? The answer may lie in Crosthwaite's remarkable earlier life.

## India

Born in 1735 and growing up in Crosthwaite, the village on the edge of Keswick whose name he shared, Peter Crosthwaite took an apprenticeship in weaving after leaving school, the burgeoning wool industry being the only major source of employment, apart from farm labour, in the area. The nature of the work was not to his liking however and being in a confined environment began to affect his health. After considering other kinds of employment it was recommended to him that he would benefit from taking a long sea voyage. So after a year of navigation training and a promise of a position with the East India Company he left for India on one of the company's merchant ships, the *True Briton*, embarking from Spithead on the Solent on Monday 8th May 1758 and not to return to his home country for another seven years. The

*True Briton*'s voyage to Bombay was to be a long and perilous one. A full century before work started on building the Suez Canal, the route necessitated sailing the length of West Africa, around the Cape of Good Hope into the Indian Ocean and northwards, via Madagascar to the west coast of India. The long voyage took nine months, five of which were spent out of sight of land. Overcrowding, sickness, and the dangers presented by the high seas, whether through changes in the weather or piracy, meant that to undertake such a trip was a life-threatening choice. Crosthwaite records in a memoir that as the result of sea scurvy many of those on board lost their lives.[1] The prospects of remaining healthy were not much improved on arrival either. Disease in various forms was common and widespread, with almost a third of those who left the Cumbrian region to work for the East India Company failing to return.[2] Given that Cumberland and Westmorland were the two English counties providing the highest number of Company employees this had a considerable impact on those from the region seeking a better life.[3]

After less than a year working as a regular sailor Peter Crosthwaite had made enough of an impression to be appointed, while still in his late twenties, as commander of a gunboat, the *Otter*. His job was to protect the East India Company merchant ships off the west coast of India, principally in the Gulf of Cambay (now Khambat) close to Surat, with the main threat coming from piracy, though given the ruthless trading practices of the company, the question of who was the greater aggressor remains an open one.

The British-owned East India Company was a trading organisation which, under an innocuous name, took commerce to an unprecedented level of control, exploitation and cruelty. The tactics it used to undermine the economy of India and the way it chose to wield its power

*Figure 1.3. A view of Surat.*

---

[1] Peter Crosthwaite's Memoir, Keswick Museum and Art Gallery.
[2] Saville-Smith, p36.
[3] Ibid, p95.

was notorious and something usually only seen in the behaviour of autocratic nation states. While India was at the heart of its operation, since its inception the company had set its sights further east to the East Indies and China, carrying cargoes of spices, silk, indigo dye, saltpetre and, most significantly tea.

Crosthwaite worked for the East India Company for seven years, rising to the position of lieutenant within their marine service, but it was neither a happy nor a distinguished period for him. In his memoirs, written in the third person, he gives accounts of various confrontations with pirate boats and also of the animosity between him and his fellow officers, which he claimed arose from envy on their part.

> From his first setting foot in the Otter...he had experienced one continued series of malice and envy, rising progressively against him as he gained money and esteem of generous minds.[4]

This friction culminated in an incident which was eventually to lead to the end of his time there. He had ordered a friendly ship to be fired upon, believing correctly that it was manned by pirates, though not realizing that they had actually been hired by the Portuguese owners. As a result Crosthwaite was charged and imprisoned, having been declared a lunatic and had his property and money taken away from him.[5] His health began to deteriorate and with his taste for warfare diminishing, once he was free to do so he made the decision to return to England.

During the time he spent in India Peter Crosthwaite had found he much preferred the company of the native Indian people he met and worked with to that of his British colleagues. The latter, he wrote,

> ....far exceeded in baseness any caste or tribe of Indians that ever [I] had connections with and they were many....40 of them being easier to manage than 5 Europeans.[6]

The feeling seems to have been mutual and, according to Crosthwaite, he was held in high esteem by the local people. For five months of the year, during the monsoon period, it wasn't possible to operate at sea so Crosthwaite took the opportunity to travel inland, where he "made excursions into the country further than others durst", travelling to one town "where they has only seen one European for 50 years...to another where never."[7] Although his writing contains little in the way of detail about the time he spent ashore, the evidence of his later activities suggests that it was this experience which left the most positive impression on him.

Peter Crosthwaite collected various objects of interest from these trips inland, some of which found their way into the exhibits on display once he opened his museum in Keswick. Whether these ever included any musical instruments is uncertain, though there were to be several musical items in the museum collection. There is no reason to think that Crosthwaite was a particularly proficient musician but there are various references, including a couple of

---

[4] Peter Crosthwaite's Memoir, Keswick Museum and Art Gallery.
[5] East India Company records, British Library.
[6] Peter Crosthwaite's Memoir Keswick Museum and Art Gallery.
[7] Ibid.

examples from his time in India, which suggest that he was drawn to music and was fully aware of its value and potential. In one he describes an episode at sea when his crew were about to board a pirate ship and called to the pirate crew for silence in order to hear a proclamation from the master of the *Otter*. The pirates responded in demonstrable fashion:

> In reply they set up a most horrid uproar, brandished their polished scimitars, belaboured their thundering tom-toms, which with their huge trumpets far exceeded the European marshall (sic) music, being much louder and much more awful.[8]

Awful as Crosthwaite might have found the sound of tom-toms and trumpets, the display seems to anticipate and perhaps influenced the way in which, years later, he chose to attract visitors to his museum in Keswick. Enlisting the help of his wife and daughter, together they would produce a comparable cacophony, beating simultaneously a drum and a Chinese gong along as well as playing a barrel-organ, with Crosthwaite also performing on his Music Stones. The memoir from his time in India records another, more low-key musical episode from the time he had been imprisoned in a dungeon by his fellow officers who had declared him to be mad: he writes of having had a flute with him, with which he "began to play away for amusement."[9]

The question remains as to whether Peter Crosthwaite's idea for the way he assembled his Music Stones originated in instruments he had seen on his foreign travels. While instruments with bars arranged horizontally in the manner of xylophones and glockenspiels were not widespread in Europe until the mid-nineteenth century and even later in Britain, they were not common in India either so it's not certain that he would have seen them there. They were however to be found in some parts of South East Asia and there has been an assumption that Crosthwaite must have come across them during a period working away from India, though this may have arisen through a misunderstanding. Contemporary reports, including Crosthwaite's own writing, refer to him travelling to the East Indies, a term which is used today to refer to South East Asia, but at that time could equally be applied to the area around the Indian subcontinent.[10]

The extensive trading area of the East India Company in this region made it likely that their seamen would have come across tuned percussion instruments in other countries. In Java and Bali there were the instruments of the gamelan, mainly metallophones but also sometimes made from bamboo, while (wooden) xylophones were represented in the garantung of Sumatra, the ranat of Thailand and the pattala of Myanmar and elsewhere. But there is nothing in the available writings of Crosthwaite to indicate that he ventured far at all beyond the waters off Surat, on India's west coast. If his job had on occasion taken him further afield, protecting trading ships on their voyages, it seems likely he would have mentioned this in his diaries and memoirs, but here is no record of him travelling further afield during the months when he wasn't employed at sea. To have done so would have been a time-consuming enterprise which his working contract would have been unlikely to allow and the monsoon weather is likely to have prohibited that anyway. If Crosthwaite himself didn't visit these places, it may, however, be that sailors who did go on trading trips brought back instruments to India and that Crosthwaite perhaps came across them for sale in markets or played by itinerant musicians. It

---

[8] Ibid.
[9] Ibid.
[10] Savill-Smith, p xiv Glossary.

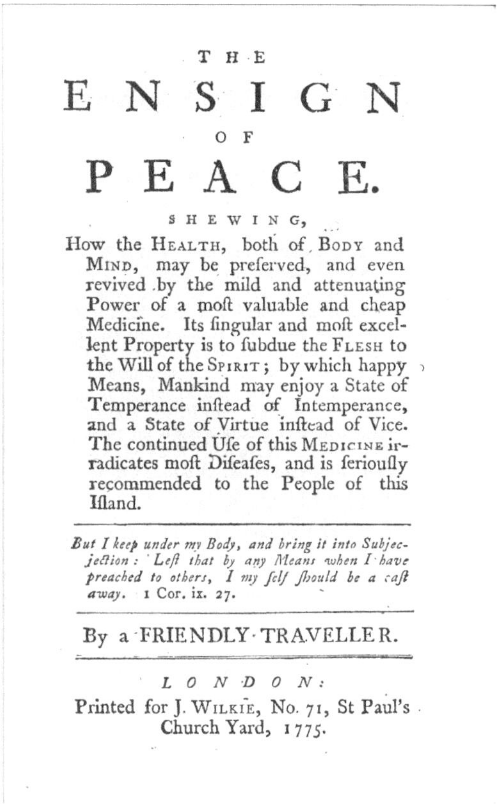
THE

ENSIGN

OF

PEACE.

SHEWING,

How the HEALTH, both of BODY and MIND, may be preſerved, and even revived by the mild and attenuating Power of a moſt valuable and cheap Medicine. Its ſingular and moſt excellent Property is to ſubdue the FLESH to the Will of the SPIRIT; by which happy Means, Mankind may enjoy a State of Temperance inſtead of Intemperance, and a State of Virtue inſtead of Vice. The continued Uſe of this MEDICINE irradicates moſt Diſeaſes, and is ſeriouſly recommended to the People of this Iſland.

*But I keep under my Body, and bring it into Subjection: Leſt that by any Means when I have preached to others, I my ſelf ſhould be a caſt away.* 1 Cor. ix. 27.

By a FRIENDLY TRAVELLER.

*LONDON:*

Printed for J. WILKIE, No. 71, St Paul's Church Yard, 1775.

*Figure 1.4. The Ensign of Peace, title page.*

has also been suggested that he might even have encountered stone instruments while he was in Asia, but this seems less likely. There were a small number of tribal groups in Vietnam who played lithophones, but they were not located in a coastal region.

### Blyth, Northumberland

Arriving back from India in 1765 Peter Crosthwaite did not initially return to Keswick, living for a while in London where he met Hannah Fisher, a former neighbour from Keswick, who he later married. They then moved to Blyth in Northumberland where he took up a post as customs officer, which he held for twelve years, during which time the couple produced three children, Robert, Mary and Daniel, only the latter two of whom survived into adulthood.

In 1775 Crosthwaite published a book *The Ensign of Peace*, born largely out of his experience in India (Figure 1.4). In this he expounded on what he saw as the shortcomings of mankind, namely lust, adultery, tyranny, war, pride, revenge, ingratitude, gaming, and injustice. But at the centre of his argument, something he felt could be the saving grace for humanity and a way to dramatically reduce the prevalence of disease, was the efficacy of good quality water. This, he advocated, was essential for drinking but also for cleanliness, washing not then seen as a regular requirement. While in India he had witnessed how people took care over the preparation of water, filtering and boiling it prior to consumption. As a result, he claimed, they suffered far less serious illness than Europeans. The value of water as a drink was also associated, for Crosthwaite, with the idea of temperance, the consumption of alcohol considered by him to be at the root of many of society's ills. In a fastidious thoroughness which can be seen to have run through each of his pursuits Crosthwaite presented an analysis of water, recording in detail its changing properties according to ingredient salts, temperature etc. and the effect this had on its quality as a drink and as an agent for hygiene. Noting the poor health of many of the people around him compared to those in India, he sought to educate them on the matter and on his eventual return to Keswick Crosthwaite constructed a device whereby water was filtered effectively by passing it through a gravel bed, which was to remain in use by local people for many years. While many of the views expressed in *The Ensign of Peace* are very much of their time, his advocacy that general well-being is fundamentally dependent on choices we make regarding diet and exercise were remarkably prescient of modern thinking.

## Keswick

When Peter Crosthwaite finally returned to Keswick in 1779, twenty-one years after departing for India, he was to find it a changed place. In that time the Lake District had become a destination for tourism, increasingly popular as more people discovered that they didn't need to travel abroad to witness dramatic landscapes and beautiful scenery. There were a number of reasons for this, one being the improved state of the roads, the introduction of the turnpike system of toll roads having reduced journey times by as much as two thirds. In addition, the continental grand tour, typically undertaken by well-heeled young men prior to settling down, was becoming a less attractive option due to the unstable political situation in Europe. With Britain itself having been in involved in various recent military campaigns, even before the onset of the Napoleonic era, there was also a prevalent feeling that exploring what the home country had to offer was the patriotic thing to do. So the Lake District became an attractive proposition and one which, being closer to home, also became affordable to a greater number of people. The area had been receiving good publicity too from the attention of poets and writers. Thomas Gray, already a known figure, largely on the strength of *Elegy Written in a Country Churchyard*, had made a visit in 1769, subsequently publishing his *Journal of a Visit to the Lake District* in which he recorded and marveled at the wonderful vistas he had seen there. More writers and artists followed his example, with Wordsworth, Coleridge and Southey soon taking up residence there and the influence of the romantic movement inspired thousands of people to leave urbanity for a short period to be enthralled by the sights on offer.

Most of the tourists travelling to the Lake District in increasing numbers were not interested in adventure climbing or long hillside walks but, like Thomas Gray, to be awe-struck by the

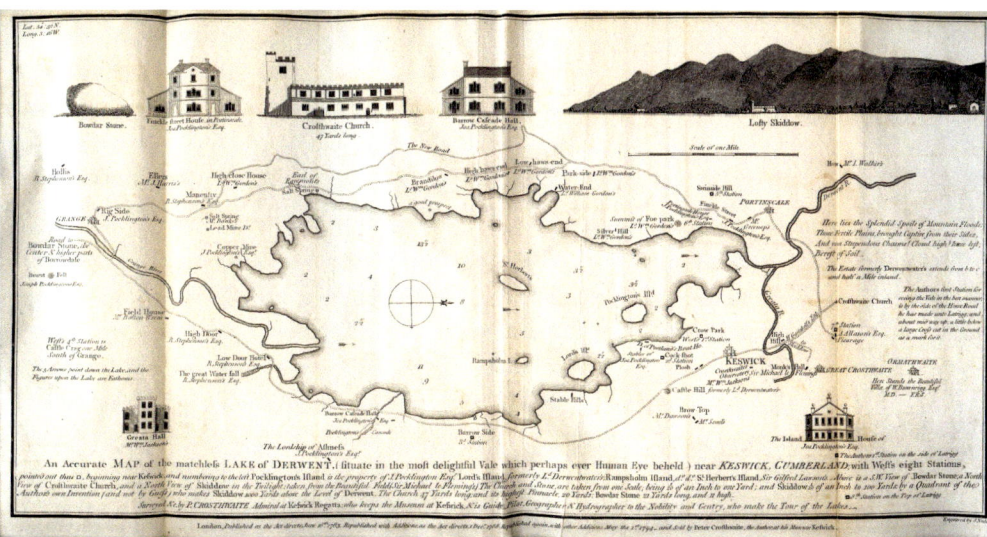

Figure 1.5. One of Peter Crosthwaite's tourist maps showing Derwentwater and surrounding attractions. Courtesy of the Cumbria County History Trust.

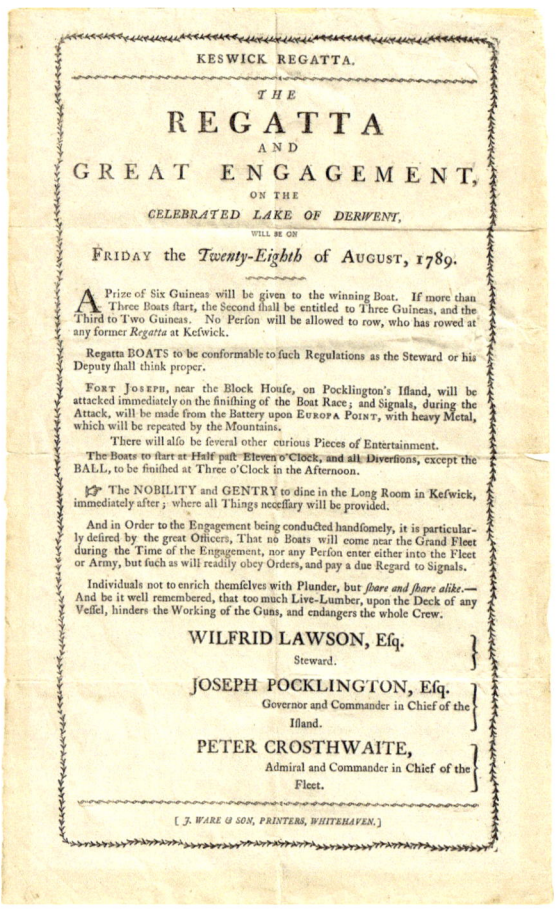

*Figure 1.6. Derwentwater Regatta handbill 1789. Courtesy of Keswick Museum and Art Gallery.*

majesty of the mountains. Taste may have been shifting from idealized, classical notions of landscape to something more rugged and natural but it was still to be viewed from a safe vantage point and there remained a notion of the 'picturesque'. In 1778 a Jesuit priest, Thomas West, produced the first popular guidebook to the Lakes in which he recommended various 'stations' from which the tourist might best behold this magnificence. This was to prove so popular that by 1812 ten editions had been published. With his knowledge of the area Peter Crosthwaite soon began generating income by hiring himself out as a guide and then, putting some of his navigation skills to inland use, he began surveying the surrounding area and produced a series of illustrated maps of the lakes, pinpointing each optimum viewpoint. They were published and printed and became effectively the first ever tourist maps, which were a great success and continue to be praised by cartographers, not just for their innovation but also their accuracy (Figure 1.5).

Crosthwaite was starting to make his presence felt in the town of Keswick, becoming known for his wide interests, expertise and undoubted eccentricity. Not shy to capitalize upon his maritime record, he accepted an offer to become Grand Admiral of the fleet at the spectacular Derwentwater Regattas. These were staged annually for ten years from 1781, on the banks of Derwentwater and on what had become known as Pocklington's Island, owned as it was by a wealthy man called Joseph Pocklington who had built himself a grand house there (Figure 1.6). The regatta was jointly organised by Pocklington and Crosthwaite and involved staging boat races, firework displays and the big attraction, a mock battle in which the island was "attacked" from the opposite bank of the lake. This was augmented by explosive sounds from cannons firing blanks and at times some musical accompaniment. In 1784 a group of French horn players were employed and a contemporary account gives the flavour:

> "Upon the retreat of the fleet, and the firing of the first *feu-de-joye*, the music began and continued till the renewal of the attack: these pleasing sounds, which softened and reverberated by innumerable cliffs, exhibit an almost supernatural tide of harmony,

*Figure 1.7. The Crosthwaite Museum, Keswick.*

were at times disturbed by the explosions of the guns. First the loud fierce report of the cannon totally drowned the music; then all was silent for a few seconds, and the music again was heard. Scarce could the ear comprehend a note when the gun was re-echoed from the surrounding precipices like a peal of thunder: when this ceased the horns again were heard, but almost instantly the uproar arose among other and more distant cliffs: which was repeated many times from each discharge."[11]

It seems likely that Peter Crosthwaite master-minded this particular display, recalling as it does Crosthwaite's description of the naval confrontation back in India which had clearly made enough of an impression for him to record it in his memoir.

In 1781 Peter Crosthwaite announced the opening of his museum, referring to it as his "Cabinet of Curiosities". Initially smaller sized items were displayed, including objects Crosthwaite had managed to bring back from his travels, such as coins and semi-precious gemstones, as well as examples of the local geology and other natural history specimens (animal, vegetable and mineral) discovered on his walks. The Crosthwaite Museum, as it became known, soon proved to be a popular place to visit. Whilst the Lake District continued to attract more tourists, the local climate presented something of a drawback as Keswick was also prone to visits from rain clouds on a fairly regular basis, so with the opening of the museum people had somewhere to visit when the weather was too inclement for hillside rambling. The collection soon grew and encouraged by the museum's success Crosthwaite was able to move it into purpose built

---

[11] Hankinson, p16.

premises in 1784. Larger items were purchased, others were donated and using his maritime connections he was able to add more exotic material, persuading a series of sea captains to bring items back from their voyages to order. These included John Wordsworth, brother of the poet William, who was also employed by the East India Company and remained so until he lost his life in1805 when his ship, the *Earl of Abergavenny* foundered off the Dorset coast.

In a relatively short period of time Crosthwaite's collection of curiosities expanded from hundreds to thousands of objects of every description. With no expectations to live up to and no format to follow, his being the first such museum in the region, he included anything he thought worth presenting. There was a range of stuffed animals including a polar bear, the heads of a walrus and a babirusa, the skin of an armadillo, a seven-foot-long alligator (suspended from the ceiling) and an albatross with a ten-foot wingspan, brought back from the Cape of Good Hope by John Wordsworth. Various ethnographic items were included, such as weapons, tattooing instruments, fish hooks, microscopes, sextants, model boats, tobacco pipes and a petrified wig.  As well as a host of items from the natural world there were also examples of the unnatural variety, stretching the credulity of visitors to the museum: a three-legged goose, a four-legged chicken, a kitten with eight legs and two tails, a calf's foot with five hooves, plus what was purported to be the unearthed rib of a twenty-one foot high giant (thought more likely to have come from a mammoth).

Last, but certainly not least, there were the museum's musical items, including the mechanical barrel organ, capable of playing seventy-seven tunes, a Chinese gong, various drums, a selection of sheet music and in pride of place the set of sixteen Music Stones, which remained, out of all of this vast collection, one of Peter Crosthwaite's most valued items. In his memorandum, written much later in his life and recalling significant entries from earlier diaries, his discovery of the Music Stones is recorded twice. The first time it is mentioned, cited earlier, he has emboldened and underlined the key words (Fig.1.1) indicating the importance it held for Crosthwaite. In the second entry he gives more detail of the location: "June 11th ,1785 found my 6 first Music Stones at the tip-end or north end of Long Tongue"[12] (Figure 1.8).

Some have disputed Crosthwaite's account of where he collected the stones, saying they are of a type which would have been found higher up on the slopes of Skiddaw, but there is no apparent reason why he should have fabricated the story. According to a newspaper report years later Crosthwaite's original intention when he went to look for a ringing stone was "for the purpose of procuring a good sounding stone to contrast with bell metal, when to his delight, he found they sounded one a note above the other".[13] If his original idea had not been to produce a melodic instrument, then finding that the first six stones he collected each

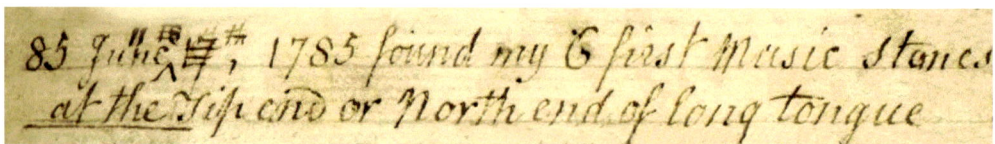

Figure 1.8. Peter Crosthwaite's second Memorandum entry referring to the discovery of his Music Stones. Courtesy of Keswick Museum and Art Gallery.

---

[12] Peter Crosthwaite's Memorandum,  Keswick Museum and Art Gallery.
[13] Westmorland Gazette, Saturday 13th November 1832,  p6.

*Figure 1.9. Peter Crosthwaite's Music Stones. Courtesy of Keswick Museum and Art Gallery.*

played a different "true" note was more serendipitous and fortuitous than has generally been thought. Once he had discovered that to be the case and understanding that he would be able to tune the ten additional stones he collected, it was presumably then that he decided to lie them horizontally. It is tempting to think he must have gained this knowledge from having seen something similar, but when and where remains a mystery (Figure 1.9).

With the Music Stones on display in the museum, Crosthwaite was not averse to giving a performance on them to anyone who would listen, though it's not known whether visitors were allowed to play them. With musical instruments playing an important role in Crosthwaite's efforts to attract visitors, the Music Stones had a particular novelty value and were often mentioned in published descriptions from attendees of the Crosthwaite Museum. Watching through the window, Peter Crosthwaite would, at a sign of potential customers approaching, then alert members of his family and they would begin to play, not in perfect harmony but, by all accounts, with a determinedly raucous vigour. A Cambridge undergraduate, William Gell (later a renowned classical topographer) gave an account of a visit to the Crosthwaite Museum in his book *A tour in the lakes 1797*. He seems to have been moderately impressed with the exhibits, including the musical ones, mentioning among other other things:

> ....a Chinese Gong which produced a most thundering sound and an instrument of the staccato kind, made of stone of which he pretends to have found six notes in the proper musical succession.[14]

But even these items seem to have been somewhat upstaged in the twenty-year-old student's eyes by Crosthwaite's daughter Mary who he describes as "an elegant woman, and more worth seeing than any thing else in this house". He then proceeds to describe the presence of Crosthwaite himself:

> He is seated in a gouty chair and drums in one corner of the room like a fool, to the noise of a barrel organ. While he has mirrors in every direction at the windows, by which he sees every carriage that comes from any of the neighbouring towns, though he sits

---

[14] Gell, p20.

not near to any of the windows himself. The organ strikes up if anyone passes and his drum is thumped, at the same time the old woman runs upstairs and rattles away at the gong, in a manner that cannot fail to attract the notice of the neighbours in the street. He has even attempted to make a larger gong than that he has already, with which he might astonish strangers, but this has not succeeded, probably owing to the too great thickness of the brass with which it is formed.[15]

Peter Crosthwaite's predilection for the combination of music and noise is once more in evidence. The barrel organ Gell mentions, whose repertoire included marches, minuets, reels and hymns, is also referred to by columnist Joseph Budworth, who described in 1792 how it was

> ….allowed by judges to be one of the finest instruments of its size that ever was heard; it is very loud, and has a sweet tone….when you leave the museum the organ strikes up and he never sees any of his customers pass his house without a tune of acknowledgement, I think we got about six."[16]

In addition to making the gong mentioned by William Gell, based on the one brought back for him from Canton, Crosthwaite experimented with constructing other musical instruments, replicating a drum he had seen on his travels and also an aeolian harp, its sound produced by the wind playing on the strings. Having presumably seen one elsewhere, he went about refining the design of the harp and constructed one which he then placed close to a window opening out on to the street so that an entering breeze would bring it to life. The idea was that the gentle and unexpected sound it produced would draw the attention of those passing and lure them into the museum. With the help of the family, in particular Daniel and his wife, he then began to produce aeolian harps to be sold in the museum along with other merchandise on display to visitors as they left the building and hundreds were purchased over the subsequent years. Partly because of their association with antiquity, aeolian harps had become a reference point in the picturesque notion of landscape tourism and one reason given for their recent popularity was that they "encouraged visitors to imagine themselves in an Arcadian scene".[17] The instrument was also celebrated in two poems by James Thomson in 1748 and in 1796 Coleridge published a poem "The Eolian Harp", which may itself have been inspired by seeing them in the Crosthwaite Museum.

These musical items were not however the only products of Crosthwaite's inventiveness. He had also come up with, among other things, a design for a fire-escape, a portable bathing-machine, a non-smoking chimney pot and a proposal for a cork-lined self-righting lifeboat, a prototype model of which was displayed in the museum. Having been persuaded that there was no point in trying to take out a patent on it, the idea was later taken up by another entrepreneur who was able to capitalize on it.

Despite putting himself at the service of people wishing to experience the glory of the natural landscape, Peter Crosthwaite could himself hardly be described as a romantic. He was a practical man who thrived on finding solutions to human problems. Much as he undoubtedly

---

[15] Ibid.
[16] Brears, p111.
[17] Lynch, p246.

had a love for the region he had returned to, he expressed this not through poetic adulation but in quantification: his notebooks contain an abundance of measurements, whether they be metrological (recording rainfall, wind direction and cloud conditions) or geographical (calculating the height of mountains, waterfalls etc). From the start, the contents of his museum largely comprised items from the natural world, reflecting his almost obsessive fascination with it, but the naming of things, whether they be rock types, fossils or shells, was always important to him. But alongside this penchant for data there is also a sense in Crosthwaite's writing of his sheer wonder at the world and its curiosities:

> ….the yelling of the ice as the water falls away…the flying of the snow like the smook [smoke] of a mighty furnace….the spray of lofty waterfalls born away with gales of winds like the smook of a mighty furnace….the wild irregularity of the sensible horizon….the small space close to the side of the falling water….and the swift motion of the water passing will probably give a very pleasing sensation.[18]

It was clearly also this sense of wonder that so delighted Crosthwaite in the discovery and collection of his Music Stones from the landscape he knew. But the way he referred to them, as "music stones", seems to reflect his utilitarian side, purely describing their function, unlike the way they later became known generically as "musical stones", a more fanciful way of describing their sonorous properties. Incidents recorded in Crosthwaite's writings showing how musical experiences clearly left their mark on him have been cited earlier and writing years later his son Daniel recalled an occasion when he was four years old and his father took the family into a field on a Sunday morning specially to listen to the ringing of the bells from Crosthwaite Church.

The Crosthwaite Museum was an undoubted success story, the first in the region and, because tourism was a new phenomenon in Britain, one of the first such provincial museums in the country. It received favourable newspaper coverage and a high number of visitors: at its peak in 1793 the museum was recorded as having been visited by "1540 persons of rank and fashion".[19] Peter Crosthwaite proudly boasted of a series of celebrated figures who had passed through its doors and duly signed the visitors book, including William Wordsworth, HRH Prince William of Orange, Viscount Palmerston, Samuel Taylor Coleridge and Robert Southey. Nevertheless there were critical voices, expressing the view that the museum offered entertainment rather than the impartation of knowledge, with one visitor calling the exhibits "more gimcrack than antiquity"[20]

Success also brought with it local rivalry, coming in particular from a man called Thomas Hutton who began offering his own guided walks. These were to prove more popular than Crosthwaite's due to Hutton's more engaging manner and the fact that they offered a less ambitious excursion into the hills than those Crosthwaite preferred to lead. Crosthwaite became incensed that much of the information his rival imparted to tourists was in fact false and his memoirs repeatedly show his indignation at Hutton's behaviour on various occasions. But the most significant threat to Crosthwaite came when Thomas Hutton decided to open his own museum in the town in direct competition to Crosthwaite, who referred to Hutton and

---

[18] Peter Crosthwaite's Memoirs, Keswick Museum and Art Gallery.
[19] Wilson, p28.
[20] Brett, Online essay: "Peter Crosthwaite". No longer accessible.

his associates as a 'junto' who were trying to drive him out of business through fair means and foul. Vandalistic attacks were made on the museum, with items sometimes stolen then re-exhibited elsewhere and Crosthwaite's son Daniel was himself subject to a physical attack. Hutton could not compete with the overall quality of the Crosthwaite Museum, but was still relatively successful and Crosthwaite felt forced to counteract with publicity denouncing the "low cunning and mischievous falsehoods" of his rivals. From his memorandum it is clear that this all troubled Crosthwaite deeply, decrying what he saw as the evil of envy, a throwback to his experience with fellow officers back in India.

Peter Crosthwaite, a truly extraordinary man, died in 1808 and to this day he seems not to have been given the credit he deserves. A man of relatively little education, he travelled to the other side of the world defending the interests of colonialism before rejecting most of its tenets. In his book *The Ensign of* Peace he offered a social philosophy advocating the pursuit of morality and health, including in the process an analytic study of water and it use for consumption and hygiene. He contributed to the community of Keswick and its visitors through developing a method of water filtering and constructing a new pathway into the surrounding hills, pioneered developments in map-making, opened one of the earliest and most successful provincial museums in the country, came up with a series of completely plausible inventions and in what was by no means the least of his achievements, produced his Music Stones. In doing this he paved the way for a succession of stone instruments to be built by others in the area over the next century and beyond and inspiring those from later generations and further afield to do the same.

In his will Peter Crosthwaite expressed the wish that his family continue the Crosthwaite Museum, which they did, with his son Daniel taking on most of the responsibility, continuing to run the museum for the rest of his working life. There does seem to have been a temporary change of plan along the way as in September 1813 the museum's contents, including the musical instruments, were put up for auction, an announcement appearing in the local newspaper.[21] Whether the sale was cancelled or insufficient interest shown is not clear but in the event it didn't happen. What were now always referred to as the Musical Stones remained a major feature of the collection as can be seen in the museum catalogue produced in 1826, where they are the very first item mentioned:

> One of the greatest curiosities is a set of Musical Stones, containing sixteen regular notes, upon which any lady or gentleman who understands music, may play any tune on the natural key His late father discovered the first six musical stones on the 6th [sic] of June 1785; and upwards of 200 ladies and gentlemen have declared them to be the first set of musical stones that ever were in the world, and one of the greatest curiosities of the kind in England.[22]

In 1830 the Crosthwaite Museum received a visit from the young John Ruskin, later to become widely known as a writer and critic. Eleven-year-old Ruskin was visiting Keswick on a holiday in the Lakes with his parents from their home in south London and, following a trip to the museum, was inspired to write in verse about the experience. Modest in poetic achievement, the verses nevertheless offer a perspective on the way the museum was arranged thematically

---

[21] Westmorland Advertiser and Kendal Chronicle, Saturday 25th September 1813, p3
[22] Keswick Museum and Art Gallery collection.

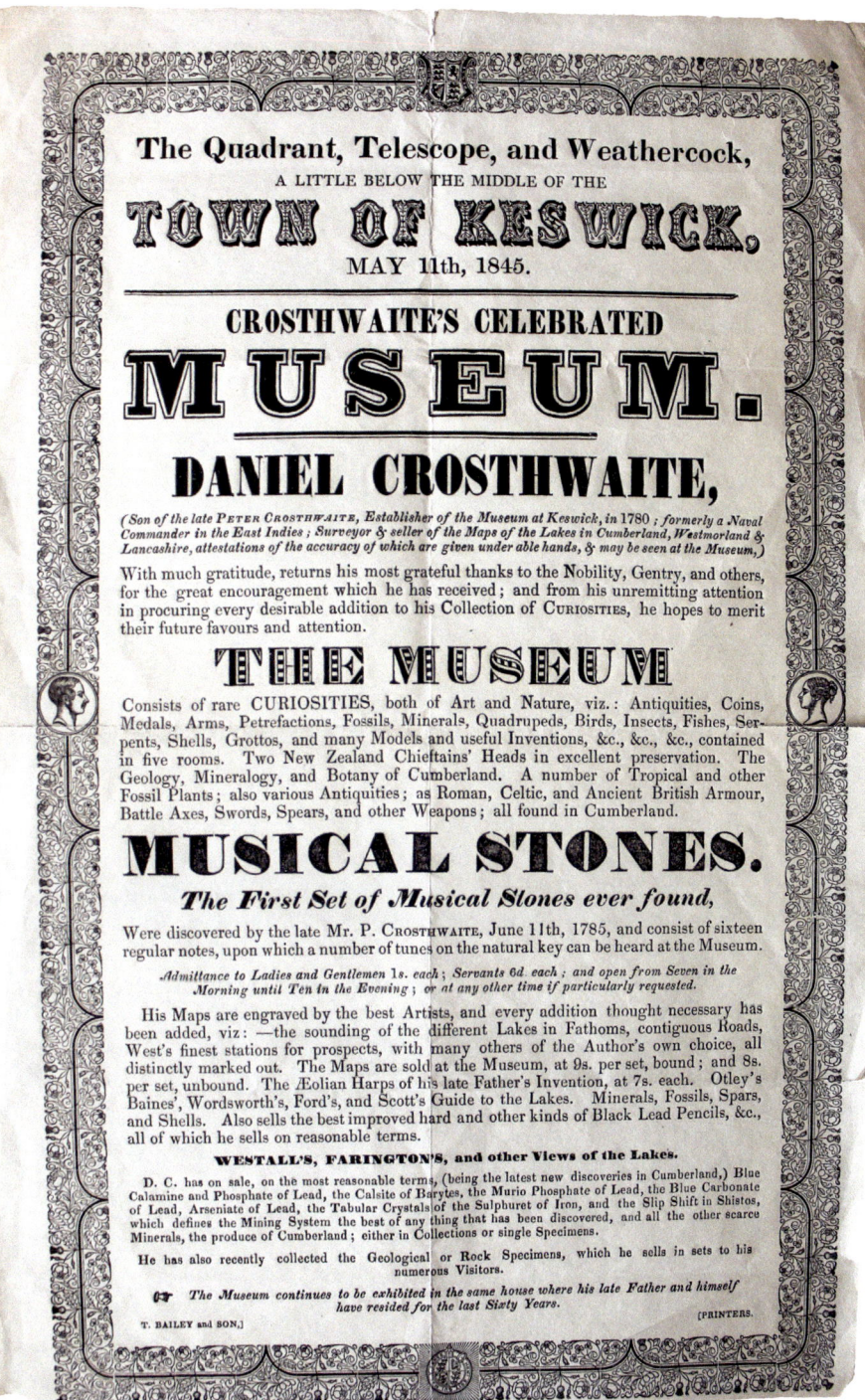

*Figure 1.10. Crosthwaite Museum poster 1845. Courtesy of Keswick Museum and Art Gallery.*

## Music Stones

with visitors invited to ascend the stairs then proceed through the five rooms housing the exhibits. Clearly Daniel Crosthwaite had continued his father's custom of providing visitors with a musical as well as a visual experience, Ruskin noting that

> ....a gong, which on high, from a roof was suspended.
> Whose noise, we all thought, was not to be ended
> I think as hard as a stone was his pate,
> And deaf as a post was Mr. Crosthwaite!
> For he thwacked, and he whacked, and he beat and he bang'd
> And the gong in our ears so incessantly clang'd
> Till we thought that at each and every knock
> We should be obliged our ears for to stop[23]

The Music Stones were in the second room.

> And next, we were shown, upon quite a new plan – O
> A kind of a sort of a stoney piano!
> Some stones in the bed of the Greta's stream found,
> Emitted, when struck, a most musical sound! ...
> But this, though was bearable, finished he soon,
> And ushered us into another small room.[24]

The memory of this presumably stayed with Ruskin as later in life, when he moved to the area, taking up residence at Brantwood on the bank of Coniston Water, he was to have his own set of musical stones.

Daniel Crosthwaite died in 1847, after which his son, John Fisher Crosthwaite, already employed as Keswick's postmaster, took over. It seems that despite his other commitments he honoured the musical aspect of the museum, judging by a piece in the Kendal Mercury in 1852 describing a visit to the Crosthwaite Museum with the instruments still being performed on the stones:

> We heard a Scottish jig and the Copenhagen waltz played upon them very neatly... [25]

In 1870 it was decided to sell the museum and its contents and once again the whole collection was put up for auction. Unable to be sold in its entirety it was divided up and the items dispersed. The Musical Stones fetched £11 but they remained in the family. At some point they were donated to the Fitz Park Museum, now the Keswick Museum, where they can be seen today, in a wooden glass-topped display case.

---

[23] Brears, p111.
[24] Ibid, p112.
[25] Westmorland Gazette, Saturday 13th November 1852, p6

# Chapter Two

# The new contenders

## Limestone, lithophones and a rock harmonicon

Peter Crosthwaite's Music Stones were on display in the family museum in Keswick for over eighty years, seen and heard by countless visitors. In time others were to take up the challenge and build bigger and better stone instruments, but for more than half a century there was nothing quite like them. It may well be that during that time others, having seen the stones in the museum, were inspired to make a set of their own, the ringing hornfels rock being within relatively easy reach. Some sets may have survived, others not, possibly discarded by a later generation, failing to recognize their purpose. Sometimes reference to musical stones can be found in advertised house sales and auction listings in newspapers from the time and as early as 1817 London's Morning Chronicle published the announcement of an auction in Covent Garden, with one item described as a "very fine and interesting cabinet of minerals [including] musical stones from Cumberland". But there were those in Cumbria who were beginning to recognize the commercial as well as the musical potential of stone instruments and acted upon it. One of those was a man called William Todhunter.

### William Todhunter

Living in Hawkshead, around twenty miles south of Keswick, William Todhunter was, like Peter Crosthwaite, a man of diverse pursuits. A hatter by trade, he also ran a bookshop, was a skilled bookbinder and would later take up taxidermy and even umbrella making, possibly with an eye on the emerging tourist market in an area becoming known for its changeable weather as well as its fine scenery. With a particular interest in mineralogy Todhunter would have had good reason to visit the Crosthwaite Museum and it gave him the idea to open one of his own, as it had Crosthwaite's rival Thomas Hutton, though in Todhunter's case the museum was far enough away from Keswick not to be in direct competition to Crosthwaite himself. The Todhunter Museum opened at some point in the 1780s, so at most only a few years after Crosthwaite's. It was housed behind Todhunter's shop, the items on display reflecting his interest in the natural world and including a range of minerals, fossils and shells.

In 1796 William Todhunter moved to Kendal, where initially he reopened the museum in a rented building, before transferring it to his own property in the main street where it occupied the upper floors, allowing him to expand the collection (Figure 2.1). Mineralogy and crystallography were becoming increasingly popular areas of study for scientists and amateur collectors and both Peter Crosthwaite and William Todhunter included examples in their museums, reflecting their own interest and the potential appeal to visitors. In time, Todhunter further emulated Crosthwaite by extending the geological content of his collection to include a set of musical stones he had assembled himself, referred to in a newspaper advertisement announcing the opening.

*Figure 2.1. Stricklandgate in the early 19th century, the location of the Todhunter Museum. Courtesy of Kendal Town Council.*

Mr Todhunter returns his most grateful thanks to the ladies and gentlemen who have patronized his museum and generously contributed to it, and informs them that he has now been able to add many valuable specimens, and has arranged the whole museum systematically in two rooms fitted up for the purpose and ornamented with shells etc...He has now collected together Minerals, Shells, Petrifications, Incrustations, Crystalisations, Spars, Marles and many curious Fossils,Mosses, Lichens, and plants of spontaneous growth and a variety of Birds, Quadrupeds, Fishes and Coins, Medals, Antiques and curiosities originally belonging to Kendal Castle, sculptures from Furness Abbey, Basaltes from the Giant's Causeway, Musical Stones from Kendal Fell and some curious specimens of mechanisms etc, etc. Admittance, ladies and gentlemen 1/- each; children of working people and servants 6d. Each. Open 7 am till 10 pm, Sundays excepted.[1]

William Todhunter's musical stones were not hornfels rock as found on and around Skiddaw but limestone collected locally. Some forms of limestone ring very sweetly when struck, but being composed of petrified fragments of sea shells they do have weak points and can crack, whereas the slate-based metamorphosed hornfels rarely breaks when struck face-on. The instrument Todhunter built is now lost or unidentified so there's no knowing how refined

---

[1] Brears, p122.

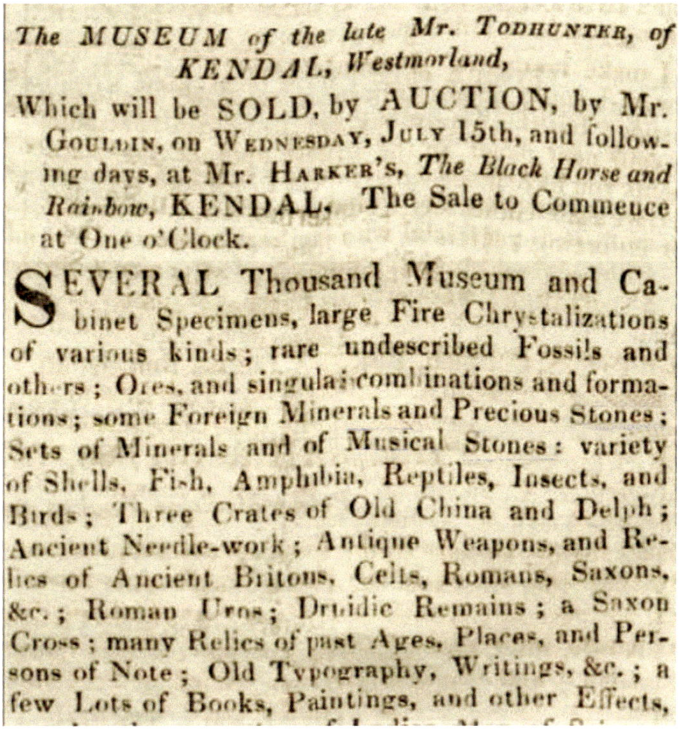

> The MUSEUM of the late Mr. TODHUNTER, of KENDAL, Westmorland,
>
> Which will be SOLD, by AUCTION, by Mr. GOULDIN, on WEDNESDAY, JULY 15th, and following days, at Mr. HARKER'S, *The Black Horse and Rainbow*, KENDAL. The Sale to Commence at One o'Clock.
>
> SEVERAL Thousand Museum and Cabinet Specimens, large Fire Chrystalizations of various kinds; rare undescribed Fossils and others; Ores, and singular combinations and formations; some Foreign Minerals and Precious Stones; Sets of Minerals and of Musical Stones: variety of Shells, Fish, Amphibia, Reptiles, Insects, and Birds; Three Crates of Old China and Delph; Ancient Needle-work; Antique Weapons, and Relics of Ancient Britons, Celts, Romans, Saxons, &c.; Roman Urns; Druidic Remains; a Saxon Cross; many Relics of past Ages, Places, and Persons of Note; Old Typography, Writings, &c.; a few Lots of Books, Paintings, and other Effects,

*Figure 2.2. Announcement of auction of the contents of the Todhunter Museum, 1835. Carlisle Journal Saturday 11th July 1835.*

or in good tune it was, but we do know that he went a step further than Peter Crosthwaite with his musical stones. Probably taking note of Crosthwaite's successful marketing of the aeolian harps, he began to produce more of his lithophones with the intention of selling them to the public. They were described as having a tone "more sonorous than notes struck on cast steel"[2], the comparison being to the sound of bells or chimes as there were few if any tuned metallophones around in Britain at that time. How many of his limestone instruments Todhunter made or sold is not recorded, but it may be that some of the musical stones turning up in house sales and auctions originated in his workshop.

Following William Todhunter's death, sometime in the early 1830s, an advertisement appeared in the local press in July 1835 announcing an auction of his museum collection (Figure 2.2). The list of items to be sold included "sets of minerals and musical stones", implying that this may have included a number of unsold instruments as well as Todhunter's own personal set.[3] It's also possible that a set was kept in the family, as in 1866 an evening of entertainment at the Workington Assembly Room was reported which included a Mr Todhunter playing Irish airs on the musical stones, but there is no clear evidence of a family connection.[4]

---

[2] Brears, p123.
[3] Carlisle Journal, Saturday 11h July 1835 p2.
[4] Whitehaven Advertiser, Tuesday 20th November 1866.

MUSIC STONES

### Joseph Richardson

Thirty miles away in Keswick, living close to the Crosthwaite Museum in the early 1800s was the Richardson family, John, his wife Dinah and their seven children. Only four of the children would survive into adulthood and the oldest of these, Joseph, was to go on to build one of the most extraordinary lithophones the world has seen. Along with three of his sons, Joseph Richardson was to present well in excess of a thousand public performances across the British Isles as well as in Europe on what eventually became known as the Rock, Bell and Steel Band, an instrument which can be still be seen today in Keswick Museum alongside Peter Crosthwaite's Music Stones (Fig. 2.3).

Joseph Richardson was born in 1792, probably in the village of Crosthwaite, moving with his family to Keswick when he was a young child. His father John was a miller and worked in the Richardson corn mill in the vicinity of the Crosthwaite Museum. Living where they did, Joseph would certainly have been aware of the raucous musical activities regularly taking place at the Crosthwaite Museum. Peter Crosthwaite was still managing his museum and seeing and hearing him play his Music Stones would undoubtedly have had a bearing on Joseph's later decision, in his thirties, to build his own stone instrument on a much larger scale. There was also another local man who the young Joseph Richardson heard playing musical stones,

*Figure 2.3. Joseph Richardson's Rock Harmonicon in its final version, showing the added upper rows of steel bars and bells. Photograph Mike Adcock, Courtesy of Keswick Museum and Art Gallery.*

an amateur naturalist called William Greenip. According to Peter Crosthwaite's grandson, John Fisher Crosthwaite, writing years later, the young Richardson had been kept amused by hearing Greenip play his set of stones which, Crosthwaite claimed, were an imitation of his grandfather's Music Stones.[5] For Joseph Richardson, in seeing these examples of musical stones the seeds were perhaps being sown what was eventually to become a remarkable musical career.

Initially the Richardson family lived in a house adjoining the museum but later moved to one opposite, but still well within earshot of the Crosthwaite family and its musical outpourings from a combination of drums, Chinese gong, barrel-organ and Music Stones, as well as the more gentle but persistent sound emitting from the aeolian harp at the open window. It may well be that hearing this assortment of sounds was itself an inspiration for Joseph Richardson's much later decision to supplement his own stone instrument with bells, metal bars and foot-operated drums.

From an early age Joseph had shown an aptitude for music. It was said that he had the ability to immediately produce something musical from any instrument he picked up and he became a relatively skilful player of the violin, flute and pipes. Whether he received any tuition isn't recorded but he was certainly becoming acquainted with a wide range of music as he grew up. One story which emerged years later illustrates an early inventive approach to musical instrumentation. Joseph had wanted to make his own violin and, in need of some suitable wood for the purpose, had proceeded to saw up a mahogany-topped table in the family home, one which unfortunately happened to be a particular favourite of his mother. If true, this endeavour might itself have been influenced by seeing Peter Crosthwaite's Music Stones, representing as they did a decidedly *ad hoc* approach to musical instrument-making, creating something from materials that were readily available. The story of Joseph's early venture into instrument-building has not been substantiated, though other contemporary reports claimed that the young Richardson did actually build a violin, but without mentioning whether the resultant instrument incorporated recycled mahogany.

Joseph Richardson was to become a stonemason by trade. There had been other stonemasons in the family including possibly his father earlier in life, so this could have had a bearing on his choice of career. As he moved into adulthood he may well have continued to pursue his musical interests in one way or another, but it was not until his mid-thirties that he began working on what was to become his major achievement, the instrument he called a rock harmonicon. Being a stonemason with musical ability was certainly the perfect skill set for anyone aspiring to build an instrument of this kind, there being an intrinsic link between the two activities. Anyone working with stone will be aware of the sound produced by the chisel and this awareness will feed into the choices being made in the stone-carving process, providing essential information about the quality of the stone being worked. The sound will change depending on the force and angle at which the chisel strikes, making listening to the stone central to the skill itself. For Richardson to now apply the skills he had acquired over the years to the construction of a musical instrument would certainly have faced him with unprecedented and considerable challenges. Precision in the use of his tools would prove essential when a small margin of error

---

[5] Carlisle Journal, Friday 2nd November 1849, p4.

would determine whether a note was in or out of tune, while at the same time he would need to rely on his own listening and judgement to assess when it rang true.

When Richardson decided to start work building a lithophone, on a scale Peter Crosthwaite had never dreamt of, he first had to establish the most suitable rock to use. Through seeking out suitable stone as part of his daily work he would have known the different types of stone available to him in the local terrain, but the specifications for the task he was taking on now were going to be markedly different from the requirements of the building work to which he was accustomed. A feature in a local newspaper gave a colourful impression of what was involved, indicating that from the outset things did not run smoothly. From the detail given it must be assumed that Richardson, or perhaps a member of his family, was the source.

> The stones which he first collected…did not suit his purpose, and thus, at the very commencement of his undertaking a large proportion of time and labour was necessarily lost. This would have almost been sufficient to have dispirited an ordinary mind; but it only served to increase Mr Richardson's efforts, and to convince him that with industry and perseverance success lay within his reach. Having discovered that the stones best calculated for his purpose were only to be met with amongst the rocks of the mighty Skiddaw, he began to explore the mountain in search of the musical treasures which it contained. The inventor bore the stones from the mountain to a considerable distance home upon his back; he had afterwards to reduce many of them, to shape them, and to try their varied tones, before he could pronounce a favourable opinion on their merits. This was a work of immense labour and time, and required much determination and industry for its accomplishment, and after many hard days' labour in the mountains, Mr Richardson denied himself the repose which exhausted nature required, and spent whole nights, after his family had retired to rest, in hammering and chiselling the rough stones, and in selecting and arranging them, ere he brought to its present state the sweet-toned instrument which cost him thirteen years of unwearied labour and perseverance, under circumstances few minds, not possessed of uncommon fortitude, could have surmounted.[6]

After a period of testing different types of stone Joseph Richardson concluded, like Crosthwaite, that the hornfels rock, sometimes referred to more specifically as horneblende, had the best sound. He would have soon discovered, however, that two pieces of the same stone found in the same location will not necessarily ring with the same quality and, for reasons which are not always obvious, some will not ring at all.

Once Richardson had settled on the best stone available for the job, and that seems likely to have come from an area called Sinen Gill, to the east of the Skiddaw slopes, he then began the process of extracting it. Unlike Crosthwaite who gathered his Music Stones where he found them in the landscape, Richardson would need to quarry the slabs from the rock face because of the number required. Although these would then need to be cut to the correct length and width, the thickness of the slabs was determined by the layers constituting the hornfels rock, whose thickness was reasonably consistent and so needed no further attention.

---

[6] The Atlas, No.789, Vol XV!, Saturday 26th June 1841, p416.

*Figure 2.4. Early photograph of the Richardsons' cottage in Applethwaite, with the byre where the rock harmonicon was built at the near end. With thanks to Tony Gibbs who photographed the picture.*

By 1827, when he started work on the new instrument, Richardson had been married for eleven years and he and his wife Elizabeth had produced six children, though a daughter, also named Elizabeth, had died in infancy and also one of twin sons. Another baby was born the same year and three more were to follow. The family lived in a cottage outside Keswick, in the village of Applethwaite which, although slightly closer to Sinen Gill than Keswick itself, still meant carrying the required amount of stone a considerable distance (Figure 2.4). Whereas Peter Crosthwaite was quite modest in his ambitions for the Music Stones, merely wishing to create a two octave instrument upon which he could play simple melodies, Joseph Richardson was planning something on a much grander scale, wishing to build a stone instrument suitable for any kind of music to be played upon it. This meant it needed to be chromatic, enabling the players to perform in any key of their choosing, and he decided it should span at least five octaves.

Richardson's plan was to set out the slabs in the same arrangement as a piano keyboard, a similar solution to the one later used for western xylophones, marimbas, glockenspiels and vibraphones, so in this alone Richardson was a pioneer. The two rows of slabs, corresponding to the white and black notes of the piano, were to lie on straw, supported by a large wooden frame (Figure 2.5). The challenge Joseph Richardson had set himself was a massive one: Peter Crosthwaite had taken six months to produce a set of sixteen moderately sized stones but Richardson's instrument was going to require sixty-one, many of them longer than Crosthwaite's, with the lower-pitched bars over a metre in length. Because of their size, each having a width of approximately 8cms, the instrument would need to have a total length of

*Figure 2.5. Close-up showing the hornfels slabs in position. Photograph: Mike Adcock. Courtesy of Keswick Museum and Art Gallery.*

nearly four metres. For an effective performance it would need to be played by three people, with music specially arranged accordingly.

The task of building the rock harmonicon was time consuming and perhaps even more onerous than Richardson had imagined. At first it was something he did in his spare time alongside his daily work as a stonemason. But as the years went by it began to take over Joseph Richardson's life, becoming something of an obsession and one which proved to be detrimental to his paid work. The family income fell, making ends meet become increasingly difficult and times became hard. The Richardson's oldest child, Ann, was born in 1817 and their oldest son John in 1819, so during that period the two siblings, by now teenagers, may have been able to provide some income to the family coffers, but there were many mouths to feed. John was the only one of the sons to follow in his father's footsteps and become a stonemason; the younger sons, Joseph, Samuel and Robert, enthralled by the new instrument as it began to take shape, were instead to share the musical path which Joseph was to take. When the first version of the rock harmonicon was completed in 1840 it was initially only Joseph and Samuel who practised with their father on the instrument, in the hope of being able one day to perform for others. The three of them learned together how to play it, and also how to play it together, the rock harmonicon being almost unique among instruments in requiring three operatives. Robert, the youngest of the boys was only twelve at that time but it wasn't long before he was a match for the others and in time became the most musically proficient of them all, eventually replacing his father Joseph in performances.

When Joseph Richardson and his two sons felt they had reached a sufficient level of proficiency playing the rock harmonicon they decided it was time to let others see it. Friends, neighbours and anybody else who they thought might be interested were invited in for a demonstration and, the reaction being decidedly positive, word soon spread and they began to receive visits from a number of eminent visitors to the area, including musicians, writers and even the Bishop of London. Alerted by the attention being paid by such dignitaries, the local press began to take an interest, noting that these visitors

> ....highly eulogised the surprising powers of the Harmonicon, and expressed their astonishment at sounds so rich and sweet being drawn from materials so rude and unmusical in their appearance. On the recommendation of several of the distinguished visitors who witnessed the performances of Mr Richardson's sons upon the Harmonicon, he was, though we believe somewhat reluctantly, induced to bring it before the public.[7]

This reluctance to perform publicly, stemming from Joseph Richardson's modest disposition, is a feature of the story which is repeated in a number of contemporary news reports, including another in the *Cumberland Pacquet*, whose editorial staff proved to be valuable supporters of the Richardsons' cause.

> Mr Richardson's modesty would not allow him to flatter himself that his labours and ingenuity had produced an object worthy of public notice, and the instrument, as far as his views went, was doomed to obscurity... The sole use of the Harmonicon was so far merely to teach his sons the performance of music, and to sweeten the hours of relaxation from severe labour by listening to its enchanting and animating tones.[8]

By all accounts Joseph Richardson was indeed a modest man, but laudable though these purely domestic intentions, "to sweeten the hours of relaxation", may have been, the lengths to which he went in order to perfect the instrument, the time it took and the sacrifices that were made on its behalf would suggest that he had his sights set on more than just home entertainment. His modesty may have prevented him from predicting national success with the instrument but his wife Elizabeth might well have had other views on reports that her husband had undertaken the project purely to benefit the family's leisure time, perhaps thinking that his time might have been better spent ensuring there was food on the table. More likely is that it was a matter of expectation management and that Richardson chose to underplay any hopes he may have had for fear of looking foolish if the whole thing was a miserable flop. However much he underplayed it, Richardson was clearly ambitious and well aware of the pioneering nature of what he was doing, in an age when a spirit of innovation was in the air and invention was celebrated. In his heart he must have believed this to be a risk worth taking, that in the long term this could pay off and that there was distinct possibility that they could achieve success. His family, it seems, were prepared to go along with that and share the dream.

---

[7] Cumberland Pacquet and Ware's Whitehaven Advertiser, Tuesday 1st December 1840, p3.
[8] Ibid.

## Messrs Richardson and Sons' Original Rock Band

Whether it was with reluctance or not, a suitable venue for the instrument to be exhibited was sought. The Crosthwaite Museum might have been an appropriate choice, but in the event it was another museum, the Hutton Museum, which agreed to display it. Thomas Hutton had died nine years earlier and the museum was now managed by one of his daughters, Hannah. Daniel Crosthwaite, still in charge of his father Peter's museum, may well have felt somewhat slighted to discover that it was the Hutton Museum, set up in opposition to his family's own establishment. which was now to present to the public a bigger and better stone instrument than the one made by Peter Crosthwaite, fifty-five years earlier. There does indeed seem to have been a continuing family rivalry between the Crosthwaites and the Huttons, illustrated by the Hutton gravestones at Crosthwaite Church which bear the inscription stating that the family members were of '*the* MUSEUM' in Keswick.[9] Joseph Richardson's choice of the Hutton Museum could also have played a part in the lead-up to a public dispute some years later between Daniel Crosthwaite's son John Fisher Crosthwaite and Richardson after the former had taken over management of the Crosthwaite Museum. For Hannah Hutton the interest shown in the new exhibit must have been very welcome as the museum's fortunes had been in steady decline and within a few years it was to close permanently.

Once installed into the Hutton Museum the rock harmonicon must have made quite an impression. Almost four metres in length, the rock harmonicon would have commanded an imposing presence with its five octave stone keyboard mounted on the timber-framed superstructure. Joseph, accompanied by two of his sons, nineteen-year-old Joseph and Samuel (fifteen), gave regular demonstrations of the instrument's capabilities to visitors and news of it spread, quickly, both by word of mouth and through the increasingly popular and influential local newspapers, happy to sing its praises.

> The largest and most complete set of musical stones that were perhaps ever collected in this, or any other country, may now be seen in the Hutton's Museum, Keswick…. Tourists no more think of leaving the capital of the Lake District without seeing these truly astonishing musical stones…than they do of leaving without seeing Flintoff's celebrated model relief map of the area, or Crosthwaite's far-famed museum. These stones…are worked by Richardson and his two sons, and they at once astonish every visitor who listens to their enchanting and perfect music. In fact, any piece of music set to the pianoforte can, with the greatest delicacy and correctness, be played upon what the collector has so happily denominated the Rock Harmonica [*sic*].[10]

Boosted by the success of the rock harmonicon's debut at the Hutton Museum where it was installed for several weeks, it was decided to take it further afield, performing on a more commercial basis. Joseph Richardson arranged for them to travel to Whitehaven, a coastal town just under thirty miles from Keswick, where they were booked to appear daily for several days in a large room above a public house, the Queen's Arms. Getting there would present a logistical challenge and, in anticipation of this, the large and weighty instrument had been designed to break down into sections to facilitate transportation and these were then to be packed into specially constructed storage boxes. Towards the end of November 1840 they

---

[9] Brears, p122.
[10] Cumberland Pacquet, Tuesday 28th July 1840, p3.

NEW MUSICAL INSTRUMENT
CALLED
**THE ROCK HARMONICON,**
WILL BE EXHIBITED IN THE
*QUEEN'S ARMS LARGE ROOM, MARKET PLACE, WHITEHAVEN.*

**JOSEPH RICHARDSON,**
*(Who is a Native of Underskiddaw, near Keswick),*

MOST humbly begs leave to announce to the admirers of Harmony, and to the Public in general, that the ROCK HARMONICON is an entirely New and Novel Musical Instrument of his own Invention, the construction of which has occupied a very considerable portion of his time during the last Thirteen Years. Although rude in its appearance, it is yet found capable of producing tones of the sweetest Harmony and Richness. The Rock Harmonicon is composed of an extensive variety of Musical Stones, selected from the remoter parts of the majestic Skiddaw, the collecting and arranging of which have been a most assiduous and difficult undertaking. It extends to a compass of nearly Six Octaves, accompanied with all the additional Semitones. Altogether it is perhaps one of the rarest and most singular curiosities ever witnessed, and as a Musical Instrument, exhibits a striking contrast to all others in the simplicity of its construction, and the rudeness of its external appearance.

J. R. and his Two Sons, who can Play a great variety of favourite Airs, &c. &c. on the above Instrument, will be in attendance at the Queen's Arms Large Room, daily, from 6 o'Clock in the Morning till 10 'clock at Night.

Nov. 20th, 1840.

*Figure 2.6. Announcement of Whitehaven residency. Courtesy of Andy Aliffe.*

Manchester April 19th 1841.
Mr Joseph Richardson
To the Directors of the Manchester
Mechanics' Institution, Dr
To use of Room for exhibiting the Rock
Harmonicon, from April 19th to 24th £2..2..0
Settled same date
Geo Lawton

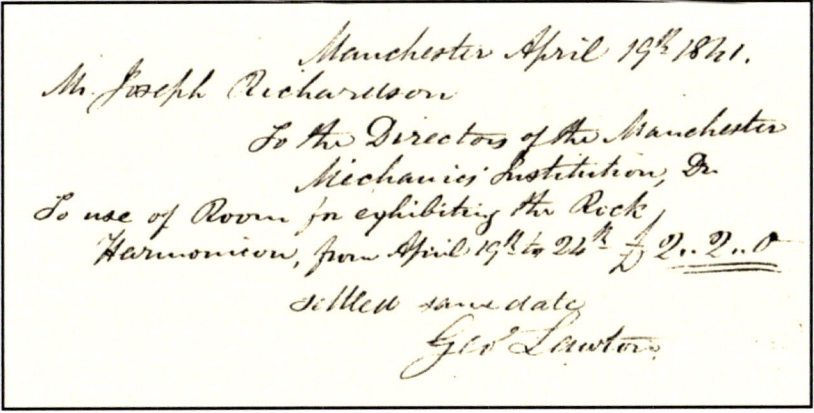

*Figure 2.7. Receipt for hire of room at Mechanics' Institute, Manchester for a six day stay. Courtesy of Andy Aliffe.*

were ready to set off, with wagon and horses, for the first professional appearance of Messrs Richardson and Sons' Original Rock Band.

As in Keswick, the rock harmonicon was on display throughout the day in Whitehaven, with Joseph and his two sons again remaining in attendance to give intermittent performances. A long day it was too, starting at a surprisingly early 6.00am and playing (presumably with a reasonable number of breaks) until 10.00 at night. In Keswick most residents would probably have been familiar with the notion of a stone instrument, Crosthwaite's Music Stones having been on display in the museum for many years, but for many in Whitehaven, and in places they were to play subsequently, this was indeed a novelty. The initial run was again so well attended and received that their residency was extended by a week, though the opening time was put back until 9.00am. The *Whitehaven Herald* was ebullient in its praise, declaring that any fears that the Richardsons' appearance might be overlooked by the public due to their lack of performing experience proved to be unwarranted, though it was prepared to express some mild criticism in respect of the instrument's tuning:

> Every spectator who has beheld the simple yet astonishing instrument has gone away delighted and wonder-struck at the notes drawn from it by the Masters Richardson, and at the skill and taste which they exercise in drawing the most delicious harmony from the rudest of nature's materials. The whole results are highly triumphant. It is probable that further experience and attention may enable the proprietor to attune the instrument to greater perfection than at present attained, but even as it remains at this moment it will be found to surprise both the unprofessional and the cognoscenti, and to amply repay inspection and a visit.[11]

The *Cumberland Pacquet and Ware's Whitehaven Advertiser*, having been the first newspaper to report the launch of the rock harmonicon, thought it warranted further coverage, extolling the virtues of the "wonderful instrument" and its inventor and advising him to "carry the productions of his ingenuity and labour to larger towns, where he will have an opportunity of exhibiting it to more refined tastes".[12] Days later, just such an opportunity arose and the Richardsons were invited to bring their rock harmonicon to Liverpool, to commence a short residency in mid-December.

The journey from Whitehaven to Liverpool was almost certainly undertaken using the steam packet which operated between the two ports, possibly an incentive in accepting that particular booking. The venue on this occasion was Miss Knibb's Commercial Warehouse, 15 Bold Street. Once again the local press was on their side, with the *Liverpool Standard and Commercial Advertiser* recommending their readers to go along.

> We were yesterday favoured with a sight and hearing of a most extraordinary musical instrument…and we most cordially recommend our readers to pay Mr. Richardson, the inventor, a visit. Several musical men in Liverpool have already heard it, and all declare it to be the most singular invention they have ever met with, not only from the novelty and singularity of its construction, but also for the strange and wild quality of its tone.[13]

---

[11] Whitehaven Herald, Sunday 8th November 1840, p11.
[12] Cumberland Pacquet, Tuesday 1st December 1840, p3.
[13] Liverpool Standard and Commercial Advertiser, Tuesday 15th December 1840, p7

Once again it proved to be success, prompting more interest in the local press, with the *Liverpool Mercury* expanding a feature on the Richardson band to include reference to the ancient Chinese use of sonorous stone and quoting a piece written by the editor of the *Liverpool Journal*, a "native of Cumberland", recalling intrepid visitors to Cumbria being treated to musical renditions on ringing stones gathered long before Richardson had the idea:

> We recollect one of much older date, situate where few amateur or professors would be likely to go in search of one, near the top of Scawfell Pike, at least 3000 feet above the level of the sea. That mountain is older than Skiddaw, consisting of a very fine sienite, which splits into long prisms, almost as hard and heavy as iron. On the site we have indicated, some musical shepherd has beguiled his time, by selecting a series of fragments, which give out tones when struck, and which are shown by the guides to the few visitors to the precipitous region.[14]

The *Liverpool Mercury* article also offered some positive criticism to Joseph Richardson, recommending some attention should be paid to the tuning of the rock harmonicon and also that one head of the mallets should be covered with leather to offer the possibility of a softer the tone. Subject to those refinements the article found further potential in the instrument and was fulsome in its recommendation:

> If the stone harmonicon can be *perfectly* tuned (of which we are by no means certain) it would be no difficult mechanical problem to render it a keyboard instrument, like the pianoforte or organ.

> In conclusion, we recommend a visit to Mr Richarson's harmonicon to all those who are fond of the "concord of sweet sounds," and all who regard ingenuity and perseverance as the proper objects of public patronage.[15]

Evidently others were recognizing the potential for this innovative instrument to reach a far wider audience and this must have come as great encouragement to Joseph Richardson and his sons. Announcements advertising the Liverpool appearances referred to the three sons playing, so evidently the youngest, Robert, not yet in his teens, was now performing alongside his older brothers. Joseph Richardson took note of the press comments made about the instrument and some variation in mallet heads was introduced.

Stone, when struck, has an intrinsically brittle sound, somewhere between the relative warmth of wooden instruments such as xylophones and marimbas and the sharp, bright metallic tone of glockenspiels, though not having the sustain of a metal bar. Having a choice of mallets, covering the head with leather and possibly felt, would have certainly broadened the potential tonal range of the instrument, introducing the possibility of a warmer, less strident sound. The Richardsons were to find that using different types of wood for the mallets also changed the tone, with ash and elm proving best for the middle notes and the extremely hard and dense lignum vitae used to play the high treble. For the bass notes a sturdier hammer-shaped beater was used. Played with commitment the rock harmonicon could be surprisingly loud and

---
[14] Liverpool Mercury, Friday 25th December 1840, p6
[15] Ibid.

the Richardsons found they needed to play with a degree of restraint for fear that windows, already vibrating, might shatter.

The Richardson band presented a varied programme of music in their performances, and in doing so presumably hoped it would appeal to a wide audience. The repertoire included popular dances from the time, such as schottisches and quadrilles, traditional airs from Scotland and Ireland and also arrangements of classical works from the likes of Handel, Beethoven and Rossini. What is remarkable about this is not only that neither Joseph Richardson nor his sons had received any significant musical training, but that they were having to invent the rules of how to play this large and cumbersome new instrument. The challenge in arranging these established musical favourites, for three players playing side by side on a five octave stone keyboard with notes about four times the width of those on a piano, was a considerable one. Their performances clearly stood up to the test and whilst early press reports picked up on initial teething problems with the instrument and commented on the humble background of the performers, there is no suggestion that their musical renditions were in any way inferior. As the three men played more together the performances would certainly have improved and they also seemed to have been happy to take advice when and where it was offered. During their stay in Liverpool, which because of a series of extensions lasted almost three months, they had the fortune to meet a professional musician who helped them to further refine their act.

John Davies was a church organist and teacher of organ, piano and violin. He attended one of the early performances given by the Richardsons in the city, was very impressed and met with them afterwards, which led to him giving advice about playing and on ways of extending their repertoire. Davies also agreed to perform publicly with the band and this was such a success that another collaborative performance was advertised for Wednesday 27th January 1841, the local press reporting the presence of a "crowded and fashionable audience".[16] John Davies continued to perform regularly with the Richardsons during the weeks of their Liverpool residency and they were to play again together the following year in Dublin.

Local journalists writing copy about the Richardsons' concerts were always glad of any opportunity to mention the appearance in the audience of the great and good, their presence presumably denoting a degree of quality and sophistication in the whole enterprise, but shortly before the final performance of their residence in Liverpool a touching open letter of thanks appeared in at least one newspaper, setting a rather different tone. It came from teachers of six different schools in the area and seems to indicate that the men from Keswick still had their feet firmly on the ground and their hearts in the right place.

> Sir, we…being the teachers of the children on connexion with the charity schools, who have benefited, and at the same time been delighted at hearing the sweet music of your admirable invention, the rock harmonicon, beg, on our own and their behalf, to return our sincere thanks for your liberality, in granting gratuitous admission to those to whom, on other terms, the pleasure must have been sacrificed. Having been made acquainted with the history of the invention, the children have had an opportunity of learning that industry and perseverance can extract sweet melody and dulcet tones

---

[16] Liverpool Mail, Tuesday 2nd February 1841, p3.

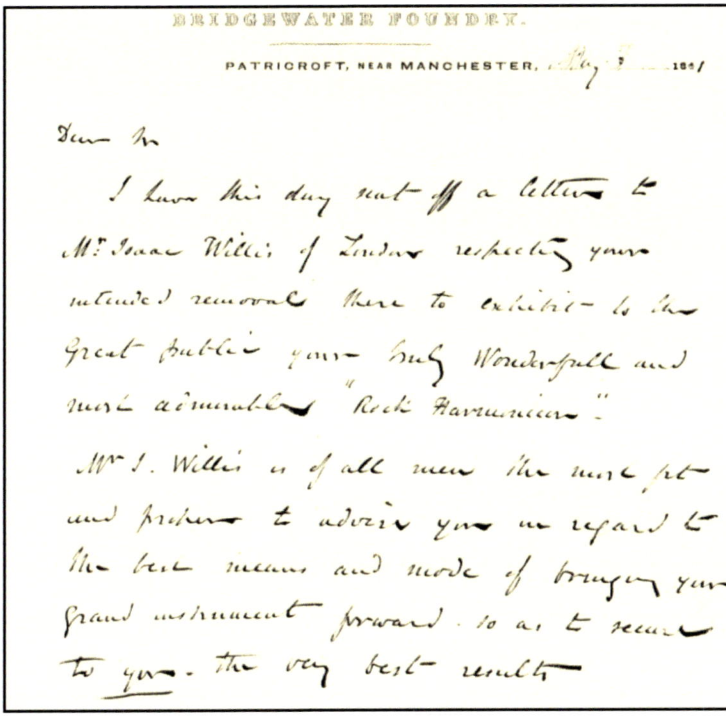

*Figure 2.8. Extract from James Nasmyth's letter to Joseph Richardson. Courtesy of Andy Aliffe.*

even from rocks. With our sincere wish that your ingenuity and liberality may meet with its just reward, we have the honour to be, sir, your obedient humble servants....[17]

After Liverpool, Manchester was next, where the Richardson Rock Band (the name tended to vary as they went along) enjoyed another lengthy residence, this time at the Mechanics' Institute. Again the rock harmonicon was on display, with daily performances stretching over another lengthy period, this time two months, once more the result of a series of extended runs. How this affected the cancelled acts they presumably replaced isn't recorded, but for the Richardsons success seemed to breed success in each location they found themselves. Word of mouth probably played a big part, but having the support of the local press, who seemed keen to promote this new phenomenon, was also crucial. While newspapers had been around for a good while, by the mid-nineteenth century they were becoming more affordable and therefore increasingly important in the dissemination of not just news but of wider cultural activities. But what also helped to spread the word further afield about the Richardson Rock Band was the practice of local newspapers to cite or reprint stories from other newspapers, both local and nationwide, through a form of syndication. So a feature on the band in the *Cumberland Pacquet and Ware's Whitehaven Advertiser* might appear shortly afterwards in the *Liverpool Standard and Commercial Advertiser*, the *Morning Post* in London or even sometimes abroad. As well as helping the Richardsons secure new bookings, this also meant there was already some awareness and

---

[17] *Liverpool Mercury*, Friday 12th March 1841, p7.

interest in what they were doing in advance of their arrival. With their performances being so well received, a growing demand and more bookings in the offing, the four men must have felt that their long and hard toil was finally proving to have been worthwhile.

The band's first appearance in Manchester was on 9th April 1841 at a private launch to which the press were invited. Again the musicians impressed, their humble background not being referred to as a way of excusing or qualifying their playing ability, but for the positive qualities it brought to the recital:

The youths are evidently clever musicians, although possessing much of their father's rusticity; but they have played their instrument from their childhood, long before it was ever supposed that the world, beyond Keswick, would hear of it; and their natural enthusiasm gives a charm to the performance which is seldom met with in public exhibitions.[18]

Four days later they performed at the Institute's 17th anniversary tea party and concert "when a very large and respectable party assembled, of members and friends, including a good sprinkling of ladies."[19] Among those attending was the renowned engineer James Nasmyth, whose particular contribution to the ongoing industrial revolution was the development of the steam hammer. He was impressed by the rock harmonicon and after the Richardsons' concert Nasmyth engaged in conversation with the performers which, following their fortuitous meeting with John Davies in Liverpool, proved again to be to their advantage. On returning home Nasmyth was moved to write to a friend of his in London, Isaac Willis, telling him about his find and suggesting that Willis might assist the performers in procuring bookings in the capital.

This new contact was to be an important one for the Richardsons. Willis was involved in the music business in both London and Dublin, coming to it through his older brother, John Willis who was a flute-maker. Isaac Willis helped to market his brother's instruments which led to him setting up in business, selling not only flutes but also pianos and other instruments, as well as publishing sheet music and promoting concerts. Having written to Willis, Nasmyth then wrote to Joseph Richardson recommending that he should endeavour to work with his friend (Figure 2.8).

> Dear Sir, I have this day sent off a letter to Mr Isaac Willis of London respecting your intended removal there to exhibit to the great public your very wonderful and much admired "Rock Harmonicon". Mr I.Willis is of all men the most fit and proper to advise you in regard to the best means and of bringing your instrument forward so as to receive to you the very best results. Mr Willis is a man of the very first respectability and honour, and whatever he recommends you may proceed with the utmost confidence, as he has been for many years the principal charge of their musical novelties which have most successfully attracted the notice of the public. I have requested him to write either direct or through me, and I would strongly advise not to commit yourself with any other party until you either hear from or see him.

---

[18] Manchester Chronicle, cited in Cumberland Pacquet, Tuesday 13th April 1841, p2.
[19] Manchester Times and Manchester and Salford Advertiser and Chronicle, Saturday 17th April 1841, p2.

The wonderful merits of your admirable instrument cannot fail to be well appreciated by the London public, who are a very musical people. But the great point to aim at, is for you to place yourself in the very best position to display the greatest advantage of your ingenuity and skill, and I know of no more certain mode of doing so than placing yourself under the advice of so excellent and able man as Mr Isaac Willis, who is at the very heart of the musical world in London. I would have given you a letter to the Polytechnic Institute, but Mr Willis is worth a thousand such. Wishing you all and ever success with which your merits deserve.

James Nasmyth[20]

The Richardsons remained in Manchester until the beginning of June 1841, performing daily at the Mechanics Institute, morning, afternoon and evening. They had already been away from home for seven months having initially left Keswick for a three-week trip and they might have been expected to now return for a well-deserved break, but it was not to be. By 12th June the band had booked into the Morlands Hotel and Tavern, 23 Dean Street, Soho, in London's West End, anticipating the next stage in their musical career, which would see them based not in Keswick but in London.

---
[20] Phillips 1, p48.

## Chapter Three

# A stonemason, a boatman and a fiddler
## Two cousins, William Irwin and the sound of slate

**William Bowe**

While the Richardson men were setting their sights on London performances there were others back in Cumbria taking up the challenge of what could be achieved by converting a set of suitably tuned slabs of ringing stone into a musical instrument. One such was a man called William Bowe, also from Keswick and who, like Richardson, was a stonemason. In what could seem like uncanny synchronicity given the thirteen years of toil Joseph Richardson had spent developing and building his rock harmonicon, Bowe, with the assistance of a friend, came up with his own remarkably similar instrument less than twelve months after Richardson had presented his to the public for the first time. A five octave instrument, approximately the same size and therefore also requiring three musicians to play it, Bowe even took Richardson's name for it, calling it a rock harmonicon. Perhaps to avoid comparisons with the original, William Bowe chose to launch his harmonicon not in Keswick but in Carlisle in April 1841. It seems that Bowe himself wasn't one of those playing, as an announcement in a local paper informed the readership that "for a few days only" Messrs Bowe and Graves "have engaged three musicians to perform on this Novel Instrument, so that they can expect to be enabled to give a Musical Treat as rare as it is delightful"[1] The venue was Mr Sawyer's Large Room in Fisher Street and was above a chemist's shop. The following month they played in Newcastle and it evidently went down well:

> The music performed upon the Rock Harmonicon consisted of Strauss's and other waltzes, and some of the favourite national and local airs, and popular ballads - music of the day, arranged for the three performers by one of their number. Although the room was very much crowded, and the sound in consequence greatly injured, the general effect of the instrument was such as to give the liveliest satisfaction to the audience, who manifested their pleasure by encoring every piece. The Messrs. Bowe, Walker & Graves have now removed the Rock Harmonicon to the Academy of Arts, in Blackett Street, where it is exhibited and performed upon daily; and we sincerely trust they will meet with the success they so well deserve.[2]

A month later, and rather surprisingly given the warm reception given to the performance, an announcement appeared in the *Cumbrian Pacquet and Ware's Whitehaven Advertiser* under the headline "Musical Stones For Sale":

> After some years of research and unceasing perseverance a most superior set of musical stones, collected upon the Majestic Skiddaw, consisting of five octaves, with

---

[1] Carlisle Journal, Saturday 24th April 1841, p2
[2] Aliffe p38 citing "Records of remarkable events, connected with the Borough of Gateshead May 22nd 1841"

all the semitones, has been collected by William Bowe, guide and boatman, by whom they are now on sale, and may be seen and heard at the Joseph Bowe, King's Head Inn, Keswick. Any further information may be obtained by applying to William Bowe, guide and boatman, Keswick, the owner of the musical stones, who will also treat for the sale thereof.[3]

William Bowe being described not as a stonemason but as "a guide and boatman" is an indication of how the story then becomes rather harder to follow. It transpires that William Bowe had a cousin who was also named William Bowe and it was he who was the mountain guide and boatman. The potential for confusion here is exacerbated by the knowledge that this second William was also in possession of a rock harmonicon, with which he later toured and continued to do so for some years to come. Why then, should this announcement of the sale refer to him, William the guide and boatman, just prior to him performing widely on it? One possibility is that the two cousins worked together on building both harmonicons and then decided to sell one of them, with the William Bowe referred to in the announcement merely taking charge of the sale, but this is purely guesswork.

## The other William Bowe

Unlike his cousin the stonemason, William Bowe the guide and boatman did perform himself on the rock harmonicon in the concerts he gave, alongside two other men, and these took place principally in the north-east of England and in Scotland. Again, it seems significant that Bowe chose new pastures to present the rock harmonicon, as his cousin had done, Joseph Richardson having not yet secured any bookings in those regions. The performances, like the instrument itself, seem to have been modelled on the pattern set by the Richardsons, with a similar repertoire of light classics, local airs and popular dance tunes, though the impression given was that this was an original idea:

> It may not be generally known that on the mountain of Saddleback, near Keswick, there are found long thin stones, possessing most musical and striking tones. A very ingenious and meritous person in Keswick, one of the Lake guides, William Bowe, has, with great labour, selected such a number of these stones that he has been able to combine such a variety of tones as to nearly equal a pianoforte, and to enable him to play with great sweetness and effect a number of tunes...Many families from Edinburgh last summer heard the Rock Harmonicon (from one of whom this notice comes). And Mr Bowe is to be very shortly in Edinburgh to exhibit the effect of these stones. We are confident that a more singular or interesting exhibition has not been in this town for many years.[4]

Whether the 1841 sale of the instrument ever went ahead, meaning only one of the cousins continued to perform, or if they both retained their rock harmonicons is unclear, a question inevitably muddied by their sharing a name. It is also uncertain as to whether the Bowe cousins had collaborated in building their instruments. The newspaper announcement of the sale cited above mentions "years of research and unceasing perseverance" which implies that one or both rock harmonicons must have been in production at the same time as Richardson was still working on his own instrument. The Bowes would have been aware of the nature of

---
[3] Cumberland Pacquet, Tuesday 22nd June 1841, p1
[4] Caledonian Mercury, Saturday 26th November 1842, p3.

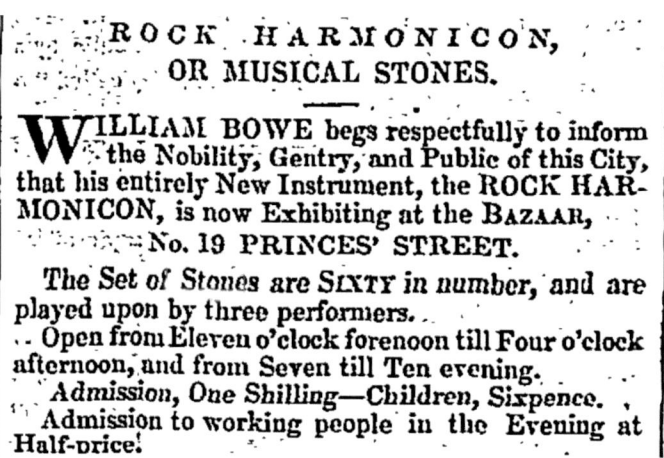

Figure 3.1. Newspaper announcement of William Bowe's appearance in Edinburgh. The Scotsman Saturday 24th 1842, p3.

Richardson's rock harmonicon and with one of them being a stonemason might well have known him personally, but whether their instruments were built with Richardson's assent or behind his back is not known. That the concept of the rock harmonicon was originally Richardson's is nevertheless acknowledged in one short item in Newcastle's *Journal* in November 1842:

> A rock harmonicon, in imitation of Richardson's celebrated instrument of that name has been lately brought to a considerable state of perfection, by Mr William Bowe, of Keswick.[5]

Whether the William Bowe referred to was a stonemason or a mountain guide and boatman was not specified.

## The Harrison Brothers

In the mid 1840s yet another instrument modelled on the Richardsons' rock harmonicon was produced, this time by the Harrison brothers from Ulverston, a town about forty miles south of Keswick, and they too were soon to be booked for concerts, featuring the now almost obligatory three male performers. It seems that their father had assembled some musical stones about thirty years earlier, possibly having seen those of Peter Crosthwaite, but there is no known account of whether he performed publicly with them or what happened to them. The Harrison brothers achieved some success by travelling south, including performances at the Royal Surrey Zoological Gardens in July 1845 where they played at a multi-media, *son et lumière* event:

---

[5] The Journal, Newcastle, Saturday 26th November 1842, p4.

> The Rock Harmonicon, by the Messrs. Harrison, will be heard at intervals during the day, and the fete will conclude with the Royal Aquatic Tableau, fifty-two feet high, in the centre of the lake, consisting of Transparencies, Illuminations, Devices, &c., and the most brilliant display of Fireworks ever witnessed.[6]

Although this report mentioned the brothers by name, press announcements began to often refer only to the rock harmonicon itself and not to who was playing it. In giving the instrument the same name that Joseph Richardson used and not naming the players there may have been a degree of ambiguity intended, leaving potential attendees unsure as to whether they were getting the originators of the rock harmonicon on stage or not.

## Sonorous slate

The various large rock harmonicons which began to be built in Keswick all used hornfels stone from the Skiddaw area, but there are two Cumbrian lithophones from around the same time which were made from dark blue-grey slate. It probably came from Elterwater Quarry or from nearby Langdale, close to Ambleside. One of these instruments, known as the Elterwater Set, is in Keswick Museum, along with Peter Crosthwaites's Music Stones and the Richardson instrument. (Figure 3.2) The other is in the present-day Kendal Museum, successor to the Todhunter Museum which closed in 1835. There appears to be no documentary evidence linking the two instruments, but they do have a visual similarity and both were machine cut rather than having been tooled by hand.

After William Todhunter's death and the sale of his Kendal museum collection in 1835, the Kendal Natural History and Scientific Society was formed with a view to opening a new museum in the town and this was realised three years later in 1838. Although some items from

*Figure 3.2. The Elterwater Set. Photograph: Mike Adcock, Courtesy of Keswick Museum and Art Gallery.*

---

[6] The Sun, London, Thursday 31st July 1845, p6.

*Figure 3.3. Lower end of slate lithophone in Kendal Museum. Reproduced with kind permission of Kendal Museum. Object accession number, KMS2016.6.*

Todhunter's collection found their way into the new museum, they did not include any of his limestone instruments and what happened to them isn't known. At some point however, the museum did take possession of the slate instrument which remains on display in the existing Kendal Museum (Figure 3.3). It would appear that this was originally a chromatic lithophone, with the notes probably set out like a piano keyboard, as with the rock harmonicons, but this is no longer the case. In its current state the slabs of slate are simply laid out on a table, supported by two lengths of rope. There are thirty-four notes, twenty-two of which represent a simple diatonic scale. The remaining twelve are insufficient to provide "black notes" for the whole instrument and anyway some of the pieces of slates are no longer properly in tune. Unfortunately there appears to be nothing in the museum's records to indicate the provenance of the instrument.

The Elterwater set of tuned slates, residing in Keswick, is smaller than the Kendal instrument, having only eighteen notes. Again the provenance is unclear, with different views on who might have owned it, with nobody sure of who assembled it in the first place. One theory is that it belonged to William Greenip, the Keswick naturalist who, according to John Fisher Crosthwaite, had played to the young Joseph Richardson.[7] This seems unlikely. John Fisher Crosthwaite described William Greenip's set of musical stones as having been "in imitation of the original" (ie his grandfather, Peter Crosthwaite's Music Stones), which would suggest they were not made from slate but from the same local hornfels stone which Crosthwaite had collected in 1785. Being a Keswick man it seems unlikely too that Greenip would have chosen to make an instrument from slate, taken from an area twenty miles away.

---

[7] Cumberland Pacquet, Tuesday 30th October 1849, p3.

## William Irwin

Another theory is that the Elterwater Set of slates had been owned by a renowned fiddler called William Irwin[8] and it is certainly on record that he owned a set of musical stones. Also from Keswick, born there in 1822, Irwin moved as a young man to Langdale, living for much of the time in Chapel Stile, close to Elterwater. Having taken an apprenticeship as a cooper he found work making barrels at the Elterwater Gunpowder Company, though it seems that much of his spare time was spent playing his fiddle at dances around the area, able to earn enough money from this for it to become half his income. Writing about his father in a private letter to folk-song collector Anne Gilchrist in 1926, his son Edwin described him as having been a "really first-rate country fiddler…for quite a long period he was the most popular fiddler in the district."[9]

Irwin also taught fiddle and wrote many fiddle tunes, some of which are still played to this day. A man of wide interests, particularly in relation to the natural world, Irwin was a collector of minerals and possessed a set of musical stones. Like others before him, his geological interests led him to explore the musical potential of the local stone, though whether he played them publicly isn't on record. Having almost certainly seen Peter Crosthwaite's Music Stones back in Keswick and then becoming a musician living and working very close to a slate quarry, it seems likely that Irwin would have been well aware of the sonorous properties of slate and perhaps been drawn to making his own lithophone from it, and yet one of Edwin Irwin's letters to Anne Gilchrist suggests that his father's instrument was not made from Elterwater slate:

> He was a Keswick man and collected, himself, one of the first sets of musical stones, from the bed of the river Greta.[10]

This was precisely the place where Peter Crosthwaite, according to his notebook, had found his Music Stones in 1785. It seems possible that Edwin Irwin, writing almost forty years after his father's death, was mistakenly recalling the details of the original find by Crosthwaite rather than the circumstances by which his father, William, obtained his musical stones. According to Edwin Irwin there was a family connection with Peter Crosthwaite: Hannah, Crosthwaite's wife, was apparently related to the Irwins and William Irwin remained in touch with Crosthwaite's grandson, John Fisher Crosthwaite, for many years, so Edwin Irwin may have heard family stories about Peter Crosthwaite's collecting stones and later remembered wrongly that it was his father who found his stones in the Greta. Something we can assume to be true is Edwin Irwin's memory of his father's musical stones having meant a great deal to him.

> My father lent his set to to a brother, who lost them. I have often heard him mourn the loss of the stones.[11]

William Irwin lived much of his life in or around the village of Chapel Stile, close to Elterwater and was buried there in 1889. He had married a woman from there called Dorothy Greenup

---

[8] The regularity at which the name William appears during this period may not be a lack of imagination when it came to naming, but a reflection of the popularity of Prince William, who was crowned William IV in 1830.
[9] Letter to Anne Gilchrist, 1st November 1926, Vaughan Williams Memorial Library.
[10] Letter to Anne Gilchrist, 24th November 1926, Vaughan Williams Memorial Library.
[11] Ibid.

*Figure 3.4. Three of William Irwin's fiddle tunes as transcribed by Anne Gilchrist. The titles of the lower two refer to the woman who was to become his wife, Dorothy Greenup. Courtesy of the Vaughan Williams Memorial Library.*

who had grown up at Baysbrown House, described at the time, for whatever reason, as a 'large manor of demons'[12] Dorothy's father Robert was a farmer (and Baysbrown Farm is still there today, with its own camping site) but records show that a man called John Greenup, also living at Baysbrown, was a slate quarry owner. A directory from 1829 mentions the area around Baysbrown as having "two extensive blue slate quarries."[13] So with the same slate as that used in the so-called Elterwater Set to be found almost literally on Irwin's doorstep there is a distinct possibility that the instrument in William Irwin's possession was made there, if not by him then possibly by someone from his in-laws' family. So without any concrete proof available, there nevertheless seems to be good circumstantial evidence to suggest that the Elterwater set in Keswick Museum once belonged to the still celebrated fiddler and composer, William Irwin.

Over a period of time the interest sparked by seeing Peter Crosthwaite's Music Stones on display in the Crosthwaite Museum had led to the production of a number of stone instruments, some known today, some perhaps forgotten or no longer in existence. By the early 1840s at least four large-scale rock harmonicons had been built in the Lake District area (and more were

---

[12] Parson & White's Directory of 1829.
[13] Glover, p76.

to follow), being used for public performances in different parts of Britain, drawing large audiences and receiving critical acclaim. However, making the running in the field was still undoubtedly Joseph Richardson's Original Rock Band. The strength of his innovative idea of an enlarged and more versatile version of Crosthwaite's Music Stones had from the start made an impression on all who witnessed it and its initial success was to continue for several years. Only a year after he had first shown it to a few people in the workshop alongside his cottage in Applethwaite, Joseph Richardson and his three sons were ready to present their pride and joy to the fashionable audiences of London itself.

# Chapter Four

# Richardson's Original Rock Band
## London and beyond

### Music in London

The London in which Joseph Richardson and his three sons, Joseph, Samuel and Robert found themselves in June 1841 was a richly musical city. Music was ubiquitous, not only in its pubs, clubs, dance halls and theatres but on the streets as well. Any thoughts that London was a relatively tranquil city before the invention of the internal combustion engine should be dispelled, music being so prevalent that while it was welcome entertainment for many it was also a frequent cause for complaint. Street-musicians were everywhere: there were ballad singers, organ-grinders, hurdy-gurdy players, bagpipers and a host of other instrumentalists, sometimes playing solo but often in groups and frequently made up of immigrant musicians, bringing a wide diversity of sounds to the city streets.

For those preferring to hear their musical entertainment indoors there was an ever expanding selection on offer. It ranged from what was becoming known as as "classical music", considered refined, synonymous with upper-class taste and heard by small and select audiences in rather grand settings, to a less prescribed "popular" music with its roots in a more vernacular tradition, typically old songs spruced up with new and often risqué lyrics. At the same time the demarcation between high and low-brow was becoming blurred and the mix of music ever richer, with this development coming about for one main reason: the rise of the middle-class. Having recently been granted male franchise through the 1832 Reform Act, the middle-class was a new force to be reckoned with: confident, affluent and having an appetite for new cultural experiences. There was a thirst for the new and taste in music was becoming increasingly eclectic with a liking for variety, a demand which would soon be served by the music halls, in which Handel arias might be presented alongside bawdy songs, dancing and other entertainment. By the 1840s there were already clear signs that barriers were breaking down and the qualitative hierarchy of music being challenged. In the words of Roland Pearsall in his book *Victorian Popular Music*, "the most prominent feature of the nineteenth century music scene was that music was not departmentalised".[1]

In 1838 the first promenade concert took place in London at the Lyceum. The standing audience paid a low price to hear a varied programme of music, just as in today's annual concerts at the Royal Albert Hall and elsewhere, and it proved a great success with similar concerts soon being staged in other venues in London, including the Crown and Anchor Tavern in the Strand and the English Opera House. In July 1841, a month after the Richardsons arrived in London, a series of promenade concerts took place at the Theatre Royal in Drury Lane, the auditorium having been specially carpeted and decorated with natural and artificial flowers, water fountains and sculptures. On the rostrum was the celebrated French conductor, Louis Jullien (Figure 4.1),

---
[1] Pearsall, p12.

*Figure 4.1. Louis Jullien*

who was soon to become something of a household name, certainly in London, at a time when the conductor of an orchestra was scarcely considered, even among the musical cognoscenti. Jullien's popularity soon changed this, with audiences beginning to attend concerts because he was conducting and not on the strength of the music on offer in the programme. Jullien himself did not come up with the concept of promenade concerts but in London he made them his own, in a way that no one else would until Henry Wood took charge in 1895, to then continue in the post for a further fifty years.

Already becoming renowned for his extravagant performances, Louis Jullien believed in giving audiences variety and entertainment, mixing symphonies with lighter works including his own compositions, often popular dance pieces such as quadrilles and waltzes. A true showman, he delighted audiences with his theatrical touches and imaginative instrumentation. Jullien would conduct a Beethoven symphony with a jewelled baton while wearing white kid gloves, all handed to him on a silver salver. The evocation of the storm in the *Pastoral Symphony* was, under his direction, enhanced by the sound of dried peas being rattled in a tin box. Never one for understatement, his arrangement of a piece from a Bellini opera featured twenty cornets, twenty trumpets, twenty ophicleides and twenty serpents and he chose to augment Beethoven's Fifth Symphony with four military bands. Audiences loved it and Jullien almost single-handedly challenged the expectations of what a classical concert could be in the capital and beyond. According to his biographer Adam Carse, the promenade concerts under Jullien were designed to appeal

> ....not to the usual cultured and limited concert-going audience of a large city, but the ordinary men and women who never went to a concert and could not afford to do so, but who wanted a pleasant evening's entertainment at a low price...Jullien was not trying to attract the limited number of upper-class people who patronised the Concert of Ancient Music, the Philharmonic, or the artists' benefit concerts...he was providing for the people who...usually went to the theatres, circuses or shows for their amusements."[2]

Louis Jullien's unique style, which much of the musical establishment found extravagant and vulgar, became widely popular because it connected with audiences and was symptomatic of the demand for entertainment as well as cultural enlightenment. In an era which brought new and exotic instruments to the concert hall, Jullien delighted in incorporating these into his arrangements, being possibly the first to include a part for saxophone in a piece for the concert hall, as well as featuring the cornet à piston, the ophicleide, the clavicor and a four metre high double bass known as an octobasse.

Jullien conducted promenade concerts in London from 1841 until 1849 and with the Richardsons based in the capital throughout that period the conductor's popularity almost certainly helped create a climate in which the Rock Band's success became possible. The Richardsons too combined classical pieces with dance tunes, something they had done from the beginning, but they may not have expected London audiences to be so receptive to their varied programme of music played on such an idiosyncratic instrument, but as things turned out they seem to have arrived in the city at exactly the right time. It's highly likely that Jullien's and the Richardsons' paths crossed along the way: they performed at some of the same venues, such as Willis's Rooms, the Hanover Square Rooms and Exeter Hall and the band performed several of Jullien's compositions. If he saw it, Jullien would undoubtedly have been intrigued by the Richardsons' rock harmonicon and it's not unreasonable to think that the Frenchman might have offered them some encouragement in what they were doing.

### The first concerts

The initial performance in London by Messrs. Richardson and Sons' Original Rock Band took place on Saturday 12th June 1841 at Willis & Co's Royal Musical Library, 75 Lower Grosvenor Street. This promotional launch was attended by members of the press and a number of reviews followed in newspapers and magazines, including one in *The Athenæum*, the noted literary magazine, which was somewhat guarded in its praise.

> We can fancy that, heard in the open air, which has a tendency to soften all discords, and to eke out or subdue inequalities of intonation, the effect of this primitive dulcimer must be more than commonly picturesque and engaging. Further experiments, we doubt not, will enable the worthy inventor of it – an ingenious mason, we believe, - still further to perfect his curious invention.[3]

Another significant literary publication of the time, *The Atlas*, was rather more positive:

---

[2] Carse, p3.
[3] The Athenæum, Saturday 24th July 1841, No. 717, pp559-60.

> Mr Richardson was not a mere craftsman – not merely a man of chisels and gavels; he treasured up his observations, he had musical feelings, exciting a wish to turn them to account, and enthusiasm of purpose for the completion of his project....As a matter of novelty of idea and successful resolve in carrying it out, and altogether as a most meritorious effort on the part of an unschooled man, we strongly recommend the Rock Harmonicon to the notice of our readers; their curiosity will be gratified by the inspection of one of the quaintest inventions of the day, and their ears will be delighted by the sweetness of its sounds.[4]

In seeking an example of another instrument with which to compare it, the article makes no mention of another tuned percussion instrument such as a xylophone, not yet a familiar sight, indicating just how novel the rock harmonicon must have appeared to Londoners at that time:

> The tones extracted from these unyielding materials are strikingly sweet and glassy in quality, and at a little distance, the whole effect resembles that of the largest kind of "musical box" with the difference, only, that the bass of the Rock Harmonicon possesses a depth and fullness unattainable from the steel springs of the machine to which we have likened it.[5]

Interestingly, and unusually in coverage about the Richardson band, the article also draws attention to, an aspect of playing the rock harmonicon which gave it a flexibility not found in other instruments:

> For the performer's convenience the arrangement is occasionally altered; as for example, if a piece be played in the key of A major, those stones representing the sharp F's, C's and G's, are transferred to the lower tier, while the corresponding natural notes are placed in the vacant spaces above.....[6]

As was now customary, it was decided that the rock harmonicon should be on show for more than just a few days and it remained in place at the Royal Music Library until September, the three brothers performing each day between 10.00am and 6.00pm. The entrance fee was fixed at an affordable one shilling for adults and half-price for children.

Having the opportunity to showcase and demonstrate the musical potential of the rock harmonicon for three months, in the prestigious and affluent Mayfair district of London, meant that the Richardsons could not but be noticed by a number of eminent and influential people. One such was Sir George Smart, one of the best known and highly regarded musicians of the time who held the post of organist and composer at the Chapel Royal, counting amongst his predecessors the likes of George Frederick Handel and Henry Purcell. Also a conductor and teacher, some years later Smart would be appointed as musical director for the opening of the 1851 Great Exhibition. Having watched one of the Richardson performances at the Royal Musical Library he was impressed enough to write a letter of commendation to Joseph Richardson which was published in several newspapers.

---

[4] The Atlas, Saturday 26th June 1841, p12.
[5] Ibid.
[6] Ibid.

> Sir - I am happy to offer my testimony in favour of your very clever invention, and think the production of the "Rock Harmonicon" does infinite credit to your perseverance and musical feeling; the tones of the instrument are powerful and beautiful, and I was highly pleased with the performance of your three sons upon it. I sincerely hope your labours will be rewarded as they richly deserve. - I am, sir, your obedient servant.
>
> George Smart[7]

Another important figure on the London music scene who came to see and hear the Original Rock Band, possibly on the recommendation of Isaac Willis, was Michael Costa, then making his name composing and conducting ballets and opera at the Haymarket Theatre. Born in Italy in 1808 Costa had moved to England as a young man and settled in London, eventually being granted both British citizenship and a knighthood. He too was impressed by what he heard and a week after Joseph Richardson had received the letter from Sir George Smart another one arrived from Michael Costa.

> Sir – I have been much gratified with the performance of your three sons, on your very ingenious instrument, "The Rock Harmonicon", and sincerely wish you may be recompensed for your wonderful discovery.
>
> M.Costa[8]

This contact was to produce early dividends: within days Michael Costa had composed a suite of Rock Harmonicon Airs for the Richardsons to perform, which was immediately published by Willis and Co. and advertised for sale in a piano arrangement. One piece in the Richardsons' repertoire which had become a favourite with audiences was their arrangement of Handel's *The Harmonious Blacksmith* and included in Costa's suite was a new piece to complement it entitled *The Harmonious Stonemason*, which was soon added to the programme.

Isaac Willis's business, which had been granted royal patronage as "Music sellers and Musical Instrument Manufacturers to the King" (Victoria only having come to the throne in 1837) was by now principally engaged with music publishing. When he began working with the Richardsons the agreement included a publishing clause which could benefit both the performers and Willis himself. In the same way that later, in the era of recorded music, merchandising at concerts was dominated by the selling of records, so in the mid-nineteenth century earnings from concerts could be boosted considerably by the sale of sheet music. Featuring pieces played in the concert, these were generally arranged for piano. The 1840s saw an exponential rise in the sale of pianos as upright models, suitable for the average home, became more available. Pianos became a status symbol for aspiring households and there was such a boom in demand that during that decade dozens of piano manufacturers opened for business in London. By 1851 there were around two hundred piano companies in the country[9] and the Great Exhibition included 102 piano manufacturers displaying their wares.[10] This interest in pianos brought of that year with it a demand for piano tuition (thought particularly suitable for young ladies)

---

[7] The Age, London, Sunday 8th August 1841, p6.
[8] Phillips 1, p54.
[9] Scott, p29.
[10] https://piano-tuners.org.

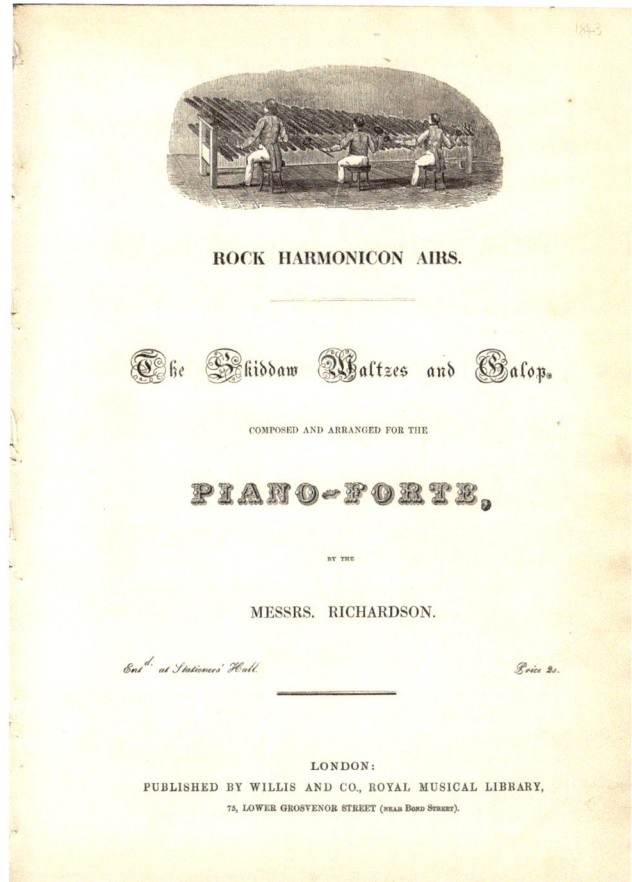

*Figure 4.2. Sheet music of a set of original pieces composed by the Richardsons, illustrated with a drawing of the three men playing.*
© *John H. Phillips.*

and also a need for suitable material to play. Musical concerts were therefore seen as prime events at which to promote pieces which could later be played in the home. and Willis and Co. not only published arrangements of Michael Costa's pieces written for the Rock Band but also original compositions from the Richardsons themselves, bringing to the fore another of their faculties (Figure 4.2). Not only was the sheet music of these pieces available for sale at the concerts but there were also sometimes special offers, which could include for a dress box ticket at 3/6d, the sheet music of a piece being performed that evening plus two other pieces selected from the ublisher's back catalogue.[11] Music in the city was becoming a commercial enterprise as never before.

Barely a year since the Richardsons had begun performing publicly on the rock harmonicon, they were already showing that they could hold their own within the music world of London,

---

[11] Aliffe, p26.

not only due to the novelty of their chosen instrument but through the quality of their performance. While their humble background and relative lack of musical experience or tuition became a feature of the story being told in the press, had they not been able to come up with the goods on the day, they would certainly not have been able to sustain the musical career they were embarking upon with some success. Indeed, they continued to go from strength to strength as noted in a review which appeared in London's *Morning Herald*:

> Since our former visit to this extraordinary invention, at the establishment of Messrs. Willis, at the Royal Music Library, in Lower Grosvenor Street, considerable progress has been made by the young Cumbrian Mountaineers, in the cultivation of their novel and singular art. They not only perform simple tunes with perfect accuracy, but have so far mastered their instrument as to be able to give entire overtures, which want nothing in fullness of tone to assimilate them to a complete orchestra. We yesterday listened to the overtures of Tancredi [Rossini] and Zauberflüte [Mozart] and were delighted, no less at the wonderful sounds which were elicited from the stones, than at the extraordinary development of memory in playing complicated pieces of music, such as these, without notes. The wild and thrilling tones of the rock harmonicon are admirably adapted to represent the melody of the Zauberflüte. It almost seems as if the spirits evoked by the composer were themselves at work to give full effect to his conceptions. So much having been done in so short a period, we may confidently predict a very brilliant result to the exertions of the inventor Mr. Richardson.[12]

## On the road

Following their three-month residence at the Royal Musical Library the Rock Band does not appear to have given any more performances in London in 1841 but in October the Richardsons travelled to Brighton for a two-week period. Here they installed the rock harmonicon in the Musical Library, part of Wright's Library and Reading Room run by Frederick Wright, an entrepreneur and songwriter and probably known to Isaac Willis. Being able to call on the expertise of Willis and Wright, men who were conversant with the commercial aspects of music, must have been greatly valued by Joseph Richardson, now in a managerial role within the band and no longer performing. But although Willis's assistance was crucial in the introductions he was able to make to various contacts it was Richardson whose job it was to pursue possible bookings, make all the arrangements and produce publicity material in the form of posters and flyers to send to concert promoters. The penny post had been introduced the previous year and the establishment of a national postal service would have made all the difference in negotiations with venues across the length and breadth of the country. He was also able to call upon the services of local book and music shops to assist in advance promotion for the band's appearances.

From Brighton the Richardsons travelled north to the Assembly Rooms in Leamington Spa where they stayed for a further two weeks, giving their final performance there on New Year's Day 1842 before moving on to another fashionable spa town, Cheltenham, where they again performed in the local assembly rooms. This was the name given to a relatively new and popular type of music and dance venue which was becoming established in numerous

---

[12] Morning Herald, Wednesday 25th August 1841, p7.

towns. Assembly rooms had been set up to appeal to the rising number of potential attendees who were happy to hear concert music being played but were also attracted to the idea of something rather more social, providing the possibility of trying out the new and increasingly popular dances which had found their way into the country. The assemblies were able to offer something with wider appeal, maintaining certain standards but without feeling too select, "the nearest parallel the Victorians had to modern ballroom dancing – classless, sober and restrained"[13]

One attraction of the new dances being introduced to Britain from Europe was that they were less formal and more lively than court dances, with the added appeal of calling upon a degree of physical contact to the paired participants. The quadrille, introduced in the eighteenth century, was particularly popular, with the waltz arriving later, followed by the polka. While these dance forms were also being taken up and transformed by a number of early to mid-nineteenth century composers, notably Weber, Chopin and the Strauss family, in Britain there was a resistance in the music establishment to such dance music as being insufficiently cerebral for serious consideration, as well as being dangerously un-British. It was through challenging such attitudes that Louis Jullien was helping to build a new fan-base for a different kind of musical event. By playing in assembly rooms the Richardsons were demonstrating that they were presenting themselves not only as a concert band for a seated audience or a novelty act, but that they could also play for dances, as did Louis Jullien. Yet the fact that Joseph Richardson had included dance music alongside concert pieces from the start was possibly not so much that he had his finger on the pulse of what was fashionable, but that he had broad taste and chose to play the music he liked. As a former tradesman, from the lower middle-class, he was not so different in his taste from many of the people who came to hear the band play, whether in Cumbria or London, so he was part of the same change which was affecting the nature of the audience and this played to his and the band's advantage.

With the agreed duration of their booking at Cheltenham Assembly Rooms coming to an end the Richardsons were invited to remain in the town by moving to another location, the premises of the Literary and Philosophical Institution and they remained there for almost a month. During that time the band performed two benefit concerts for local institutions, something they began to do from time to time when they felt there was a worthy cause to be supported. From Cheltenham they travelled to Oxford where they played at the Holywell Music Room, a fine eighteenth century building thought to be the first purpose-built concert venue in Britain and still in use today. The Richardsons then moved on to Reading for a two-week stay before returning to London in May. This time they set up stall in the Stanley Auction Rooms which had started to diversify its business by staging musical events. The band's reputation was by now well-established in London and during their stay there, which lasted until early August, they were afforded a lengthy article in the prestigious *Illustrated London News*, which included a new engraving showing the three Richardson brothers sitting playing the rock harmonicon (Figure 4.3). In describing the instrument an effort was made once more to find something with which to compare it:

---

[13] Pearsall, p187.

*Figure 4.3. Drawing from article on Richardson and his Rock Harmonicon in Illustrated London News, 28th May 1842. © John H. Phillips.*

Those who are acquainted with the toy harmonicon, consisting of pieces of glass laid on tapers, to be struck with a cork hammer, will readily form an idea of this singular instrument, and the mode in which its sounds are elicited.[14]

Almost sixty years after Peter Crosthwaite first assembled his Music Stones, tuned percussion instruments of this type, of whatever material they were constructed, were still not widely known in Britain, except, it seems in the form of a relatively expensive child's toy. Whatever this tells us about the market for musical instruments, it also serves as a reminder of how far ahead of the game Peter Crosthwaite had been in 1785.

## Ireland

In the summer of 1842 the Original Rock Band seem to have taken a summer break, most probably returning to Keswick, the first extended period of time the Richardson family would have spent together since leaving to play their first concerts in Whitehaven. Following that they embarked on their first visit to Ireland, sailing from Liverpool to Dublin at the end of September where they played at the Music Hall before moving to another major Dublin venue at the time, the Rotondo. There they were joined on stage by John Davies, the musician they had befriended in Liverpool two years earlier. The previous month Davies had taken part in some other concerts featuring a rock harmonicon back in his home city, but although his name was given in announcements printed in the Liverpool papers, "the two other professional gentlemen" taking part were not named.[15] It is possible that it had been two of the Richardson men, but more likely is that it involved at least one of the Bowe cousins capitalising on the

---

[14] Illustrated London News, Saturday 28th May 1842, p7.
[15] Liverpool Standard and General Commercial Advertiser, Friday 12th August 1842, p1.

Richardsons' earlier success in the city, and by not being specific allowing the ambiguity referred to earlier to imply that it might be the Original Rock Band making a return appearance.

To make the trip to Ireland worthwhile there clearly needed to be a well-planned and substantial block of bookings and presumably Isaac Willis, by now the band's *de facto* manager, would have had good knowledge and contacts to help with that, having maintained a business interest in Dublin. In the event the band generated enough work in Ireland to stay for several months, travelling on from Dublin to play in the counties of Cork, Limerick, Kilkenny, Tipperary and Waterford. They also managed to fit in a return visit to the Dublin Music Hall where they were to play on Boxing Day, supporting a celebrated ventriloquist known as Mr Gallagher. He was considered by the local press to be an even greater attraction than the Original Rock Band, something reflected in the unusually high prices charged for the more expensive seats and private boxes. This particular engagement was itself to continue for almost a month.

## England and Wales

Finally returning to England at the end of April 1843 the band continued to tour with unrelenting regularity. Becoming far more widely known and facing ever increasing demands for them to play in cities and towns throughout the country, it became essential to arrange blocks of bookings on a regional basis to keep travel to a minimum. There was also talk of trips to Europe and while they were in Ireland this started to be mentioned in their publicity with subsequent references in the press that Joseph Richardson had "been induced to postpone his engagements for the Continent." They were to play abroad, but not for a number of years.

In May and June the Rock Band were in Bristol, Bath and Salisbury and Southampton before making their way back to London. Once more they took up a two-week residency in Old Bond Street in the now refurbished and renamed Stanley's Music Saloon before going on the road again with a series of dates in the south of England, finishing the year with performances around Kent. In reporting their forthcoming appearance at the Assembly Room in the Star Hotel in Maidstone the local newspaper noted that "the proprietors of the <u>real</u> Rock Harmonicon are about to pay this town a visit", going on to mention a disappointing performance given on a previous occasion by performers playing a rock harmonicon who they had assumed were the Richardsons, an account which confirms that audience indeed had been misled, whether deliberately or not.

Coming back to London in April 1844 the Original Rock Band had its most prestigious booking to date, playing at the Queen's Concert Rooms in Hanover Square for several weeks presenting performances described as being "very fashionably attended"[16], as well they might have been in a venue which had in the past hosted names which included Haydn, Mendelssohn, Paganini, Clara Schumann, Liszt and Berlioz. Then, after a few weeks break the Richardsons were off again, pursuing a life-style a touring musician today would find hard to fully comprehend. At some point they would have been able to start making use of the developing rail network, but for the most part they would have been dependant on horse-power. Travelling with an extremely heavy quota of equipment, they were never entirely sure of how long their stay would be in each town or city they visited or when there might be a long enough break from

---

[16] Bell's Life in London and Sporting Chronicle, Sunday 28th April 1844, p1.

*Figure 4.4. Egyptian Hall, Piccadilly, London. Courtesy of Andy Aliffe.*

playing for them to return to their home and family. This time it was Midland towns which were introduced to the sound of musical stone: Northampton, Coventry, Leamington, Leicester, Nottingham and Derby, finishing the year on the east of the country with several concerts in Lincolnshire. 1845 saw them continue travelling from one county to another, mainly in the south, pausing only to carry out some improvements and maintenance on the rock harmonicon before spending another few summer weeks in London, this time playing at another popular concert hall, the Egyptian Hall in Piccadilly (Figures 4.4 and 4.5). The band name now changed again, to Richardson's Monstre Rock Band, as they continued their seemingly endless itinerary, introducing the rock harmonicon to one small town after another throughout the country as well making return visits to the sites of previous successes.

1846 saw the first major change in the specification of the Richardsons' instrument, with the addition of a row of tuned steel bars, supplementing the sound of the hornfels stone to provide a greater variation in tone. They called this new element the Chinese Steel Band and the first engagement announcing its arrival was in Salisbury on 30th September, the act now billed as "The Magnificent Chinese Steel Band and Richardson's Original Monstre Rock Band". Sometimes the publicity mentioning the new addition referred to it as the Chinese Sacred Steel Band with an announcement in a Bristol newspaper, in advance of their appearance at Clifton's Victoria Rooms, mentioning "the brilliant and beautiful-toned Chinese Steel Instruments, used

*Figure 4.5. Poster for Egyptian Hall summer residency, 1845. Courtesy of Andy Aliffe.*

in China for the performances of Sacred Music, for which they are admirably adapted."[17] It can be said with certainty that these particular steel bars did not originate in China and they were not based on any particular instrument from there, Chinese tuned percussion taking the form of suspended chimes. The name seems to have been more a suggestion of exoticism, something welcomed for its novelty value. The nature of the music the Richardsons chose to play on the steel bars is not known, though they were for the most part kept as a separate instrument in performances, tending only to be used being in conjunction with the rock harmonicon for one piece in the set. Reviews following the introduction of the expanded instrumentation make a distinction between the material played on the rock harmonicon and that played solely on the steel bars, but how far the music on the bars was intended to evoke something of the east is hard to ascertain.

With the extended tonal range brought about by the added steel bars the reception received by the Richardson Band seems to have been even more enthusiastic. Continuing to travel across the south of England and parts of Wales for the remainder of 1846 and into the following year, local press reports seemed impressed by the range of sound on offer:

> No one could help being delighted with the sweet harmonious sounds of the novel instrument cut from solid rock, and with the sonorous though melodious strains of the Chinese Steel Band.[18]

---

[17] Phillips 1, p109.
[18] West of England Conservative and Plymouth and Devon Advertiser, Wednesday 23rd December 1846, p3.

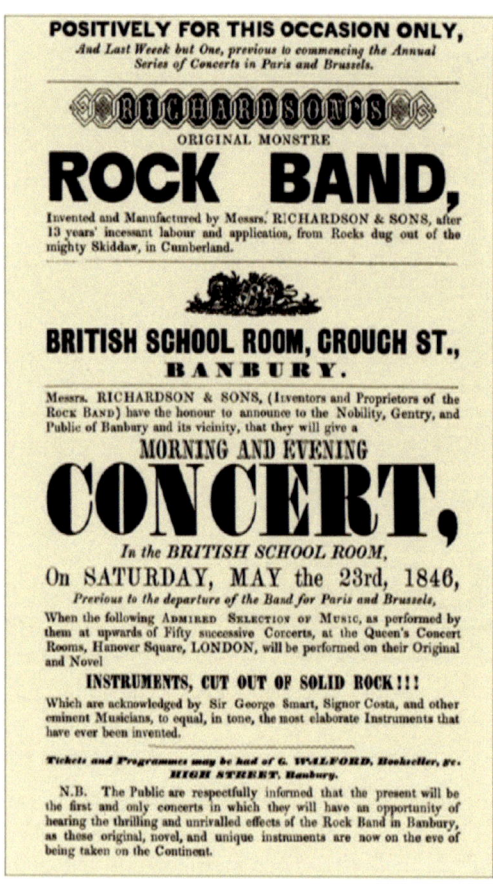

*Figure 4.6. Poster for concert in Banbury on Saturday 23rd May by Richardson's Original Monstre Rock Band. Courtesy of Andy Aliffe.*

Another review, submitted to a Shropshire paper by an "intelligent amateur" recounted the performers' ability to evoke the sound of other orchestral instruments through their playing of the stone and steel bars:

Occasionally we could fancy we heard the brilliant tones of a pianoforte, now the liquid warbling of the flute, but the lower tones of the rockband assimilate so nearly to the pizzicato notes of the violoncello, that it would take a most critical ear to perceive the difference. The programme contained a pleasing selection of sacred and secular music. Handel's well known "Harmonious Blacksmith" was deliciously rendered on the steel band, the deep bass notes of the rock band blending with the steel in a manner producing a perfectly novel and beautiful effect".[19]

The following year, 1847, twenty years since Joseph Richardson had first embarked on the collecting of stone to build the rock harmonicon, he decided to expand the tonal range even further by adding a set of so-called Swiss Bells and pedal-operated drums (Figure 4.7). The tonality of any tuned percussion instrument is limited, which is why they often tend to be used in conjunction with other instruments. In choosing to extend the rock harmonicon to include metallic sounds Joseph Richardson was acknowledging this shortcoming and acting upon it. Even ringing stone will only sustain momentarily, making long notes only manageable with good use of tremelo technique and these additions would have introduced the possibility of some more sustained sounds, with the drums adding a rhythmic pulse.

The Swiss Bells were not cowbells and had no clapper attached, being struck with a beater as with the rock harmonicon and steel band. They seem to have been a form of something called Swiss staff bells, a set of which Percy Grainger was later to possess in his collection of instruments, specifying their use in some of his compositions. James Blades describes staff bells as being mushroom shape, whereas the Richardson bells have a greater visual resemblance to bicycle bells, but varying in size relative to individual pitch. Presumably their manufacture was commissioned by the band, though who made them is not recorded.

---

[19] Eddowe's Journal and General Advertiser for Shropshire and the Principality of Wales, Wednesday 12th May 1847, p3.

*Figure 4.7. Showing additions to the Rock Harmonicon: steel bars, Swiss bells and one of the drums. Courtesy of Keswick Museum and Art Gallery.*

The foot-pedal mechanism for the drum is thought to have been designed by an engineer called Cornelius Ward.[20] Some years beforehand Ward had patented a cable-tuned kettle-drum as well as devices for tensioning side and bass drums and the same principles were used on the rock harmonicon, attached to a foot pedal. This could have been the prototype for the mechanism later employed to operate the kick-drum foot-pedal of the type found on any drum kit today, pedal-operated bass drums not having been in use at that time.[21] The design for the modern-day bass drum foot-pedal, usually credited to W.F. Ludwig, was not to come for another sixty years, but whether it was based on Ward's design for the Richardson instrument is uncertain. Keswick Museum has four drums used by the Richardsons and the foot-pedal mechanism has been designed to have two beaters, presumably enabling two drums facing each other to be played simultaneously.

---

[20] Blades, p490.
[21] Ibid.

# Chapter Five

# Playing by Royal Command
## Richardson's Rock, Bell and Steel Band at Buckingham Palace

The fully augmented version of the Richardsons' rock harmonicon, which was soon to be promoted as Richardson's Rock, Bell and Steel Band, sometimes with slight variations, made its debut in September 1847 in what was planned to be a short series of concerts in the Home Counties, around London. Predictably, what was intended to be a two-week tour came to be extended by three weeks, an indication of its success. As was always the case, audience numbers varied depending on prevailing factors, generally relating to the time of day or the weather, but the enthusiasm of those attending seemed never in doubt. But soon they were to play to one of their smallest audiences, yet one of great import. There had been a number of indications that a possible royal performance was in the offing and an invitation, indeed a Royal Command, arrived in due course, the date set at Wednesday 23rd February 1848 when Messieurs Richardson and Sons were to perform before Her Majesty Queen Victoria and His Royal Highness Prince Albert at Buckingham Palace. The select audience may not have been of a size to which the band had become accustomed, but was by no means limited to the royal couple themselves. The *Cumberland Pacquet and Ware's Whitehaven Advertiser*, the newspaper which had continued to report faithfully on the national successes of their four local musicians, gave an account of the occasion some days after the performance, including an incomplete but formidable list of those in attendance:

> The Messrs. Richardson had the honour of attending at Buckingham Palace, by express command of Her Majesty, and performed in the presence of Her Majesty the Queen, Prince Albert, the Duchess of Kent, their Royal Highnesses the Duke and Duchess of Saxe Coburg, Count Arthur Mensdorff, His Excellency Baron de Beust, the Marquis and Marchioness of Clanricarde, Lady Fanny Howard, Madame la Baronne de Wangenheim, Baroness de Speith, the Earl of Aberdeen, the Right Hon. W. Lascelles, Baron Fritsch, &c.[1]

The pieces played at the Palace included a selection from Bellini's opera *Beatrice di Tenda*, Handel's *The Harmonious Blacksmith*, Voigt's *The Nightingale*, Jullien's *Scotch Quadrilles* and Costa's *The Harmonious Stonemason*. Prince Albert asked for the latter piece to be repeated and the Queen herself requested *The Harmonious Blacksmith* as an encore, a requisition which was subsequently noted in the band's publicity pronouncements. A Court Circular, distributed a few days later, reported that the Rock Band were well received by the royal party:

> At the close of the performance, Her Majesty and Prince Albert were graciously pleased to express their entire approbation of the music selected for the Evening's Entertainment, as well as the brilliant manner in which the pieces were executed, and entered into a most familiar conversation with the Messieurs Richardson, as to the

---
[1] Cumberland Pacquet, Tuesday 29th February 1848, p2.

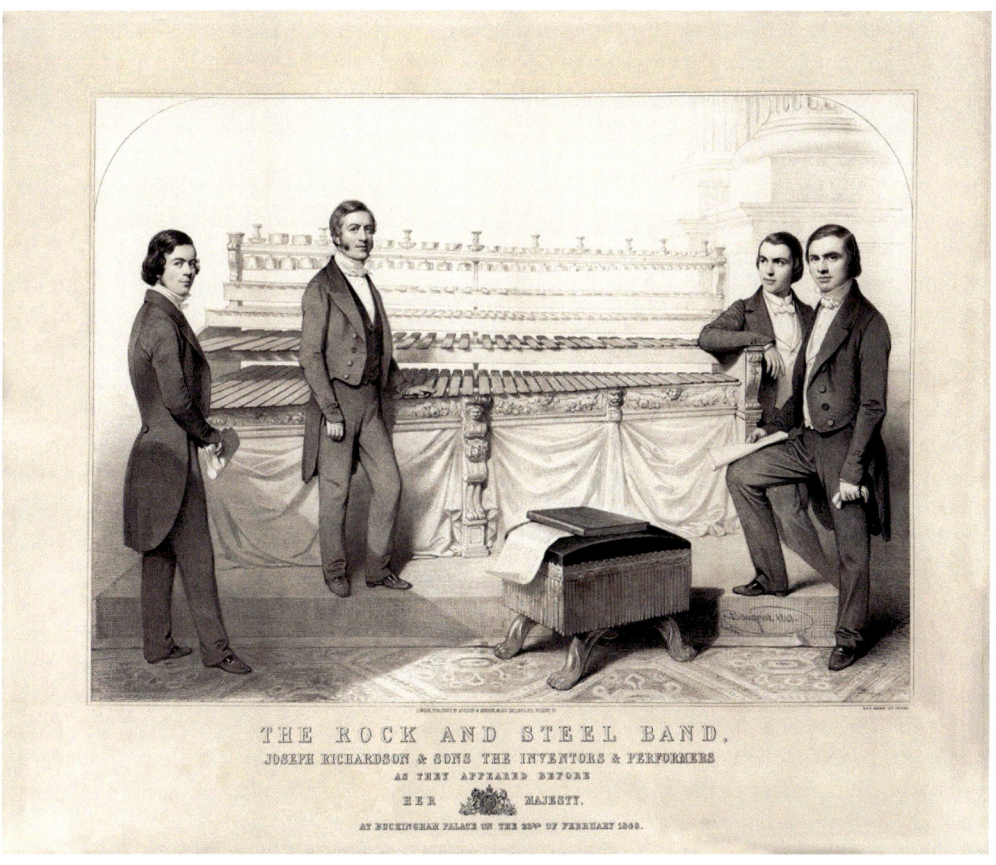

*Figure 5.1. Lithograph of the Richardsons at Buckingham Palace by Charles Baugniet. © John H. Phillips.*

invention and arrangement of their instruments, to all of which queries these Musical Gentlemen gave full and explicit answers.[2]

Queen Victoria's personal diary entry for the day of the performance at the Palace begins by expressing her anxiety upon reading in the Daily News of the battles which had taken place the previous day on the streets of Paris between "troops out in great force" and "the mob"[3]. This apparently coincided with "the day on which there was to have been the Banquets which had to be postponed"[4]. The day's diary entry closes with the comment:

> A Rock Band played after dinner in our room, - it is a curious thing.[5]

It was reported at the time that Queen Victoria did not approve of the additions to the rock harmonicon, a story which may have fed the contention that she had heard the Rock Band

---

[2] Phillips 1, p115.
[3] Royal Archives: http://www.queenvictoriasjournals.org/home.do. This was 1848, the year of widespread revolutionary activity in mainland Europe.
[4] Ibid.
[5] Ibid.

on an earlier occasion, before the addition of the Chinese Steel Band and Swiss Bells. James Blades in his definitive book *Percussion Instruments and their History* mentions a previous royal command performance,[6] but there is nothing in the Royal Archive to suggest that this ever took place.

Following their appearance at Buckingham Palace the Belgian artist Charles Baugniet was commissioned by Joseph Richardson to portray the Richardson band and a lithograph was produced with an inscription noting the occasion.[7] Baugniet had been a court painter to the Belgian royal family but moved to London in 1843 where he became a society portraitist, one of his subjects, in 1846, being Louis Jullien. His picture of the Richardsons shows them standing in front of the rock harmonicon, complete with the recently added Chinese Steel Band and Swiss Bells, though not the drums (Figure 5.1). A limited number of lithographic prints went on sale and the picture was used in subsequent publicity. In addition to its intrinsic quality, the print is particularly significant in that it is almost certainly the best representation we have of what Joseph Richardson and the three of his sons actually looked like. They began performing publicly at the very advent of photography, yet although its use and popularity grew rapidly over the next decade, there appears to be no known photograph in existence showing the four once celebrated musicians.

On the 14th June 1848 the Richardsons presented the Rock, Bell and Steel Band in its completed state in London for the first time, to an invited audience. The event was staged in the Exeter Hall in Piccadilly and was attended by the press as well various luminaries from the music business. The general reaction to the new, expanded version of the instrumental set-up, judging by reports following this event, was that the sound of steel in combination with the stone brought a greater richness to the sound. *The Literary Gazette*, while commending the way in which "difficult overtures, and airs with full accompaniment,waltzes, polkas, and quadrilles, are all executed capitally"[8] nevertheless did make the interesting observation with regard to the Chinese Steel Bars that "the tone emitted is not so vocal as that from the stone."[9] A fairly lengthy review in *The Tablet* gave qualified approval, noting that "the excellent manner in which the various pieces were executed elicited much applause from the audience" but also expressed the view that "we doubt whether the instrument is capable of becoming a popular one; the hammering on these anvils is not very graceful, and the instrument is necessarily very large."[10]

## Julia Gould

For all the variety the Richardson band was now able to offer in terms of sound and repertoire, one thing it lacked was any vocal element to their performance. It was also an exclusively male band, as were the other rock harmonicon bands operating up to that point, but both of these issues were soon to be addressed when they enlisted the talents of a young soprano, Julia Gould, to perform with the band. Gould (Figure 5.2) was from a musical family and had begun her musical career in her teens, touring with her mother, also a singer, plus her brother and

---

[6] Blades, p84.
[7] John Phillips, personal communication.
[8] The Literary Gazette, Saturday 24th June 1848, No.1640, p429.
[9] Ibid.
[10] The Tablet, Saturday 17th June 1848, p13.

*Figure 5.2. Julia Gould. Courtesy of Andy Aliffe.*

her stepfather. In 1841 Julia Gould had begun to sing regularly at the recently opened English National Opera off the Strand, so Joseph Richardson may well have known of her for some time, but it was not until 1848, possibly after hearing her perform at Exeter Hall in a concert with her mother and brother, that he invited her to join the band. She agreed and, after some rehearsals, began what was to become a five-month period of touring with the Rock, Bell and Steel Band. The posters distributed to promote what was billed as "Messieurs Richardsons' Tour Musicale" brought the public up to date with the new improved version of what was on on offer:

> In engaging Miss J.Gould for their Concerts, the Messieurs Richardsons cannot avoid remarking to the Amateurs of Music that first-rate Vocalists are generally accompanied by a Pianoforte only; this system generally injures the effect of pieces written by the great composers for a grand Orchestra, which advantages are now secured to Miss Gould by being accompanied by Messrs. R's Band. The Messrs. Richardson beg to state that by having recently made great additions to, and improvements in their Band, it is now more complete than ever; and that for the first time in the Provinces, the Cavatinas of Bellini, Rossini, and Verdi, will be sung by Miss Gould, accompanied by the Rock, Bell, and Steel Band.[11]

---

[11] Phillips 1 p125.

The trip into the provinces began at the White Hart Inn in Romford on Friday 18th August, followed by concerts in six more Essex towns. The band then proceeded to take its music back and forth from one English county to another: Suffolk, Cambridgeshire, Hertfordshire, Norfolk, Lincolnshire, Huntingdonshire, Rutland, Bedfordshire, Buckinghamshire, Northamptonshire, Oxfordshire, Warwickshire, Leicestershire and Nottinghamshire; all of which took them to the end of the year and beyond into 1849.

The singing of Julia Gould was well received by audiences. Although a trained opera singer, her musical interests spread wider than the classical canon, which was probably a reason why she was considered right for the job. As well as being completely at home performing operatic arias, if required she was also happy to sing popular ballads and airs. When she sang *Ye Banks and Braes*, Robert Burns' song set to the tune *The Caledonian Hunt's Delight*, she did so with a guitar accompaniment. While today that would be considered unsurprising, it was then thought by some to be a step too far:

> Spanish ladies wail the loss of their lovers to the tones of the guitar; but in the hands of a Scottish maiden it is quite out of place, and destroys the effect of the song.[12]

The reviewer went on to criticise Gould's use of vibrato in such songs, in this case a view with which many listeners today might concur:

> Miss Gould should also eschew all shakes in ballad singing: they are as foreign to the ballad as to the psalm.[13]

Another review also found the guitar accompaniment problematic:

> "Ye Banks and Braes", which Miss Julia Gould sings so well, if sung slower, and accompanied not by guitar, which has no effect whatever after the Rock Music, but by the Rock Music itself taking the parts...would be exquisite in itself, and form a new and excellent feature in their programme."[14]

Who was providing the guitar accompaniment to the song is not stated in the reviews; if it had been Julia Gould it seems likely it would have been mentioned. It could be that Julia's brother, Napoleon, who both played and taught guitar, was involved in some way. He is said to have moved to the USA in 1848 in which case he would not have been able to join them on tour, but it may be that he helped in rehearsals, possibly teaching one of the Richardsons an accompaniment.

After a short new year break, the Rock, Bell and Steel Band, including Julia Gould, travelled north for an extensive tour of Yorkshire towns and cities. The band were there for two months, from early February through until April with around thirty bookings. Most of these were for one day only, so there would have been no let-up in the schedule, their days alternating between travel and setting up and delivering the next performance. The final engagement of the Yorkshire tour, in Richmond on the 3rd April, was also the last concert that Julia Gould

---

[12] Cambridge Independent Press, Saturday 28th October 1848, p3.
[13] Ibid.
[14] Phillips 1, p134.

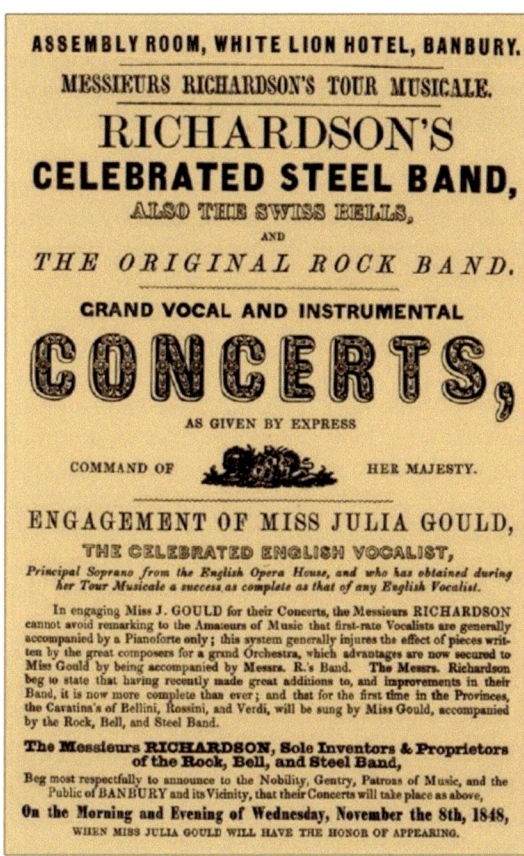

*Figure 5.3. Poster for concert in Banbury featuring Julia Gould as vocalist. Courtesy of Andy Aliffe.*

played with the band. She was soon to join her brother in the USA where she continued working in opera while also performing with him in blackface minstrel shows. In 1858 Napoleon Gould contributed to the first copyrighted and published version of the song *The Yellow Rose of Texas* for which he wrote the guitar arrangement.[15]

### The final years

Carrying on performing without their vocalist, the Richardsons made their first trip into Scotland the following month, May 1849, and began an extensive tour there which lasted until October. Who arranged this tour into a hitherto untested region is unclear. The previous year Isaac Willis had ceased trading, having been declared bankrupt following a period of decline in his business, meaning he had probably been less involved with the Richardson band for a while. Joseph Richardson himself was probably best placed to make booking arrangements, having long been in a supportive role, but how he was able to manage that whilst presumably being on tour himself with the band for months at a time is hard to imagine.

Judging by the press reviews in Scotland the Rock, Bell and Steel Band were as well received as ever and the tonal variety they were able to produce from their new set-up continuing to confound the ear:

> Had the orchestra been enclosed with a screen, the hearer would have been puzzled to determine whether the melody proceeded from harp, flute, organ or all combined.[16]
> [*Perth Courier*, 16th August 1849, p4]

Finally travelling back south of the border, the Richardsons then returned to their home region of Cumbria, playing in a number of towns including Keswick and Whitehaven for the first time since making their debut appearances nine years before. *The Cumberland Pacquet* was delighted:

---

[15] https://digitalcommons.conncoll.edu/sheetmusic/1242/
[16] Perth Courier, 16th August 1849.

> Time has reversed what is too generally found to be the order of things with him. Instead of impairing any of their powers, and leaving something to be explained and apologised for, he has added new charms, and powers which before had not been calculated upon; and we were agreeably surprised to find that our warmest eulogies in former times were more than merited by the perfection attained during a long course of experience, and under the judicious encouragement and criticism of the public. They have not been buoyed beyond their depth by applause, nor rendered careless or negligent by the fame they have won; but believing that they were capable of achieving still greater victories than hose with which they set out...they continued their exertions, and have produced the most effective combination which probably ever thrilled the ears and animated the feelings of an audience.[17]

One consequence of the triumphant homecoming of the Rock, Bell and Steel Band and the publicity surrounding it struck a rather more sour note. John Fisher Crosthwaite, grandson of Peter Crosthwaite, wrote a lengthy and indignant letter to several newspapers. He began:

> Sir, Having seen a circular printed by you, in which you describe yourself as the sole inventor of the Rock Band, I think it my duty to show to the world that you have not the remotest claim to whatever credit may be due to the inventor of that instrument.....[18]

Having quoted from the article which had appeared in the Illustrated London News he then proceeds to chide Richardson for this claim, providing the evidence that his own grandfather had first come up with the idea of producing a stone instrument and had proceeded to do so some sixty four years earlier, which the young Richardson would have known, living in the vicinity of the Crosthwaite Museum. This is the letter in which, as cited earlier, Crosthwaite also refers to Richardson having been amused by hearing the stone instrument which William Greenip had played to him. Although Joseph Richardson made no response publicly to the letter, which ran to over a thousand words, the editor of *The Cumberland Pacquet* did print a reply, also at some length, presenting the case that notwithstanding Peter Crosthwaite's achievement, Joseph Richardson had developed the idea to such a degree that he could justify being called its inventor.

The Rock, Bell and Steel Band continued its relentless touring schedule with more bookings in the north of England, where they stayed until the new year, before moving south again, working their way through the Midlands, into Worcestershire and Gloucestershire. By the beginning of May they had arrived in Wales where they remained for most of the month and it seems possible that shortly after that the Richardsons may have travelled abroad.

For some time the band's publicity had indicated that foreign trips were planned and as early as 1845 it was reported that they were imminently to be leaving London with the intention "to visit Paris, Brussels, Vienna and other cities of distinction on the continent"[19] yet a string of subsequent UK bookings show that this trip did not take place, certainly at that time. John H. Phillips, a direct descendant of Joseph Richardson, has logged virtually all performances given

---

[17] Cumberland Pacquet, Tuesday 23rd October 1849, p2.
[18] Cumberland Pacquet, Tuesday 30th October 1849, p3.
[19] Phillips 1, p161, Cited from Cumberland Pacquet, 29th July 1845, p2.

*Figure 5.4. Poster for concert in Chard, Tuesday 4th February. Courtesy of Andy Aliffe.*

by the Richardson Rock Band over the twelve year period from 1840[20] and this shows that their schedule during that time was so full that there are very few periods when they could have undertaken the number of foreign bookings that have sometimes been claimed. In May 1850, publicity for the Rock, Bell and Steel, Band mentions the Swiss Bells having been being introduced for the first time at concerts in London's Exeter Hall and later played "before the Imperial Court at St Petersburg."[21] Considering the distance involved and the limited number of ways of getting there at that time this seems barely credible, particularly as there seems to be no documentary evidence to substantiate the claim and that more was not made of it by the band or the press.

Joseph Richardson was capable of a degree of hyperbole in his promotion and perhaps that should be taken into account when trying to piece together a chronology of events. Concert programmes for the band do refer to a number of "Extracts from Continental Journals" but as Phillips points out, what is not clear about these translations is whether they relate to local concerts in the country in which they were published or from foreign correspondents writing about a performance in Britain. There is, however no reason to think the band did not play abroad and, in Phillips' view, one period when it is likely that this happened was in the early summer of 1850, possibly between the beginning of June and the end of July. Although there is no specific information about where they played, the band do refer in publicity from August 1850 to "Messieurs Richardsons' First Musical Tour since their return to this country" and "Messieurs Richardsons' First Musical Tour since their return from the Continent"[22] One city where the Rock, Bell and Steel Band were supposed to have played is Vienna and there is anecdotal evidence which supports this claim. Writing in 1979 as part of a correspondence on the subject of the Richardson instrument,

---

[20] Ibid, p232ff.
[21] Hereford Times and General Advertiser, Saturday 18th May 1850, p5.
[22] Phillips 1, p163.

another descendant of Joseph Richardson, Judy Francis, noted her mother's recollection of her grandfather showing her a programme for a concert by the Richardson Band in Vienna.[23]

However far they were able to travel in the summer of 1850, the Rock Band was certainly back in August to begin another prolonged period of touring, this time scheduled to occupy them for a nine-month period which would take them well into the following year. Some of the publicity referred to plans for further foreign travel, this time across the Atlantic, referring to it being "last musical tour in England, previous to their departure for the United States and the Canadas".[24]

1851 was the year of the Great Exhibition, which took place at the specially built Crystal Palace in London. With its brief of championing innovation, the exhibition, which had a daily programme of music, would seem to have offered an ideal opportunity to showcase the ingenuity of the Rock, Bell and Steel Band. Sir George Smart, who had published the testimonial letter to Richardson some years earlier, was musical director for the opening of the exhibition, and would have been in a position to arrange for the band to perform there, but it didn't happen. In the event it may be that the innovation they offered was not what was called for. While music was certainly represented at the exhibition, the emphasis was on hardware, the focus being on manufactured, affordable instruments, a laudable enough aim at face value, but one particularly geared to commerce, "an unprecedented celebration of commodities"[25] and in that field a large rock harmonicon was never going to compete with a cheap upright piano.

In terms of the music which was performed at the Great Exhibition, the success of the opening event seems to have been gauged by the organisers not for any premiere performance of a major composition (there was none), but by the great number of musicians and singers involved. But magnificent though the vast glass building was, its acoustics rendered the music that was played there virtually inaudible. It seems that despite the impressive quantity of participants enlisted to perform they could not be heard, Queen Victoria noting in her diary that "200 instruments and 600 voices…seemed nothing."[26]

The Great Exhibition opened on Monday 1st May, but as things turned out the Rock, Bell and Steel Band may not have been able to play there anyway, as the band was forced to take a break from their touring schedule. Robert, the youngest of the Richardson sons, had for some time been in bad health. Sickness had been prevalent in Britain, with the worst ever cholera epidemic, which had claimed many lives and it may have been feared that he had succumbed to this, but that was not the case. Robert Richardson's illness was instead rooted in a prostate condition and it's thought he may have also contracted pneumonia, which came to a head towards the end of April 1851. The planned trip to the USA and Canada, due to commence in August, was cancelled and although this was probably because of Robert's health, there may have been other factors involved. Instead, another trip to Ireland was arranged and by August, with Robert having recovered considerably, they set off.

---

[23] Newsletter of the Geological Curators' Group, Vol 2 No.7 December 1979, p423ff.
[24] Hereford Times and General Advertiser, Saturday 18th May 1850, p5.
[25] Davies and Lockhart, p235; Flora Willson, *Hearing Things: Musical objects at the Great Exhibition 1851*
[26] Ibid, p241.

Considering that the trip was planned at relatively short notice and that there must have been a question of whether it was wise to go at all, a surprisingly long list of dates were arranged. Starting off with a six-week tour of the counties of Ulster, the Richardsons then worked their way across the country, not to return to England until at least the end of the year. By the time they did return Robert's health had deteriorated once more and the decision was made, not least because Robert's musical strengths were crucial to the band, that it was time to finally call it a day. After close to twelve years of playing together, introducing the sound of stone to thousands of people throughout the British Isles and beyond, the Rock, Bell and Steel Band came to an end.

Some months before this, perhaps mindful of the way things were going, Joseph Richardson had begun thinking about the future and had purchased a public house in London, the Green Man on the Edgware Road. When they returned to England from Ireland with all their imminent bookings cancelled, it was decided that this new venture would be where they must now focus their energies. The amount of intense touring the Richardsons had been undertaking over the preceding years would have amassed a very considerable amount of money and the purchase and refurbishment of the Green Man was clearly seen as a sound investment. So it proved, and also one to the sons' liking as over the following years Joseph, Samuel and Joseph junior bought other pubs which they ran individually or jointly. Joseph's wife Elizabeth moved down from Keswick with their three youngest daughters, so for the first time since 1840 they were together as a family, except for the eldest of the children, Ann and John who remained in Cumbria. It seems that Joseph Richardson senior did not settle well into the new life however, becoming ill with bronchitis and in 1855 the inventor of the rock harmonicon died at the age of sixty-three. Robert, his youngest son survived him by three years, but was only thirty-four when he died. John, the eldest son moved down to London with his wife and daughter and, following his father's and brothers' example, became a publican. Samuel, who seemed to be the most business-minded of the family went on to have his own licensed establishment built and, in acknowledgement of where he came from, named it the Skiddaw Hotel.

The fate of the instrument known as the Rock, Bell and Steel Band was to be a mixed one. It survived, which most of the other rock harmonicons did not, but its touring days were pretty much over. It had taken pride of place at the Green Man, with Samuel taking possession of it after his father's death. At some point, however, it passed to his older sister Ann, still living in Applethwaite. Once the instrument had returned there, Ann's husband, James Henderson, had the idea that he would like to have it playing again, so he teamed up with some friends to see if they could make a go of it. Unfortunately, for one reason or another it didn't work out and the mighty instrument remained standing in silence.

The Henderson's son however, who they had named Richardson, seems to have inherited his grandfather's musical genes and in time took to playing the rock harmonicon rather more successfully. Once he had left school Richardson Henderson travelled down to London to stay with his Uncle Samuel at the Skiddaw Hotel and remained there for a while, setting up a business in the music trade. He would have undoubtedly become acquainted with the Rock, Bell and Steel Band during the period he spent in London and much later, when he and the instrument were back in Cumbria and he had opened his own music shop in Keswick, Henderson began playing it with some seriousness, along with a friend of his, William Tangye, who brought along his son as the third player (Figure 5.5). The plan was to practise a repertoire

*Figure 5.5. Richardson Henderson (centre), William Tangye (left) and Tangye's son (right) in their revival of the Rock, Bell and Steel Band. © John H. Phillips.*

of material which would enable them to revive an interest in the instrument which half a century earlier had proved such a success.

In July 1889 the three musicians made their debut playing together at the reception for Henderson's sister's wedding and it went well enough to encourage them to do more. The Derwent Hall in Keswick was therefore hired for several days the following month and they performed to the public for the first time. In addition to the Rock, Bell and Steel Band there were singers, piano solos and duets, a violinist, a comic turn and William Tangye's son played the musical glasses. The evening was well received and as a result Richardson Henderson became increasingly ambitious for this new venture, commissioning at some expense an artist friend to paint a series of large landscape views to be presented as a diorama in conjunction with the performance, with shifting light effects adding to the atmosphere. Henderson also engaged the services of an agent and a series of concerts was arranged, starting off with two well-attended nights in Keswick, presenting another varied line-up of performers. This was followed by sixteen more concerts throughout December in different towns within reasonable travelling distance. But without the support of home audiences numbers were down and however well the music may have been received by those who did turn up it seems that Richardson Henderson did not have enough confidence in this new enterprise for it to continue.

The Rock, Bell and Steel Band, having fallen silent again, was taken back to Henderson's music shop where the instrument was to remain for several years. Richardson Henderson, it seems, was a broken man, perhaps in part caused by not having been able to emulate his grandfather's success.[27] In 1917 he and his wife decided to move to Edinburgh and the instrument was donated to the museum in Keswick's Fitz Park where it has remained to this day, called upon for the occasional public performance, but during museum opening times available for visitors to discover its unexpected charms for themselves.

---

[27] Correspondence with John Phillips, January 2024.

# Chapter Six

# The Till Family Rock Band
## Following in the footsteps

The same year that Joseph Richardson began building his rock harmonicon, 1827, Daniel Till was born in Lancaster. Exactly fifty years later, he and his family were to present their own version of a rock harmonicon to the public for the first time, initially calling themselves the Skiddaw Rock Band. Following in the footsteps of Richardson and his sons, the Tills introduced a new generation of concert-goers across Britain to the wonders of musical stone and, putting their own stamp on the idea, were then to travel across the Atlantic where they were able to play to even larger audiences than they were able to command in their own country.

Daniel Till had begun his working life in agriculture, on the outskirts of Lancaster, before moving to Keswick in 1856 to assist in the construction of a waterworks. Once the job was completed he returned to Lancaster, but years later was invited back to take up a permanent position at the Keswick Waterworks Company and appointed its general manager in 1868. It was not long after that, however, that another activity began to occupy his thoughts.

One story goes that soon after taking up his post at the waterworks Till was with some employees at the reservoir, breaking up a section of rock with pickaxes, when he noticed that it rang with a musical tone when they struck it. This set him thinking about the possibility of building an instrument and decided to start collecting pieces of rock for the purpose. Another version of the story has Daniel Till walking on Skiddaw as a child (presumably on a trip from

*Figure 6.1. Daniel Till and sons Daniel and William with their rock harmonicon. Courtesy of Dr. Michael Till.*

Lancaster with his parents), accidentally striking his foot against a stone and being surprised to hear it ring. Whichever account is true, and conceivably both are, by the time he decided to build an instrument he would have almost certainly have known of the Richardson family rock band's achievements. Although they hadn't been active for many years, it's quite possible that Daniel Till saw the Richardsons playing in his younger days and that it was the memory of this which influenced his decision later in life to build something similar himself. He would have been thirteen when the Original Rock Band played their first concerts and over the following twelve years there would certainly have been opportunities to see them, although there is no record of them having played in Lancaster.

Daniel Till and his two sons, William and Daniel, began to collect pieces of rock from the Skiddaw slopes in the summer of 1868 and from small beginnings an instrument would evolve, over a period of nine years, to become a rock harmonicon of a similar scale to that of the Richardsons. A telling contemporary account of the lengthy and arduous nature of the task involved, probably the result of an interview with Daniel Till or one of the family, was published in the English Lakes Visitor of October 1879:

> Each collector, when in search, carried with him an ordinary hammer and chisel, and when a stone was found that had a sufficient tone, he set to work and reduced it to the size and shape required to fit the frame. Much labour was absolutely necessary, as on the average only about one stone in twenty proved to be of any use. When the stones had been carried down to Keswick, a distance of five or six miles, they were tuned to proper pitch with very fine chisels, but often when tuning a stone it was accidentally broken after the manipulator had been at it many hours. At the end of the first year, Messrs. Till & Sons, with considerable labour, had succeeded in collecting ten stones, upon which, with wooden hammers, one player was able to play simple tunes. They kept adding to the set at regular intervals during eight years until, after encountering many difficulties and numerous adventures amongst the mountains, they had the pleasure of seeing, as the result of their labour, the now celebrated and valuable instrument.[1]

While such reports placed Daniel Till at the centre of the story, years later William Till, who was to take charge of the Till Family Rock Band after his father had retired, wrote (in the third person) that it was actually he who had been the prime mover in the early days, both in finding and collecting the rocks, and in the construction of the instrument, albeit with Daniel's help:

> Mr Till [William] for many years explored the Palaeozic rocks of the Cumberland Mountains and at length found a series of which, when struck, produced musical sounds. The idea of a perfect instrument followed as a natural consequence. He, assisted by his father, continued to work on it and devoted eleven years in completing the instrument of five octaves which now is in his possession.[2]

William had been better educated musically than anybody in his family and became the main one responsible for the musical direction which the Tills were to take. While the initial idea to build a rock harmonicon may have come from his father it was William who seems to have been the prime mover in taking things forward.

---
[1] English Lakes Visitor, Saturday 4th October 1879, p5.
[2] 1903 letter from William Till cited by Till, p20.

The similarity between the Till and Richardson instruments suggests that at some point Daniel Till saw the Richardson harmonicon at close quarters. At that time it was in the possession of Richardson Henderson, not having been donated to the Fitz Park Museum until 1917, but Till may well have known Henderson and might have seen the instrument at his house, possibly learning the methodology of playing the instrument from the grandson of Joseph Richardson.

From the start, the Till's instrument, like the original, had three players (father and two sons) performing alongside each other (Figure 6.1) and there was also a strikingly similar repertoire, mixing classical pieces, both old and new, with traditional airs and popular pieces. In particular, both bands chose to play Handel's *The Harmonious Blacksmith*, which, while having no obvious connection with the blacksmith's work musically, did offer the opportunity to simulate the process, striking stone rather than iron. A review of a concert the Tills were later to perform in Leamington Spa was of the view that "the tones emitted by the stones under the percussion of the mallet suggests the clink of the hammer on the blacksmith's anvil more than any other instrument"[3] and William Till was to write in a publicity note that in their arrangement of the piece "the strokes on the anvil are unmistakable".[4] It certainly became a favourite with the Tills' audiences as it had been with the Richardsons' and it could even be that the Tills' rendition was based on the Richardson's arrangement which Richard Henderson may have passed on to them. Henderson had by that time become disillusioned with the idea of ever playing the Rock, Bell and Steel Band and was perhaps prepared to see another band continue the legacy.

The Tills' instrument had begun as a modest proposition, comprising only one and a half octaves, but by the time it had reached its finished state it spanned five octaves, comprising around sixty stone slabs. It may even have gone through a process of downsizing at some point, as in the publicity for their early public performances the rock harmonicon is described as being "composed of upwards of eighty musical stones", implying its range was at least seven octaves, so it may be that the highest and lowest notes were deemed to be too poor in quality and were discarded. One significant way in which the Till instrument differed from that of the Richardsons was in having tin resonators which were suspended below the lower notes to amplify their sound, due to them not cutting through as much as the higher frequency notes. Metal resonators are a feature of vibraphones, but they were not developed until the twentieth century, so it could be that Daniel or William Till got the idea from seeing somewhere another instrument such as a balafon from west Africa, which has gourds suspended below its wooden bars for the same reason. As this feature is only known about from notes made by William Till years later it's not certain whether the resonators were installed from the start or were added later.

By the summer of 1877 the new rock instrument was ready to present to the public and the Till rock harmonicon was exhibited in the Keswick Court Buildings. Daniel and his two sons, William and Daniel junior, were there to demonstrate its capabilities, and a new generation was able to witness the musical potential of stone slabs collected from the slopes of the mountain overlooking the town. In August they gave their first public performance when they

---

[3] Leamington Spa Courier, Saturday 30th December 1882, p5
[4] From Till Family Rock Band archive. Courtesy of Dr. Michael Till.

played at a bazaar raising funds for the building of a Sunday school in connection with the local Wesleyan Chapel.⁵

The bazaar took place at Keswick's Oddfellows Hall, not the first or last time this venue would host a performance on a locally built rock harmonicon and the Till family were back there in full force in October for a properly promoted debut concert appearance of the town's latest rock harmonicon. The evening was billed as a Grand Musical Entertainment and in addition to the debut of the new instrument the concert offered a varied musical programme. This included Daniel's two daughters, Lizzie and Annie singing, three other singers, a cornet duet by two local bandmasters and William Till also playing the piano. The evening was well attended and the audience were, according to a subsequent press report, "attentive and appreciative":

> On Tuesday evening last, the Messrs. Till, assisted by a few friends, gave a miscellaneous entertainment in the Oddfellows' Hall, Keswick, which was crowded throughout with a most attentive and appreciative company. The chief feature of the evening was the performance on the "Rock Harmonicon" or musical stones, which was introduced for the first time before a public audience. The Messrs.Till have for several years been engaged in the collection of and perfection of this series of stones, which at present constitute a marvellous musical novelty, comprising upwards of eighty stones, collected in the district, and which takes three performers to play, so that it is not too much to say is superior to anything of the kind ever attempted in this neighbourhood, if not in the kingdom. During the past summer the "Rock Harmonicon" has been exhibited in the Court Buildings, and musical selections have been given to illustrate its capabilities; but it was not until Tuesday evening that it was fairly submitted to the approval of a public audience. In order to give variety to the programme vocal and instrumental pieces were interspersed, and the result far exceeded the most sanguine expectations of the promoters.⁶

The report goes on to give an account of the performance, crediting those taking part and noting that during the second half of the concert a piece on the harmonicon "was also vociferously encored by the insatiable 'gods' at the back of the room, who beat a 'hoof' accompaniment in testifying their approval."⁷

**The Skiddaw Rock Band**

The effort the Tills had put into building the instrument now went into promoting their act, negotiating a series of concerts in other local towns. Billed as the Skiddaw Rock Band, for the next couple of years or so they proceeded to play throughout the Cumbrian area, an announcement in the English Lakes Visitor in September 1879 listing forthcoming concerts in Cockermouth, Workington, Maryport, Whitehaven. Keswick, Penrith and Carlisle. Although the rock harmonicon was the focal point of their performances, they continued to develop the sense of variety in their act which had been there at the outset, with songs playing an important part and an increased use of other instruments, some of them unusual. The music was a mix of operatic arias, popular songs and instrumental favourites, the *The Harmonious

---
⁵ West Cumberland Times Saturday 11th August 1877 p5
⁶ From facsimile of uncredited news report. Courtesy of Dr Michael Till.
⁷ Ibid.

*Figure 6.2. The Skiddaw Rock Band as they appeared at the Crystal Palace in 1881. Courtesy of Dr. Michael Till.*

*Blacksmith* proving to be a favourite with audiences as it had been for the Richardsons. There was also an evident wish to inform as well as to entertain with a programme for sale which, in addition to listing the pieces to be played and the lyrics to the songs, presented information on the history and geological character of the rock harmonicon.[8]

While William Till was the most accomplished musician of the family, already having some ability as a pianist, the others seem to have had a reasonable singing ability and their evident skills in playing a number of instruments were to develop as time went on. Their father Daniel's musical abilities were sufficient to receive mention in a published list of Keswick's "public men" and their roles and activities, in which he is described as "town's surveyor, inspector of nuisances, collector of water rates and player on the musical stones and bass fiddle."[9]

## Crystal Palace

In 1881 the Tills were presented with the opportunity, as the Richardsons had been, of presenting their rock harmonicon to London audiences. How this came about isn't clear but it enabled them to play to far greater numbers than had been possible in their concerts closer to home, though it was only Daniel Till and his two sons who were involved (Figure 6.2). The trio, still going under the name of the Skiddaw Rock Band, were booked for a series of concerts over several weeks at the Royal Polytechnic Institute in Regent Street and afterwards went on to play at the Crystal Palace, relocated to its new home in Sydenham following the 1851 Great Exhibition. There they played in the Opera Theatre for five days a week from February through until Easter alongside other attractions which included orchestral concerts, organ recitals and a skating rink. With special events being staged to mark the thirtieth anniversary of the Great Exhibition, the Crystal Palace was attracting large crowds as a place to see and be seen and

---

[8] From Till Family Rock Band archive. Courtesy of Dr Michael Till.
[9] West Cumberland Times, Saturday 17th May 1879, p5.

Figure 6.3. Publicity for the Skiddaw Rock Band performances at the Crystal Palace in 1881. Courtesy of Dr. Michael Till.

records indicate that on Good Friday alone that year there was an attendance of well over 25,000 people. Whether the acoustics had improved in thirty years is doubtful.

Inevitably, through word of mouth and press coverage, the Tills soon received offers of further engagements, later that year travelling to Middlesbrough and Darlington for a series of concerts and over the next few years the band, now back to its full line-up (Figure 6.4), were to perform to capacity audiences in a number of prestigious venues, including Birmingham Town Hall, St George's Hall in Liverpool and Glasgow City Hall as well as visiting many other towns around the country. Although their transportation would have still included the use of horse and carriage, the rail network was now far more established than when the Richardsons were touring the country, so it seems likely that they would have travelled by train when possible.

While the Till Family Rock Band (as it begun to be more generally known) clearly resembled the original Richardson Rock Band in a number of ways, with three male protagonists

MUSIC STONES

*Figure 6.4. The Till Family Rock Band. Courtesy of Dr. Michael Till.*

standing playing the rock harmonicon and presenting a similar range of material, the Tills offered a different kind of entertainment. The variety which characterised their first appearance in Keswick was extended and became their hallmark. Annie and Lizzie continued to sing, sometimes being joined by their father and brothers in a cappella part songs. William accompanied his sisters when they sang and also sometimes played solo pieces. The number of other instruments on stage increased over time and while audiences would have recognized the violin and cello, many of the additions were far more obscure, the Tills showing a distinct taste for the exotic. A mixing of different musical sounds became a characteristic of the Tills' performances to a much greater extent than it had been for the Richardsons, but with the rock harmonicon still remaining at the heart of proceedings. Again it was the defiance of expectation of what such an instrument was capable of which impressed audiences and critics, captivated by the joy of hearing sweet music being drawn from such unpromising stone slabs.

## On tour

1883 proved to be a particularly busy year for the Tills, travelling the length and breadth of the country, starting off in the south of England. There's no evidence that they had a manager or agent working for them to secure bookings and it seems likely that the job was shared between Daniel and his son William, who was to later prove to be particularly adept in such matters. According to local newspaper reports, they were well-received wherever they went, just as the Richardsons had been forty years before. A few extracts serve to convey the flavour, a press notice in advance of the band's appearance in Redhill in January showing that they could now expect to draw a sizeable crowd:

> So much interest has already been excited in this novel entertainment at the Market Hall this evening, that little further recommendation is needed from us. We will,

however, say, that those who have not obtained tickets will do well to be quick about it; and those who have no tickets will run a strong risk of missing a place.[10]

In Hastings the men's musical ability on the rock harmonicon in particular was commended:

> The executive dexterity displayed by the Messrs Till is something to call forth the wonder of all present, more especially when one of the performers was seen to be managing as many as three hammers at a time.[11]

In Whitstable it was the suitability of using stone for the playing of *The Harmonious Blacksmith* which the reviewer applauded:

> To our thinking this is the instrument upon which Handel's famed exercise should always be played...the metallic tones emitted by the stones under the percussion of the mallets, suggesting to us much more the clink of the hammer than any instrument of string or wind upon which we have heard it played.[12]

The following month they travelled to Oxfordshire, where the advance publicity for their concert in Witney pronounced, with a degree of hyperbole which was to become common, that their rock harmonicon had been "acknowledged by the London, Glasgow, and Provincial Press to be the most wonderful musical instrument in the world, and capable of producing the finest music."[13] A subsequent review of the same concert, appearing in Jackson's Oxford Journal a few days later records what was to become the band's customary way of finishing their concerts:

> At the close of the performance the company present were invited on the platform to inspect the instrument, and many were the exclamations of surprise at finding that the bell-like sweetness of tone which characterised all the pieces was produced by narrow rough slabs of dark stone arranged like the notes in a grand piano.[14]

In March the band moved up to North Wales where their performance in Mold was praised, along with the sound the rock harmonicon itself which was found to be

> ....more perfect than a piano, and the music is sweeter and more liquid in its tone... There was a good attendance each evening, and the entertainment was perhaps the most enjoyable and certainly the most novel that we have had here for some time.[15]

A trip to Scotland followed and then in the summer of 1883 the Tills spent two weeks in the Isle of Man where they had been booked to play consecutively at Grand Festival Week and Grand Carnival Week at Derby Castle in Douglas. As something of a variety show in themselves, the Till Family Rock Band would frequently find themselves playing alongside a miscellany of other performers, with different skills and of different ages. But here they found themselves sharing

---

[10] Surrey Mirror and County Post, Saturday 20th January 1883, p5.
[11] Hastings and St Leonards Observer, Saturday 27th January 1883, p2
[12] Whitstable Times, Saturday 27th January 1883, p4.
[13] Witney Express and Oxford and Midland Counties Herald, Thursday 22nd February, 1883.
[14] Jackson's Oxford Journal, Saturday 3rd March 1883, p7.
[15] Chester Chronicle, Saturday 17th March 1883 p6.

*Figures 6.5 and 6.6. Concert tickets. Courtesy of Dr. Michael Till.*

the stage with probably the youngest, and perhaps one of the more unusual acts they had been paired with, Lotto & Lilo, the Champion Infant Bicyclists. Lilo was only two years old and her older brother Lotto, twice her age at four years, was apparently renowned for "his marvellous feat of riding backwards...the only artiste Artiste in the World that ever accomplished this wonderful feat.[16]

## John Ruskin

Around this time, writer and critic John Ruskin, who as a twelve-year old had visited the Crosthwaite Museum and written the verse about the "stoney piano", comes back into the story of Cumbrian lithophones and that of the Tills in particular. In 1872 Ruskin, by now in middle age, had moved to the Lake District, having bought a large house called Brantwood, on the edge of Coniston Water, where he was to live for the rest of his life. Some reports say that Ruskin had seen the Tills playing in London at Crystal Palace, but by 1884 he was certainly in touch with William Till and they lived not far apart. On a day when Till was to give a solo home recital on a rock harmonicon, smaller than the one used for concerts by the family, Ruskin drove by carriage to Keswick to inspect the instrument at close hand and to hear it played. Versions differ as to what happened next. The standard account states that Ruskin then commissioned William Till to build a similar instrument for him which he could have at Brantwood, keen to be able to play it to visiting children. Commissioning something in this way was the kind of thing Ruskin was wont to do, keen to encourage local crafts. However, an American newspaper article from 1935 suggests that the instrument was in fact presented to Ruskin as a gift. Written following an interview with William Till, who by then had been living in the USA for many years, the article tells of Ruskin attending the concert in Keswick and being so impressed by the instrument that Till later arranged to have it delivered to him. It then states, wrongly, that after Ruskin's death the small rock harmonicon eventually became the property of the Metropolitan Museum of Art in New York and that "a card, telling of Mr. Till's gift to the famous man of letters, is beside it."[17] It seems that through some misunderstanding the museum had believed that the Till instrument being exhibited was the one which had been in Ruskin's possession, whereas that one had in fact remained in Coniston in Cumbria. Nevertheless, the content of the erroneous card still serves to reinforce the claim, which the proprietors had presumably also heard from William Till on another occasion, that John Ruskin's lithophone had been presented to him as a gift.

---

[16] Isle of Man Times and general advertiser, Saturday 25th August 1883, p8.
[17] From facsimile of article in Sunday Call, Newark NJ, 10th March 1935. Till archive, courtesy of Dr Michael Till.

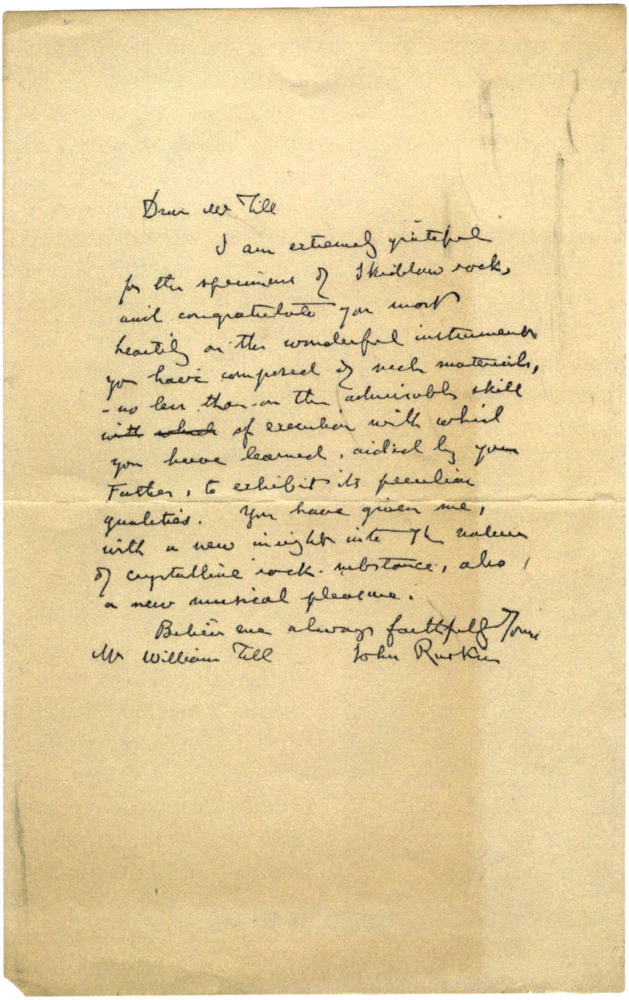

*Figure 6.7. Facsimile copy of letter from John Ruskin to William Till. Courtesy of Dr. Michael Till.*

In the 1935 interview, William Till also recalled receiving a letter from Ruskin acknowledging receipt of the instrument and expressing his appreciation, which became "one of the proud possessions of the Till family."[18] What happened to Ruskin's letter is not known, but William Till had facsimile copies made of it which were used in publicity for the Till Family Rock Band (Figure 6.7).

Brantwood, Coniston, Lancashire.
9th September 1884

---

[18] Ibid.

> Dear Mr Till,
> I am grateful for the specimens of Skiddaw rock, and congratulate you most heartily on the wonderful instrument you have composed of such materials, no less than on the admirable skill of execution with which you have learned, aided by your Father, to exhibit its peculiar qualities. You have given me, with a new insight into the nature of crystalline rock substance, also a new musical pleasure. Believe me always faithfully, Yours, John Ruskin[19]

In addition to his other pursuits, John Ruskin had a passionate interest in geology and became one of the country's leading authorities on the subject, possessing a collection of over 5000 mineral specimens. For Ruskin, rock was not an inanimate material and he saw in its slow but constantly shifting character a powerful life-force, tantamount to a kind of spiritual energy. In this context, given the value he placed on the relationship between art and nature, it seems probable that discovering the musical potential of natural stone would for him have represented something quite profound.[20] For his part William Till wrote years later:

> John Ruskin took great interest in this instrument and it was mainly due to his encouragement that the Till family known as the "Rock Band" was induced to exhibit publicly its wonderful musical properties.[21]

*Figure 6.8. Ruskin's lithophone as shown in a postcard from Ruskin Museum in the 1900s. Courtesy of Dr. Michael Till.*

Following Ruskin's death in 1900 a museum was set up in Coniston as a memorial to him, with his set of musical stones put on display where they can still be seen, though in a rather sorry state. At some point in the 1950s the stones were stolen from the Ruskin Museum, eventually to be discovered in a nearby hedge, but unfortunately with some stones missing. To prevent this from happening again the curator at the time drilled holes in the stones and secured the slabs to a board with a mixture of nails and screws in such a way that they no longer rang so sweetly.

### A new opportunity

Every year the town of Keswick hosts a large summer convention centred on Christian worship and teaching, evangelical but non-denominational. The Keswick Convention was first staged in 1875, so the Till family, who were themselves Methodists, would have been aware of its activities and in 1884

---

[19] Till archive
[20] Conversation with Howard Hull, Director of Brantwood, April 2024.
[21] From letter written by William Till in 1903. Cited in Till p20.

*Figure 6.9. Ruskin's lithophone as it is today, with several stones missing. Photograph by Mike Adcock. Courtesy Ruskin Museum, Coniston.*

they performed there, possibly not for the first time. One of those attending, visiting from the USA, was the Reverend F.E. Clarke an eminent clergyman who some years earlier had founded the Christian Endeavour movement. Clarke was particularly impressed by the Till Rock Band and suggested to them that they travel to America where they would have the opportunity to play at similar events to large audiences. Later he was to write:

> "I heard the Till Rock Band in Keswick, England last summer and was very much charmed with the artistic and swift effect of the Rock Music entertainment. It was one of the most melodious affairs I ever attended. I think that they will draw immense audiences on this side of the waters."[22]

Daniel Till had by this time resigned from his managerial job at the waterworks to concentrate on promoting the rock band and the family decided to take up the offer and made plans to travel there the following summer. Having completed another series of bookings, including a return trip to Scotland (Figure 6.10), the Tills (Daniel, his wife Margaret, William, Daniel junior, Annie and Lizzie) set off for America. It was to be a long stay. Later newspaper reports claimed that they had initially intended to stay for only one season but publicity dating from before their departure from England suggests otherwise:

> The TILL FAMILY have accepted Important Engagements on the Continent, at the termination of which they will spend some years in America.[23]

As for the engagements on the continent, it is uncertain whether these took place. As with the Richardson band, there is a degree of mystery about the extent of the Till's European travels, or whether they ever materialised at all. If they did take place in 1885, then it's possible that they

---

[22] Cited later in The Indiana Progress, Wednesday 4th September 1895, p13.
[23] From programme note in Till archive.

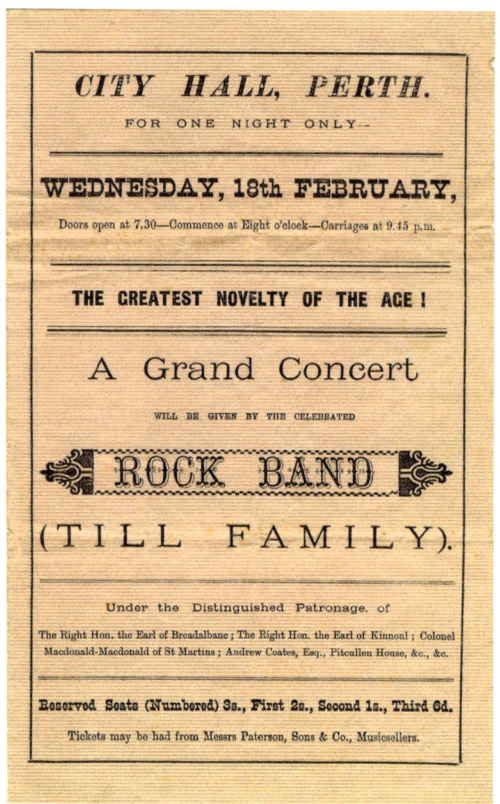

*Figure 6.10. Handbill for concert in Perth, Wednesday 18th February 1885. Courtesy of Dr. Michael Till.*

went there *en route* to the USA. Be that as it may, in June that year, exactly a century after Peter Crosthwaite had collected his first Music Stones from the foot of Skiddaw, the Tills arrive in New York, along with their five-octave rock harmonicon, and were given accommodation in the city of Bayonne in New Jersey. This was to remain their base, though they were soon to begin a busy schedule of performing, travelling widely and on a scale that must have made their former touring in Britain seem parochial by comparison.

# Chapter Seven

# The Tills in the USA
## The rise of the rockophone

**The Chautauqua Institute**

Reverend Clarke was correct in his prediction that the Till Family Rock Band would draw large crowds in America. Once they had settled into their new home they began working for a religious organisation called the Chautauqua Institute which organized annual events known as the Chautauqua Assemblies. These were initially intended as summer camps for training Sunday School teachers and were so named because the first one took place on the banks of Chautauqua Lake in New York State in 1874. Like the Keswick Conventions they combined religious teaching with broader cultural and recreational activities, with an emphasis on the arts, and were attended by large numbers of people. When the Tills performed at the 1886 Assembly they were honoured by receiving what was known as the Chautauqua Salute, which meant that after they had been introduced to the attendant crowd "10,000 handkerchiefs were waved in the air."[1]

The Till band also played at other smaller gatherings arranged by the organization, which took place in different parts of the country and these could also draw large crowds. Musical performances always played an important part at these events, with a deliberately broad range of styles on offer from opera to lighter, more popular forms including vaudeville, spirituals and rural traditional music. It's easy to see how the eclectic repertoire of the Till Family Rock band would have fitted the bill perfectly. The band also undertook a number of long concert tours, playing at religious venues and civic halls to large audiences: a single performance at the Union Square Methodist Hall in Somerville, Massachusetts in October 1885, a few months after they had arrived in the country, was reported to have attracted an audience of around 1400 people.

Most of the Till band's American bookings were made through the Redpath Booking Agency, who were connected with the Chatauqua organisation, as was a theatrical agent called H.J. Norman who effectively became the band's manager. The distances covered by the Till Family during the five years following their arrival in the USA were vast with concerts given in over thirty states, made possible by a railroad system which was by then linking all major cities as well as many towns in between. They also made at least two visits across the border into Canada and the undoubted success they had enjoyed in their home country was surpassed wherever they found new audiences, judging by the attendance numbers for their concerts and the almost unanimously glowing reviews which appeared in a host of local newspapers.

During their stay in America, the Tills continued to develop their act, adding yet more instruments and novel features. Something which became a highlight of their performances

---
[1] Altoona Times, Pennsylvania, Monday 21st January 1889, p1.

*Figure 7.1. The Till Family Rock Band, probably taken soon after they arrived in the USA. Courtesy of Dr. Michael Till.*

was the playing of musical glasses, their haunting sound put to use on popular pieces such as *Nearer my god to thee*, *Abide with me* and Gounod's *Ave Maria*, based on J.S Bach's *Prelude in C*. Using the principal of the glass harmonica, musical drinking glasses had became a quite popular form of entertainment in the nineteenth century and became known as tumblericons, though the Tills referred to theirs as Belgian glasses. Another instrument which may not have been known to many in the audience, and played in a manner familiar to even fewer, was the German streichzither. This was a relatively modern bowed instrument and the idiosyncratic playing of it by Daniel Till (probably the son, not the father) was described in newspaper review from 1888:

> Mr D.Till used an instrument with strings drawn over a sort of rectangular hollow box, to give what he said was an imitation of of chimes of Westminster Church, London and Trinity Church, New York, but no chimes were ever heard so sweet. In playing the instrument he kept it in motion all the time by swinging it over his head, making the notes sound like those of bells a long way off.[2]

While the rock harmonicon remained the star of the show, both visually dominant and the principal talking point, there were soon around twenty instruments on stage competing for attention. In newspaper reports presumably sourced from the band's publicity, the impressive claim was made, in a potential hostage to fortune, that "they carry $50,000 worth of musical instruments."[3]

---

[2] Spirit of Jefferson, Charles Town, West Virginia, Friday 3rd February 1888, p3.
[3] Altoona Times, Thursday 17th January 1889 p4.

*Figure 7.2. The Till Family Concert Band: William, Daniel jnr., Annie and Lizzie, their father no longer performing with the band. Other instruments, including a pair of ocarinas and the musical glasses visible in addition to the rock harmonicon. Courtesy of Dr. Michael Till.*

## The Till Family Concert Company

With the number of instruments increasing and vocal contributions continuing to play a significant part, the family decided, soon after their arrival in the USA, to change the name of the band to the more inclusive Till Family Concert Company. But, like the Richardsons before them, they hedged their bets, perhaps always aware that it was the rock harmonicon which remained their unique selling point. So sometimes they would revert to the old name, and on occasions combine the two. After the family had been in the country for a couple of years or so Daniel Till senior stepped back from performing, for at least some of the time, and a review of a concert from 1888, which gives a fuller account of the details of their performance than most, indicates that one of the daughters, probably Lizzie, joined her brothers at the rock harmonicon:

> The principal feature of the entertainment was their performance on the rock harmonicon, in which Miss Till and Messrs. William and Daniel Till took part...The Ocarina, which is one of the instruments used, is made of clay and modeled from an instrument recently found in the ruins of Pompeii. Solos and quartets are played on the ocarinas, accompanied on the zither. The streich zither is a German stringed instrument played with a bow, in duets with the concert zither. Their other instruments

are the gigilera, a Swiss instrument of wood, musical glasses, Indian buguen, musical nails. etc. The vocal part of the programme consists of new songs and quartettes, with accompaniment of rocks, zithers and fairy bells. That part of the performance with glass tumblers was an interesting feature. Fine cut glass tumblers of different sizes, partially filled with water were used. The music was made by moistening the tips of the players' fingers with a sponge and then rubbing them over the tops of the glasses. The "cat duet" by Miss Till and D.Till, in which they imitated a midnight caterwauling serenade, was heartily encored....[4]

The identity of some of the instruments listed may require some clarification, not in all cases an easy task. The Swiss gigilera was simply a xylophone under another name. At that time the xylophone was still relatively uncommon and the name used for it was sometimes taken from where that particular example originated, in this case presumably Switzerland. The so-called "fairy bells" were a simple form of box-zither made by Daniel Till, held vertically and producing a pleasant tinkling sound, as their name might suggest. The Indian buguen is harder to identify and may not have been Indian at all, linguistically sounding closest to a begena, a type of box-lyre from Ethiopia, and while that can only be speculation it would correspond with the other stringed instruments whose possibilities the Tills were beginning to explore. The musical nails may refer to another of the Tills' chosen instruments, the musical jack-boot, which according to the Till's own publicity, "produces music beyond description."[5] Creating music from a device designed for easing the removal of footwear was not unique to the Tills, it cropping up as instrument of choice for other performers around that time, allegedly having been invented by Joseph Seebold of the Jungfrau Kapelle from Switzerland. It constituted a boot-jack which had been customised by having different length nails driven into it, each presumably producing a different note. These were then struck, possibly with a hammer, though one description in a review of a performance by Seebold in Cardiff suggests that he may have used a bow, playing it "as he would upon the strings of a violin."[6]

## Thomas Edison

Also living in New Jersey at that time, and not far from the Tills, was America's most famous inventor, Thomas Edison (Figure 7.3). As well as living in the same neighbourhood there was another connection which brought them together, resulting in an unlikely collaboration. In 1886 Edison, who had lost his first wife two years before, married nineteen year old Mina Miller who was the daughter of Lewis Miller, one of the founders of the Chautauqua Institute. Lewis Miller and Thomas Edison were already friends and Edison then struck up an acquaintance with Mina. As their relationship developed there were some reservations within the Miller family, not least because Mina Miller was only half Edison's age, but the marriage went ahead anyway.

Edison was then developing a refined version of his phonograph, whose main use was initially seen as a recording device for office dictation. He was also mindful of the possibility of it being used domestically for playing commercial recordings, but he could hardly have imagined the extent to which that would eventually become its primary and most universal use. Edison first

---

[4] Savannah Morning News, Wednesday 21st March 1888, p8.
[5] The Grand Island Independent, Nebraska, Friday 5th November 1886, p3.
[6] Western Mail, 20th December 1890, p3.

*Figure 7.3. Thomas Edison with an early version of his phonograph.*

introduced his new phonograph to the public at a Chautauqua Assembly and, wanting to raise awareness of his invention in the hope of making the phonograph a commercial proposition, it was agreed that it could be demonstrated at concerts by artists associated with the Chautauqua organisation. So demonstrations of the phonograph then became a feature at performances by the Till Family Concert Band, showing how it could be a device for both recording and playback. The Tills' practice of inviting audiences to inspect their array of instruments at the end of a show now became extended, allowing those who came up on stage to watch and partake in the recording of voices on the Edison machine and also listen to other prepared material. Reviews of the band's concerts frequently mentioned these demonstrations and in one there is a suggestion that the Till band were themselves recorded, though no such recording seems to have survived:

> After the entertainment nearly the whole of the audience viewed the harmonicon, examined the stones, sounded the various notes and looked with astonishment upon the crude instrument from which such agreeable music was produced...some choice pieces were then likewise rendered on the phonograph.[7]

Another review, attended by around 800 people, describes one of the Tills demonstrating the phonograph.

---

[7] Detroit Free Press, Saturday 3rd May 1890, p5.

> Perhaps not fifty persons in the audience had seen a phonograph, and it was looked upon with great curiosity as Mr Till opened the box and attached a large funnel-shaped sound collector, the trumpet. The audience dared hardly breath as the little cylinder began to turn. With a feeling of awe all looked at the little wonder, waiting to hear the first word from the marvel of the 19th century. Then from way off in the distance came a merry school girl's song. It broke in so quietly that at first people did not realize that it was the phonograph singing. Then a selection was played that had been played into it some months ago. A bagpipe was imitated with wonderful shrillness.[8]

A few weeks earlier, a performance in a hall filled with students from the nearby college, which also concluded with a demonstration of the Edison phonograph, received a review in a local newspaper which struck a more sceptical and somewhat world-weary tone:

> The programme consisted of vocal selections by the family quartette, familiar airs worked out upon sticks of wood, rocks, glasses and other instruments of torture, and an exhibition of one of Edison's improved phonographs. The phonograph was run with a treadle like a sewing machine and seemed superior to the old crank arrangement. The machine reproduced band and other music that had been blown into it distinctly, and also repeated conversation so that it could be understood by those of the audience who knew what the thing was supposed to say.[9]

Whether Thomas Edison himself ever appeared on stage with the Tills is not known. It seems unlikely that he would have travelled on tour with them but they would certainly have met, with members of the band possibly learning how to operate the phonograph from its inventor, but it is tantalising to think that there may once have existed a recording of the Till Family Concert Band playing.

### A return to England

The fact that the Tills were playing for a religious organisation and frequently performed in churches did not mean that the work was not lucrative and an indication of their popularity is that after a few years they were said to be commanding the highest fees of anybody on the circuit. How many concerts they played in North America is impossible to say with any accuracy, especially since their publicity tended to err on the side of exaggeration, but some estimates suggest a figure of over three thousand. The band's periods of long-distance touring mainly took place over the first three years of being in America, but towards the end of that period it was starting to take its toll and the family decided to try and limit themselves to working more locally. Another factor was that a few years earlier William had met and married an American woman, Elizabeth Grieves, and with three young daughters they felt it was time to settle down. A couple of years later at least some of the family were thinking it was time to return to their home country. There had been intermittent return visits to England, but towards the end of 1889 a series of concerts was billed as the end of their current season in the country and on 12th June 1890 the Tills gave a farewell concert at the First Reformed Church in Bayonne. The following week the city's Office Journal published a piece about the concert which had apparently been graced with an "immense audience".

---

[8] Tyrone Daily Herald, Pennsylvania, Thursday 16th January 1890, p1.
[9] The Tribune, Scranton, Pennsylvania, Friday 6th December 1889, p5.

The church was literally crowded to the doors by our very best people, as well as by many friends from New York, Brooklyn, Jersey City and other places, who had braved the storm (one of the worst of the season) in order to be present. The Till Family are too well known here to make it necessary to criticise the performance, suffice it to say, that it was, as usual, a grand success in every way....They have remained for five seasons, during which time they have traversed the greater part of our continent playing from Florida to Prince Edwards Island, and from New York to the Rocky Mountains, their engagements embracing thirty one of the United States and the whole of the Canadas, and necessitating an amount of travel exceeding 100,000 miles. In these five seasons they had given over eleven hundred concerts, entertaining over half a million people, and neither during this time, nor during the five years previous, when they were giving their concerts in Europe, have they ever missed a single engagement, a very singular and creditable fact which will be best appreciated by those who understand the accidents of travel, and the exigencies and possibilities of the amusement world.[10]

The Till Family Concert Band had come to an end, at least in its present form and for the time being. Daniel Till and Margaret Till, Daniel junior and his two sisters Annie and Lizzie set sail back to England on 17th June. It had been a family band and a very successful one, yet of the mother of the family, Margaret, little is known. She was apparently a pianist and had played with the band on occasion though no further details have come to light. Margaret and Daniel's oldest son William, his wife Elizabeth and their daughters, Mabel, Mildred and Esther stayed in Bayonne. Following the rest of the family's return to England Daniel Till senior was only to live a further two years, dying in Keswick in 1892 at the age of 64.

## The next generation

William Till settled into his new life with Elizabeth and their family, initially continuing to live in Bayonne. Although the rock harmonicon was set to one side, he continued to play, becoming part of the musical community of Bayonne and in 1892 was appointed as organist at the First Reformed Church, where the band had given its farewell performance. William also became musical director of the Bayonne Musical Society and taught organ and piano at home, the instruments he had himself studied as a young man.

William and Elizabeth's family grew in size and number, with the arrival of three further children: two sons and a daughter. Names given to two of them show their father to have retained fond memories of his earlier life back in Cumbria: one daughter was named Greta (after the river running through Keswick) and one of the sons was called William Derwent, the latter name taken from that of the lake closest to Keswick. He soon came to be known as just Derwent, to distinguish him from his father. William senior's recollections of the past would also have doubtless returned to more recent times when, with the Till Family Concert Band, he had travelled far and wide, witnessing the very different landscapes of his adopted country and achieved considerable success, performing to many hundreds of appreciative audiences. So when it was suggested to him by a friend that he should revive the idea of a family rock band he seemed not to need much prompting to decide to give it another go. After a period of rehearsal with his daughters Mildred and Esther, neither of whom had yet reached their

---

[10] Re-published in The Bayonne Herald and Greenville Register, Saturday 21st June 1890, p1.

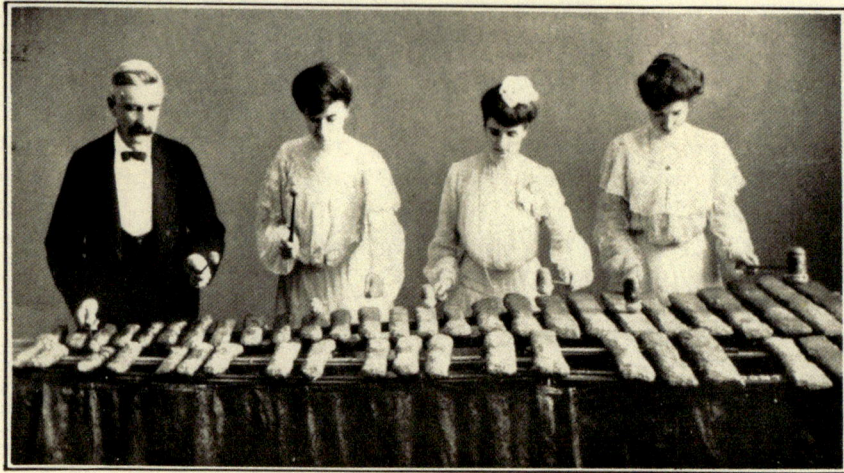

*Figure 7.4. The Rock Band Concert Company. Courtesy of Dr. Michael Till.*

teens, the Till Family Rock Band, in a new form, returned to the stage in 1897, performing as a trio. The name continued to change and for a while it was known as the Rock Band Concert Company, keeping the reference to the stone instrument at the heart of things but implying a sense of variety as well.

Only seven years had elapsed since the original band had made its final performance, meaning that the name was still well enough remembered to ensure that once more their concerts would soon be filled to capacity. Although they spent more time in the family home than in the old touring days, the Rock Band Concert Company soon began to play further afield, with concerts in the first year taking place in New York, Michigan and Ohio. In 1898 they travelled to Indiana and Kentucky and the following year to Pennsylvania in February and then across to Indiana once more. A short review of a concert there, in the town of Waterloo in the local newspaper indicates that the idea of a family rock band still had some mileage and that this latest manifestation could also deliver the goods:

> The Rock Band concert on Monday night was a complete success and everyone was well pleased. The entire performance was of the first order of merit. It is very seldom that our people have the opportunity to hear the equal of the Till Family Rock Band.[11]

In October the same year, 1899, the band made a return visit to Canada where the original Till Family Rock Band had played almost fourteen years earlier.

---

[11] The Waterloo Press, Thursday 30th March 1899, p5.

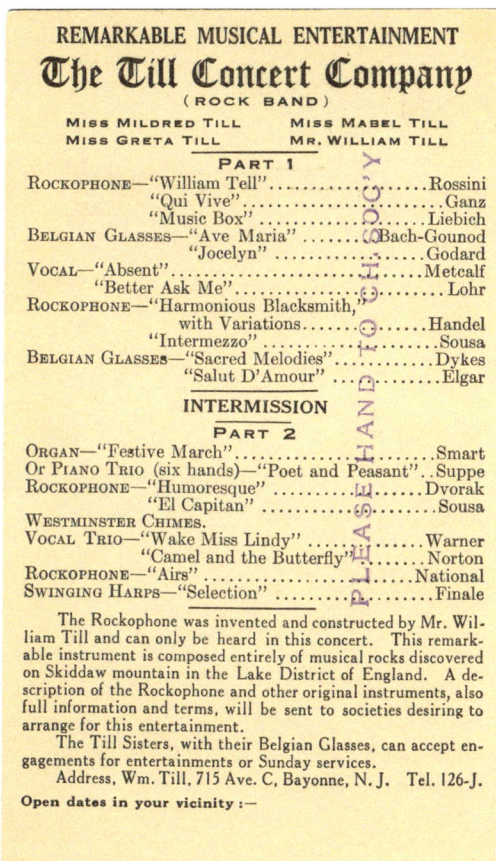

*Figure 7.5. Till Concert Company Programme. Courtesy of Dr. Michael Till.*

Despite being a pared down version of the former band, the format remained similar, combining performances on the rock harmonicon, now generally referred to as a rockophone, with a growing collection of other instruments. The two daughters, like their aunts, both sang, Mildred contralto and Esther soprano. Esther's particular specialism, however, was the recitation of verse and stories, so the way she appeared in the billing varied between being a humorist, a dramatic reader or an elocutionist. William, Mildred and Esther remained the mainstay of the band, but in time their younger siblings also took part. Mildred who, following on from her aunt, had become adept at playing the Belgian glasses, began playing them in a duet with her sister Mabel (Figure 7.4). Their act had its own technical requirements, with an insistence that only pure rainwater should be supplied for using with the glasses, its softer, less chalky character presumably giving a better sound. This was referred to in a review of a concert, with a suggestion that the request may not always have been well received:

It is said that Mr Wm. Till, manager of the Rock Band Co. raised some consternation by asking for rain water with which to fill the musical glasses. Several cisterns in the town were canvassed before satisfactory returns were obtained.[12]

Another feature which the Tills had introduced to their performance, which became popular with audiences, was what they called their "swinging harps", also known as "fairy bells", featuring William and two of his daughters playing together. They employed the same technique that Daniel Till had used with the streichzither, but using instead the box-zithers which Daniel Till senior had made. With the three of them standing holding and playing the fairy bells in front of them, this must have been a quite striking trio performance to behold. Swinging the instruments around in a circular motion gave the sound an added dimension, a type of phasing which created an impression of hearing church bells ringing from a distance, the sound naturally processing as it passed through the air. The idea was something they had almost certainly borrowed from seeing elsewhere, the same effect being used by music hall entertainers using concertinas. Such additions, as well as providing more musical variety,

---

[12] *Middletown Daily Argus*, New York, Wednesday 5th September 1894, p5.

# Music Stones

*Figure 7.6, 7.7. Two-sided handbill. Front (Left), reverse (Top). Courtesy of Dr. Michael Till.*

would also have contributed an added visual element to the performance (Figures 7.5, 7.6 and 7.7).

William Till remained centrally involved in the direction of the band, though a manager, D. Adna Brown, was taken on to assist with bookings and promotion. In 2010, archive material relating to the Till Family Rock Band came to light, discovered in a suitcase given to a charity shop in Florida.[13] It includes a scrap book containing newspaper cuttings and handwritten notes of William Till, publicity photographs, concert tickets, letters and documents. The contents give an indication of how scrupulous Till was, both in the day-to-day management of the band and in the things he clearly felt important to keep for posterity. Of particular interest are the typewritten notes showing exactly how the rockophone should be packed for transportation and instructions for it to be assembled (Figure 7.8). Because the whereabouts of the rock harmonicon used by the Tills are unknown (if it still exists at all) we cannot know exactly how it was constructed, but it is these notes which tell of the added tin resonators mentioned earlier.

---

[13] Aliffe, p106.

```
              Instructions how to set up the Rockophone
                      Five flat boxes and four horses
                      -------------------------
First-:  Take the four horses which support the frame (see that they
         are screwed  and made firm & safe) Place about 3 ft apart with the
         large horse at left (bass end)

Box No.1  12 rails (straw attached) Place as indicated in four rows
              Resonators (tin) suspend between rows 1 & 2 and 3 & 4
              for the lower notes only
              Manuscript Music, arranged for three players
              Six Mallets.   The 4 boxes below contain rocks
Box No. 2  Six rocks, No.1 to 6.   F to F   Top of resonators about
                         one inch below the note, move up or down to
                         get the best tone
Box No.3  Thirteen rocks, No.7 to 19. G to E & 25 to F1,E to G
 ..   4   Twelve       ..  No.13 to 24,  F to D
 ..   5   Sixteen      ..  No.1 to 16.   A to A

William Till, 157 Park St.  East Orange, N.J.  Phone ORange 5-9370
```

*Figure 7.8. William Till's instructions for setting up the rockophone. Courtesy of Dr. Michael Till.*

## Family spin-offs

It seems that although this later phase of the band's history continued for several years there were fallow periods and with William's other musical commitments it could not be the full-time enterprise it had been before. But this did mean that members of the family could pursue other opportunities: Mildred and Mabel performed with their Belgian glasses, advertising their availability for performing on them "for entertainment or Sunday services", Esther's recitations were always popular and and there were also different vocal groupings. When the three younger siblings, John, Derwent and Greta began performing in the family band, as both singers and instrumentalists, it probably helped to ease the pressure on the others, the changing personnel seen in publicity photographs suggesting that the number appearing varied. Derwent and Greta became particularly noted for their vocal abilities, both within the family band and outside it.

As before, the bookings the family band took on tended to be mainly at churches or at religious events. This may have come from the network of venues they had built up from the earlier years of touring as well as from a degree of contact being maintained with the Chatauqua Institute. That connection may have led to them being invited to play at a large religious event in 1903 at the Auditorium in Ocean Grove, on the New Jersey coastline, where they were "so enthusiastically received by the thousands present that a repetition of the same was demanded."[14]

In February 1907 the Till Family Rock Band were booked to perform at the Chautauqua Winter Assembly in Binghamton, New York and an eleventh hour drama ensued when they were asked to play a few days earlier than planned, as the intended guest speaker was unwell. They eventually agreed, on condition that the organisers would arrange for their equipment to be transported to and from a concert already arranged in Harlem the following day. A newspaper report about the story, which sounds very much as if it was fed by the Till Family themselves,

---
[14] Bayonne Herald and Greenville Register, 31st October 1903, p4.

MUSIC STONES

*Figure 7.9. William Till, in later years, at home with his rockophone. Courtesy of Dr. Michael Till.*

gives an indication of how they assessed their own value and status at the time, managing to make capital from their appearance at both events.

> The Rock Band concert is the most novel musical organisation in the world. Mr Till has the only rockophone in existence. He and his daughters have appeared more than 100 times in New York. Their engagements there and in its vicinity are sufficient to keep them busy the year round. Tomorrow night they will appear in the Calvary Church, Harlem, the largest Methodist Church in the world, for the seventh successive concert. Mr Till commands a higher price than any other concert company before the American public. The highest figure ever paid by the Winter Chautauqua is given Mr Till.[15]

The Till Family Rock Band continued to perform intermittently for another decade or so, mainly close to their home in the Bayonne area, before the family decided that the time had come to discontinue, playing their last concerts in 1918. The following year a short article about rockophones appeared in the prestigious American music magazine *Etude*, marking the fact that the Till Family Rock Band was no more. The article, which was syndicated nationally to other newspapers, noted that "perhaps the most unusual instrument of modern times is the rockophone which was used for many years by a family of performers known as the Till family, now engaged in church work in New York."[16]

That year, 1919, William Till also retired from his position as church organist and as musical director. He was sixty-three, a few months younger than his father Daniel had been when he

---

[15] Press and Sun-Bulletin, Monday 11th February 1907, p2.
[16] Lancaster New Era, Pennsylvania, Wednesday 16th July 1919, p8. Originally published in The Etude.

died, but William was to carry on living in Orange, New Jersey, for another twenty-five years, dying in 1945 at the age of eighty-nine.[17] When possible he and his wife Elizabeth would visit De Bruce, New York close to the Catskill Mountains where he spent much of the time trout-fishing. William Till's scrapbook of pictures largely comprises photographs and postcards showing scenes from there or from the English Lake District where he had grown up and there is a marked visual similarity between them.

## Postscript

Although there are no known sound recordings of the Till Family Rock Band from their association with Thomas Edison and his phonograph, there remain a good number of photographs of the band in its different manifestations. Unlike the Richardsons, who left us no evidence that a camera was ever pointed in their direction, by the time the first Till Family Rock Band began performing in 1877 photography was well established across the country and the Tills took advantage of this new medium, using it for publicity material and also to produce picture postcards of the band to sell at concerts. The photographs are virtually all posed, studio-style pictures, showing the subjects formally attired, the men in morning suits and the women in floor-length dresses or skirts and all displaying a serious countenance, with no hint of the novelty and humour promised in their act.

This straight-laced manner is of course a familiar characteristic of photographic portraits from the Victorian era and largely a consequence of the subjects' need to keep as still as statues, due to slow shutter speeds. From a present-day perspective, however, there is a clear disconnect between the formality and seriousness in the way the Tills presented themselves and the far from conventional nature of certain aspects of their performances. The overwhelming impression given by reviews, unearthed from online archives, is that the band displayed a high level of musicianship, a distinctly varied repertoire and were extremely well-received, often by very large audiences, especially during their time in the USA, with one concert being so well-attended that 300 were turned away. What isn't so clear is the tone of the entertainment they were offering. Were they attempting to subvert, or at least challenge, accepted conventions or merely offering amusing titillation well within the bounds of acceptability? Was their formal attire a deliberate foil to the unconventional nature of their performance or were they merely conforming to what was expected of musicians in their position?

When, early in the band's career the Skiddaw Rock Band, with Daniel Till and his two sons, appeared as a trio in Brighton in 1881, two reviews of the same performance (quite possibly written by the same hand), refer to the manner of the spoken introductions to the items in the programme.

> On Monday evening I dropped in to hear Messrs. Till's Rock Band give some very pretty selections; they are well worth a visit if only to note how rapidly they deliver their blows on the stones. It is very droll, too, to hear the solemn way in which the numbers of the selections are given out, in a tone suggestive of a clergyman announcing "the next hymn."[18]

---

[17] Bayonne Times, New Jersey, Friday 1st June 1945, p3.
[18] The Brightonian, Friday 1st April 1881. Newspaper cutting from William Till's scrapbook in Till archive.

> Till's Rock Band is very good, and the "instrument" quite interesting...I would advise the leader not to announce the numbers of the tunes in so solemn a manner; I quite expected to hear him add, "No.18 in the old books."[19]

Perhaps these reviews missed the point, and the Tills' dead-pan demeanour was adopted to accentuate, by way of contrast, the sometimes bizarre aspects of their performance? Or did their timid introductions merely indicate a lack of confidence in speaking publicly? Was the wearing of highly respectable tails and bow-ties by the men and and long skirts and lacy blouses by the women ironic or were they merely conforming to social norms? Disappointingly, the latter was perhaps more likely to have been the case. Much of the Till's work was associated with religious events and activities, where there was probably an accepted code of how one should appear on stage. The band publicity was careful to dissociate themselves from coarse forms of entertainment and in doing so chose an interesting mixture of adjectives to recommend what they were offering. Whilst frequently referring to themselves as a novelty act and mentioning the humorous songs in their repertoire, they also described what they were doing as "refined, varied and remarkable."[20] A press release from the second version of the Till Family Rock Band, presented the band as being

> the most unique, artistic and chaste entertainment ever presented to the American public, and is endorsed by the leading clergy, musicians and the press.[21]

Others seemed to agree:

> The entertainment is one of the most unique to be found on the American platform and is so refined and clean as to make it please both man, woman and child.[22]

Yet even if they did wish to be thought of as presenting wholesome, respectable entertainment, with none of the bawdiness of the music hall or vaudeville, the Till Family Rock Band were nevertheless undoubtedly breaking new ground in a number of ways. That a group of musicians could fill concert halls wherever they went, playing a wide genre-bending selection of music on an assortment of around twenty instruments, many of which would be unknown to most of the audience, and finding at times unconventional ways of playing them, remains, from a twenty-first century viewpoint, astonishing. The catalyst in making this happen was, of course, the rock harmonicon or rockophone as it became known once it crossed the Atlantic. The Till family, despite a conventional and unspectacular background in music, became motivated by the possibilities of the stone instrument they had created, inspiring them to experiment further, investigating a range of other instruments as well as everyday objects which could be transformed into musical ones. That they considered themselves to be breaking new ground is illustrated in their claim, cited earlier in relation to the boot-jack, to be producing "music beyond description". By doing this they were, in their own way, celebrating experimentation in music and proving that wide-ranging audiences, irrespective of background, could relate to it and enjoy it. Novelty, while sometimes a byword for something merely cheap and frivolous, might also be thought of as a synonym for innovation, but without pretensions.

---

[19] The Dolphin, Friday 1st April 1881. Newspaper cutting from William Till's scrapbook. Till archive.
[20] Daily News, Frederick County, Maryland, Friday 16th April 1886, p2.
[21] From Till archive.
[22] Courier-Post, Camden, New Jersey, Wednesday 13th November 1907, p2.

Taken individually, the items in the Till's programme can scarcely be thought of as groundbreaking. What might be broadly termed the classical items they chose to include in their repertoire were the more popular, less challenging works by established composers such as Bach, Handel, Verdi and Rossini. Many of the contemporary composers whose works they performed have since been largely forgotten, along with their music, but the Tills did feature pieces such as *Humoresque* by a then relatively young Antonin Dvorak and *Salut d'Amor*, from an even younger Edward Elgar. The latter work was originally composed for violin and piano, but the Till sisters adapted it to be played on the musical glasses. In addition to these concert pieces the band's repertoire included traditional airs, popular songs and comic pieces, though unlike the Richardsons they do not appear to have played dance music, possibly on religious grounds. So what is striking today is the sheer breadth of repertoire. It's very hard to conceive of an act today becoming extremely successful performing such a wide range of material on an even broader assortment of instruments, one of those constructed from stone bars. This is what they achieved and a review of an 1886 concert in Canada is worth quoting at length in order to illustrate just what an evening with the Till Family Concert Company at its height entailed:

> The concert was probably the most varied ever listened to in Brantford, the parts being mostly instrumental, the music exquisite, and performed on a great variety of instruments. The programme opened with a quartet, *Spring Song*, by the Till family, sung without any instrumental accompaniment. This and another quartet in the second part of the programme, which elicited a hearty recall, were all the vocal selections given. The pieces rendered on the rock harmonicon, the xylophone, the streich zither, the fairy bells, the ocarinas, the musical boot-jack, the musical glasses and other strange instruments delighted the audience for two hours. The selections were the old familiar pieces which everybody enjoys, well known Scotch tunes, Irish selections, Moore's melodies, such American pieces as the Swanee River and Yankee Doodle, English and Welsh song tunes and sacred pieces. The musical part of the evening was most thoroughly enjoyed. Miss Ida M. Brown gave a reading in the first part of the programme which was well received; but her humorous selection in the second part caught the humour of the audience and she was twice recalled. Mr D. Till explained the instruments performed on and at the close of the programme the greater part of the audience passed across the platform at his invitation and examined the musical museum. The Star Course Course Committee are certainly furnishing a good class of entertainment.[23]

---

[23] The Brantford Weekly Expositor, Ontario, Canada, Friday 19th February 1886, p8.

## Chapter Eight

# Honoré Baudre

## Antediluvian music and a geological piano

"For a million years the sound of making hand-axes provided the percussion of everyday life."[1]

Keswick played a major part in the story of nineteenth century lithophones and it didn't end with the Till family. But before others from the town were to throw their hats into the ring a Frenchman called Honoré Baudre quite independently came up with a rather different instrument of his own, which he was to call his *piano géologique*. In 1875 Baudre took it with him from his home in the central area of France to stay in London for several months, where he played it regularly, introducing the instrument to British audiences, when it became known as a geological piano (Fig. 8.1). The name seemed to fall into favour and a couple of years later, when the Tills were making their first public appearances as the Skiddaw Rock Band, their publicity sometimes used the term "geological piano" to describe their own instrument, but ultimately the name remained associated with one man, its inventor Honoré Baudre.

*Figure 8.1. Honoré Baudre with his geological piano. Engraving used in article about Baudre in l'Illustration, Saturday 13th July 1901.*

Baudre had built his instrument some years before from pieces of flint, most of which he collected close to the small town where he lived, Ardentes, in the French département of Indre. He had first visited Britain in 1866 with an earlier version of the instrument, which he called his antediluvian piano, but it was only when he revisited the country nine years later, that it took on its new name. This time he gave daily presentations at London's Royal Polytechnic Institution. Regular announcements were placed in newspapers advertising performances by the Frenchman and his geological piano, raising awareness that there was such a thing and no doubt a curiosity as to what exactly that constituted.

---

[1] Neil MacGregor, A History of the world in 100 objects, BBC Radio 4, 2010. Also in book of the same name, Allen Lane, 2010. Edition Postcript Bpooks, Penguin, 2015 p13.

Little is known about Honoré Baudre's early life, or indeed when he was born, though it was probably sometime in the first decade of the nineteenth century. The limited number of articles written about him make no mention of how he made his living, though he does seem to have acquired a knowledge and understanding of music, reviews of his performances noting his considerable playing ability. The way he was to speak about his geological piano and perhaps his choice of name for it, suggests that Baudre also had an interest in scientific matters, but whether that had been reflected in his professional life is not recorded.

Baudre first began collecting flints for his self-styled piano in 1851,[2] but it was not until 1865, when he would already have been well into middle age, that he felt ready to introduce it to the public. He was another man for whom the building of an instrument from pieces of rock became a preoccupation, possibly to an even greater extent than Joseph Richardson, who had toiled for thirteen years in the pursuit of achieving his dream. Like Richardson, he continued to develop the instrument, though in Honoré Baudre's case this was not to build on its proven success but from the frustration of not being able to finalise his original idea. For Baudre the geological piano remained a work in progress for the rest of his life.

Accounts vary as to exactly how the idea of making a lithophone first came to Honoré Baudre. Some say that he was taking a country walk, picked up a piece of flint which he had struck with his foot and, hearing the pleasant tone it emitted, took the idea from there. But another version, whose added detail gives it greater credibility, is that he was walking through a construction site for the laying of a new railway when he came to some labourers shovelling pieces of flint. As they dispersed it, the sound of the pieces falling on top of each other caught the attention of Baudre and it was then that he began to think of the musical possibilities it offered, going on to devise a way in which he could use such flint to construct his own musical instrument.[3]

Flint is formed from a type of silicon, often alongside beds of chalk. A process takes place in which this silicon-based acidic material dissolves and replaces areas of chalk. Pieces of flint then become coated by the chalk and over time this tends to break up, giving us the blueish black or grey flint partly covered with a whitish layer which can be seen ploughed up in fields. But in some places pieces of flint remain almost completely coated with chalk and it was these which Honoré Baudre chose to collect. From the ones which rang with a bright attractive tone he selected only examples already emitting the right pitch, exactly corresponding to the notes he needed to assemble a two-octave chromatic scale. He chose not to tune the pieces of flint he found, having discovered that tampering with it in any way would destroy the tone. So for him the stonemason's skills of a man like Joseph Richardson were unnecessary, his time being spent solely in gathering the required number. Initially he confined his search to the local area where he had first encountered the ringing flint, but the difficulty in finding examples which matched his exacting requirements meant he had to spread his net wider and the quest proved to be an extremely slow process:

> To create his orchestra, the collector, once he had exhausted the neighbouring quarries, widened his search further afield, then further still. He travelled thus from place to place to try to make the stones sing as he went along, and when, once or twice a year he encountered the perfect flint, which rang out musically and fully, he was happy and all

---

[2] Cincinnati Enquirer, Saturday 6th December 1879, p10.
[3] Gabriel de Mortillet in Matériaux pour l'histoire positive et philosophique de l'homme, 1865 pp 109-111

that long effort felt worthwhile. Then he would wrap the stone in cotton wool and hold on to his treasure jealously, with love.[4]

As he began working on his new project it occurred to Honoré Baudre that just as he had been struck by the beauty of the sound produced by many of the flints he picked up, so those working with flint in ancient times would also have been aware of its extraordinary sonic property and must surely have chosen to use it themselves in some musical way. Baudre was aware of the developing interest in researching the ancient past and this was to influence the direction he was to take in presenting his musical instrument, giving a didactic purpose to this new musical journey.

**Paris**

By the autumn of 1865 Baudre had managed to assemble enough suitable flints to complete the construction of his geological piano. There were still some notes missing and he had to resort to using a different rock type, schist, for two of them, but he was satisfied that it was ready enough to present to the public. He arranged to exhibit the instrument in the centre of Paris, a distance of almost 200 miles from his home, and received the support of a man there called Abbé Moigno. Moigno was a priest who, following his ordination, had gone on to study maths and physics and was later appointed professor of mathematics at a college in Paris. He also became known for staging events at which he would introduce new scientific ideas to the public and it was at one of such occasions that Honoré Baudre presented what at that time he was still calling his *piano antediluvian*.

A Paris correspondent for London's *Morning Advertiser* wrote at some length about the presentation by Baudre, his rather world-weary style failing to disguise the fact that he was clearly quite impressed.

> We have a certain scientific priest in Paris, an Abbé Moigno , who is much addicted to hunt out all sorts of useless marvels, which he brings before the public, to whom he lectures… The Abbé convoked his disciples yesterday to listen to his laudations of a newly invented stone piano… This curious instrument, on which the inventor, M.Baudre, played several airs from the *Enchanted Flute* and other operas with wonderful accuracy, is formed of two parallel bars about five feet long, resting horizontally on supports at each end.[5]

Honoré Baudre's lithophone was exhibited in a public room at 154 Rue de Rivoli and attracted enough interest to warrant a short article in a monthly bulletin dedicated to historical and prehistorical discoveries. In it reference is made to a leaflet produced by Baudre in which he expressed his belief that what he had done in assembling these fine-sounding flints was only what our ancestors would have done in prehistoric times.

> Starting from the principle laid down by M. Boucher de Perthes that man, having always been the same, must always have had the same needs, the same instincts, Mr. Baudre admits that primitive man must have loved music. Knowing only stone, it was with

---
[4] Translated from L'Illustration No.3046 13 July 1901 p19
[5] Morning Advertiser, Thursday 9th November 1865, p5.

*Figure 8.2. Engraving of Honoré Baudre by Louis Poyet.*

stone that he fashioned his first instruments. Mr. Baudre believes he has rediscovered, if not the instrument of the true stone age, at least primitive harmony, as his leaflet says! This may be true; but who can confirm it?[6]

Jacque Boucher de Perthes, the pioneering archaeologist mentioned in the article, had several years earlier unearthed prehistoric tools and other implements, and the conclusions he drew from that, predating Darwin's *Origin of the species*, flew in the face of the widely accepted version of the dawn of mankind, as expounded in the Book of Genesis. The idea that music might have been produced on earth in prehistoric times, quite possibly using ringing stone, was not something which had been seriously raised by others involved in the building and playing of lithophones at the time and would most likely not have been entertained by a devoutly Christian family such as the Tills. But to Honoré Baudre this possibility had come as something of a revelation.

Baudre's geological piano, which seems not to have survived, was a distinctive looking instrument. Although there is no known photographic record of it there are a few drawings, plus an engraving (Figure 8.2) which pays considerable attention to detail. An iron frame, with cross pieces and a central decorative star facing forward, supports the flints, which are suspended on double loops of string. Underneath them runs what appears to be a flat shelf, but is actually a sounding board, amplifying the resonance of the stones.[7] Honoré Baudre is shown playing the instrument, using two small flints to strike the notes. Édouard Forestié, who attended a later performance on the antediluvian piano provided a first-hand description of how it looked and sounded:

---

[6] Matériaux pour l'histoire positive et philosophique de l'homme  Gabriel de Mortillet  1865 pp 109-111.
[7] Cincinnati Enquirer, Saturday 6th December 1879, p10.

To get an idea of the instrument, imagine an embroidery loom, surmounted by two transverse and parallel wooden bars, to which burnt stones are attached to strings. These are arranged in such a way that the semitones are interspersed between the tones, as in the piano keyboard. The number of stones is 25, from *so* to *so*, comprising two chromatic scales, to put it better, a fourth, a complete octave and a fifth.

The sound of flint is more beautiful than that of quartz and indefinable. This sound, soft and mellow in the bass and medium, sharp and almost deafening in the high notes, is obtained by striking the flint in a certain part with another stone, in the manner of the xylophone, the playing of it being much more difficult as the beater is shorter.[8]

## England and Ireland

In March 1866 Honoré Baudre presented his antediluvian piano at the highly prestigious Royal Institution in London. Committed then, as now, to the propagation of scientific knowledge, the appearance within its walls of a French amateur musician and instrument-builder is another indication that a concordance between arts and sciences was considered crucial at the time. In particular, it reflects the serious consideration being afforded within different scientific lines of enquiry to Baudre's ideas, touching as they did on aspects of mineralogy, archaeology and anthropology.

The following month Baudre travelled from London to Dublin, where he demonstrated what the press there referred to as his "stone piano". Again there was great interest in the often peculiar looking flints, some of which were later noted as resembling (and by implication, being) recognizable items from prehistory, such as a petrified fish and a stone axe.[9] Baudre also took with him other stones which he considered of interest and displayed those alongside the stone piano. Close attention seems to have been paid to both the sounds the flints produced and their visual appearance:

> One of the pieces of flint yields two notes - viz, its tonic and harmonic third. In another of the stones is embedded a very beautiful fossil.[10]

The same article reported that M.Baudre had declined large sums of money for his collection of stones.

Flint produces a quite different and purer sound than the hornfels used in lithophones from Cumbria and the attractive tonal quality of the flints is referred to in different press reports. One declared that "some emit sounds sweeter than could be obtained from any piano",[11] while another recorded the reception it received:

> The audience expressed the utmost surprise and pleasure at the sweet and resonant tones which were elicited from the instrument, and the wonderful facility with which complicated passages were executed.[12]

---

[8] Translated from Courrier de Tarn-et-Garonne, Friday 15th September 1871, p2.
[9] L'Illustration, Saturday 13th July 1901, p19.
[10] Cork Constitution, Thursday 19th April 1866, p3.
[11] Meath Herald and Cavan Advertiser, Saturday 21st April 1866, p4.
[12] Dublin Daily Express, Thursday 26th April 1866, p2.

A review in the Dublin Daily Express the previous week went into more detail than most, while also providing another colourful impression of how the instrument sounded:

> The performer employs two flints when playing, which is done in the same manner as a dulcimer, and indeed the harmony produced strongly resembles the music of that instrument. It possesses a compass of several octaves, the tones and semi-tones being all perfect, and capable of rendering the most intricate, and what is more peculiar, the most varied description of music. Thus, what could be more opposite, distinct, and characteristic, than the "Miserere" from "Il Trovatore" and "St Patrick's Day"? And yet each of these pieces is given with a manual dexterity, a clearness, and umistakeable individuality – if such a term may be used - that are really surprising. The "Fideste Fideles" [sic], also, is given with a dulcet softness, a fullness and exquisite harmonization equal to any piano. It is on an ordinary instrument easy enough of execution, but few could better display the powers of M. Baudre's invention, in as much as the notes must be sustained to impart a gliding effect, and thus that expression, pathos and devotional feeling for which the Portuguese hymn is so justly celebrated. The "Carnival of Venice," selections from "Norma" and a variety of dance music were also performed with sweetness and perfection.[13]

In addition to providing entertainment, there remained in Honoré Baudre an almost evangelical determination to spread the word about the historical implications of what he had found. His views were aired in a journal article five years later, published while he was exhibiting and performing on his geological piano in Toulouse. The uncredited writer of the piece is complementary about Baudre's musical performance and we learn that on this occasion this "consummate musician" was joined by two assistants in executing part of the programme. Like the Cumbrian rock bands from England, Baudre seems to have had a varied repertoire which included items from Mozart's *Magic Flute*, Rossini's *William Tell*, popular airs, and *The Marseillaise*.

The author of the article agreed with Baudre's view that distant ancestors might well have used the sound of flint to produce music, but the conclusions the writer drew from this idea were rather less enlightened:

> This hypothesis is justified: we remember having seen, in a report, a musical instrument that would be similar to M.Baudre's piano. But, as we know, primitive music is very simple and consists only of the very few notes that the savage repeats with a monotony which delights him and which we could not bear.[14]

Three weeks later a newspaper from the same area published the article by Édouard Forestié, then Secretary General of the Tarn-et-Garonne Archaeological Society. He is fullsome in his praise of both the instrument, Baudre's performance and the issues raised in his address to those present. In particular Forestié mentions the apparent lack of any correlation between the size and weight of a piece of flint and the pitch of the note it produces, yet another example of the connections being made in between music and science and what one discipline might learn from the other.

---

[13] Dublin Daily Express, Friday 20th April 1866, p3.
[14] Journal de Toulouse - Politique et Litteraire, Friday 25th August 1871, p1.

As the artist points out, without being able to explain, the sound produced is neither in direct relation nor in inverse relation to the size: thus two flints of the same weight, of the same volume and of equal density give the octave interval, while the low G and its octave have between them considerable differences in weight and often the high note weighs more than the low note. These are just some of a hundred other no less interesting problems that Mr. Baudre poses to modern science and which he listed in his session.[15]

## Belgium

The following year, 1872, Honoré Baudre accepted an invitation to attend the biennial International Congress of Anthropology and pre-Historic Archaeology which was taking place in Brussels. Here he demonstrated the geological piano to the assembly present and again used the opportunity to expound his view that the sound of flint would have been known and used in ancient times. Baudre ended the session by playing *La Brabançonne*, the Belgian national anthem.[16]

At what seems to have been a separate event in the city, Baudre also attended a meeting of the Belgian Prehistoric Archaeological Society and following an afternoon session which included discussion about different flint discoveries, Baudre brought the proceedings to a fitting conclusion by performing on his own collection of flints, once more finishing with a rendition of the host country's national anthem.

Honoré Baudre's search for flints emitting the right note continued. The preservation of the pure tone deemed only possible by preserving each piece of flint intact became more than a purely musical choice. The issue referred to in Forestié's article, regarding the size, weight and density of the flint continued to preoccupy Baudre and became a matter of interest to the scientists he met. In general the principle governing the pitch of a roughly rectangular bar, whether the material be stone, wood, metal or a synthetic material, will be determined by its length and its thickness, but the pieces of flint used by Baudre were amorphous and varied in shape, making the notes they produced far less predictable, suggesting a far more complex internal structure. It was the sonorous consequences of this complexity which impressed Baudre as well as the geologists and other scientists who he talked to. The known scientific principles underlying the design and production of musical instruments seemed not to apply and it was from these unknowns, these discrepancies which the flints were revealing, which it was felt science could learn.

## A return to England

By 1875 Baudre had found all but two of the pieces of flint he needed for his two-octave geological piano. It was in November of that year that he made his second trip to Britain for what was to be a seven-month stay. Being offered a prolonged residency at the Royal Polytechnic Institution in London was another indication of interest from the academic world in his achievements and his daily appearances once more combined musical performances with talks and discussions.

---

[15] Translated from Courrier de Tarn-et-Garonne, Friday 15th September 1871, p2.
[16] Syndicated report appearing in Leigh Chronicle and Weekly Advertiser, Saturday 31st August 1872, p8.

His presence at the Institution was publicised through regular press announcements, some of them referring to him not as a musician but as "the Discoverer".[17]

In February 1876 Honoré Baudre moved on to Oxford where he took up another residency, at the plush Clarendon Hotel. There he again gave daily presentations, attended by various eminent academics including Joseph Prestwich who, having been president of the Geological Society, was now professor of geology at Oxford University. According to a report from one of the sessions, published in the Oxford Times under the heading "Antediluvian Music", Baudre played a selection of music, spoke of his discoveries with regard to the flint, and also showed examples of fossils from his collection. Baudre told those assembled that in collecting his stones from various parts of France he had tried upwards of 200,000 in order to find the twenty-eight he needed to complete the instrument.[18] However much of an overstatement this colossal number may have been, it gives an indication of the kind of task he had undertaken.

The following month Baudre was in Birmingham for performances at the Exchange Assembly Room in New Street and in June he was back in London with, inexplicably, an appearance at the Great Horse Show in Alexandra Palace. During Baudre's stay in England he worked almost continually and is likely to have spoken and played to more people during that time than he did over a period of years in France, there being no evidence of him touring extensively in his own country in the way the Richardsons or the Till family had done in theirs.

## The USA and Canada

The twenty-eight flints in Honoré Baudre's geological piano gave him a chromatic instrument of a little over two octaves, but his lack of success in finding two particular notes, the lowest *do* (C) and the highest *do*, troubled him. Having broadened his search beyond the local vicinity in which he'd gathered his first flints, he heard that a similar type of flint was to be found in Canada. Now convinced, if irrationally, that flints giving these two notes did not exist in France, Baudre therefore used a large portion of his life-savings to take the required trip across the Atlantic in a bid to complete the set.

In accounts published years later, presumably based on Baudre's own recollections, there emerge two different versions of the outcome of his Canadian quest. In one syndicated report which appeared in many newspapers internationally the story had a happy end:

> [M. Baudre] relates that his greatest difficulty consisted in finding the low C of his octave. For more than ten years he searched for it, when last fall he came across it in Canada. He says none can appreciate the joy he felt at its discovery.[19]

Yet in a lengthy French article about Baudre in the French publication *l'Illustration* in the same year, 1901, things concluded rather differently:

> For this *do* he travelled by ocean liner to Canada. But the earth of the New World did not conceal the first note of the octave. Tired, weary, resigned, M. Baudre returned

---

[17] Broad Arrow, London, Saturday 20th November 1875, p28.
[18] Oxford Times, Saturday 26th February 1876, p5.
[19] Daily Standard, Red Bank, New Jersey, Saturday 31st August 1901, p2 (syndicated report).

*Figure 8.3. The Old South, Boston, Massachusetts.*

from his long voyage, persuaded that he would die without having heard one stone sing this notorious note, when one morning, taking a walk in Berry, hopeful again, yet also despairing, he discovered a marvellous flint which resonated with a *do* of the finest quality. That day, the collector experienced a moment of superhuman joy; such as could only be compared with the absolute bliss which awaits pure souls in heaven.[20]

The only available information from the time about Baudre's transatlantic trip comes again from newspaper archives, which show that his visit was not limited to Canada and was a lengthy one, lasting around three years and starting off in the USA. During that time he made himself known to many people, through a series of engagements similar in nature to those he had undertaken in Europe.

It seems that Baudre sailed to New York in 1879, taking his geological piano with him and was soon exhibiting it in the city. In October he gave public performances at the Charlier Institute, a school located in a prime location on the edge of Central Park and set up by a Frenchman, Elie Charlier. A reference to Baudre as "an inventive genius" in a subsequent newspaper report suggests he made a good impression on the American audiences.[21] How he procured his bookings is not known but the French diaspora seems to have been targeted as, following his appearance at the Charlier Institute, he gave presentations at the Catholic Church of St Vincent de Paul on 23rd Street, built to serve the local French community living in the Chelsea area of Manhattan. Repeating his conviction that he was merely following in the footsteps of those who would have played on flint thousands of years before, Baudre offered a biblical reference, perhaps thought appropriate for the ecclesiastical setting, suggesting that "the first musical sound Adam heard might have been from one flint falling on another", adding that "flint was the first weapon, the first source of fire, and the first musical instrument", and promising to give a lecture in the same church the following Friday.[22]

In the spring of 1880 Honoré Baudre was in Boston, performing at the Old South (Figure 8.3), formerly an important meeting house in the period leading up to the American Revolution, where the strength of feeling of 5,000 in attendance had led to the episode known as the

---

[20] Translated from l'Illustration, Saturday 13th July 1901, No.3046, p19.
[21] Burlington Free Press, Monday 20th October 1879, p2.
[22] The Cincinnati Enquirer, Saturday 6th December 1879, p10.

> **MUSICAL STONES.**
> THE PRIMITIVE MUSIC OF THE RACE OF MAN.
> Tunes will be played on these stones by M. Baudre, each hour from 10 to 4 o'clock, at the OLD SOUTH.
> tf ap26

*Figure 8.4. Newspaper announcement. The Boston Globe, Thursday 20th April 1880 p2.*

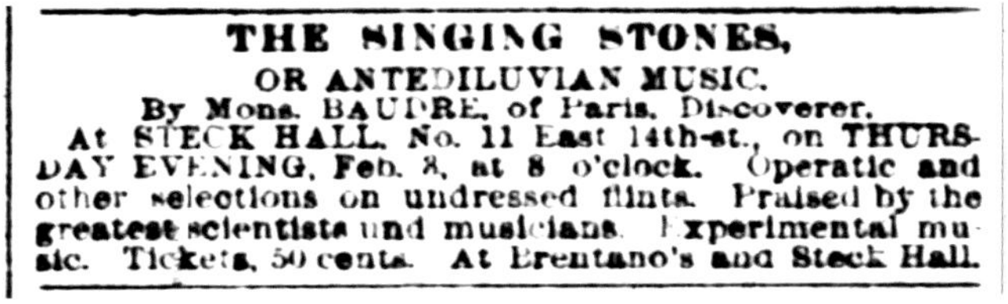

> **THE SINGING STONES,**
> OR ANTEDILUVIAN MUSIC.
> By Mons. BAUDRE, of Paris, Discoverer.
> At STECK HALL, No. 11 East 14th-st., on THURSDAY EVENING, Feb. 8, at 8 o'clock. Operatic and other selections on undressed flints. Praised by the greatest scientists and musicians. Experimental music. Tickets, 50 cents. At Brentano's and Steck Hall.

*Figure 8.5. Newspaper announcement. The New York Times Sunday 30th January 1881 p11.*

Boston Tea Party.[23] The central message of historical importance which Baudre believed he was carrying was given more prominence in the promotion for him there than it had been in Britain, his presentation being described as "Musical stones, the primitive music of the race of man" (Figure 8.4).

Baudre's theories began to attract the attention of American academics in the fields of archaeology and geology just as they had in Europe. Around the time he was in Boston, one of the leading geologists of the time, Professor J.S. Newberry of New York's Columbia College (now University), who had seen one of Honoré Baudre's presentations, wrote him an open letter:

> "The use of sonorous stones for the production of musical sounds is a novelty to our civilization, but in all probability the resonance of sonorous stones constituted all the music of the man of the stone age, so that yours, while it is the latest form devised of musical instrument is specially interesting as perhaps but a modification of the very first."[24]

In 1881 Baudre was back in New York, appearing at Steck Hall on 14th Street, a building owned and run by the piano company George Steck & Co and a venue for musical recitals and talks. This time the press announcement was even more colourful.

> THE SINGING STONES
> OR ANTEDILUVIAN MUSIC
> By Mons. Baudre, of Paris. Discoverer.
> At STECK HALL, No.11 14th-st., on THURSDAY, Feb 8th at 8 o'clock.
> Operatic and other selections on undressed flints. Praised by the

---

[23] Old South Meeting House website: *https://www.thefreedomtrail.org/trail-sites/old-south-meeting-house*
[24] Scandia Journal, Saturday 29th May 1880, p7 (syndicated report).

greatest scientists and musicians. Experimental music. Tickets 50cents.[25]

Again there was press coverage of the event and unusually it contained a transcript of part of Honoré Baudre's lecture. His view that scientific understanding can be enhanced by the discoveries of people such as himself, coming to the mysteries of nature from a different, musical direction is evident:

> "Geology, archaeology, chemistry, physics are all branches of science which find in these stones a new element. Melodies, religious music, opera airs, dance music, may all be deliciously rendered on this harmony of the first age of man. I draw my attention to a fact in physics which I think may give some clue to the solution of the problem of the vibrations of the flint. As a rule it is necessary to strike the stone on the smoothest surface to obtain the perfection of the note, the sides opposite to the smooth side produce disagreeable multiple vibrations. This may be said of the round flints; but it may be also said of the flat, that the purity of sound is only obtained when the flint is struck on the flat side and not on the aspirated. If we only look at it from a physical point of view we enter a new domain, and perhaps the recognition of the laws of the vibration will lead to unforeseen discoveries in applying to industry under other forms the said laws. Let us not forget that the notes here are entirely the work of nature, while other instruments have all been shaped and constructed with conditions unforeseen by man, and always in these industrial products weight, length or volume are observed as the basis of the effects which it is proposed to produce."[26]

The extent to which Baudre's contribution to scientific knowledge was actually valuable is hardly the point. What is significant is his recognition, shared with others at the time, that the arts, and in this case music, can share common concerns, each having something to learn from the investigations of the other. Notable in the press announcement is the use of the term "experimental music", one not much used in 1881 but from the mid-twentieth century onwards becoming a musical genre in its own right, and, coincidentally, with its first home in New York. Seeing the term applied to the music of Honoré Baudre might raise an eyebrow today, but it does signify a recognition at the time that he was involved in an ongoing enquiry, akin to scientific investigation, and in doing that he might indeed be seen to have anticipated the approach taken by John Cage (whose own scientific research included spending time in an anechoic chamber) and others who rejected what they saw as the "mainstream" avant garde's adherence to a particular musical aesthetic. Just as they were to do seven decades later, Honoré Baudre saw his involvement in music in a broader context than the aesthetic appreciation or creation of a piece of music. It seems that his choice of repertoire was actually fairly arbitrary and that for him the important issues underlying what he was doing lay elsewhere. His way of putting his point across seems at times to have been quite radical too, ensuring his audience sat up and paid attention and would surely have gained the approval of those New York experimental musicians further down the line:

> Besides the stones, M. Baudre had a number of bits of wood about the size of an old fashioned clothespin, which he threw on the marble floor one at a time, and they produced the regular notes of the scale with remarkable correctness.

---
[25] New York Times, Sunday 30th January 1881, p11.
[26] The Daily Graphic, New York Friday 4th February 1881, p3.

Nevertheless, the writer goes on to note that…

…the singing stones, however are the more interesting of M. Baudre's discoveries.[27]

By the end of 1881 Honoré Baudre was in Quebec, giving a talk entitled "Singing Stones, or Music before the Deluge" at the Parochial Lecture Room in Notre Dame Street, Montreal. While he was there Baudre met up with the distinguished writer Louis Fréchette, playing pieces for him on his geological piano. Fréchette then composed a sonnet about Baudre which he performed for him accompanied on a lyre.[28] Where in Canada Baudre went in search for flints to complete the complement required for the geological piano is uncertain, but he was in the country for several weeks, certainly until March 1882 when he performed in Ottawa, then sometime after that he returned to France.

Honoré Baudre was to receive the greatest amount of public attention paid to him towards the end of his life when he exhibited the geological piano at the *Exposition Internationale* in Brest, Brittany in 1901, by which time he would have been in his eighties. The exhibition, a large scale event of the type favoured at the time, declared itself to be devoted to commerce, industry, science and the fine arts. In a bid to attract a wide range of visitors it offered the added draw of theatres, casinos, competitions, as well as the opportunity for sea-bathing and the use of a

Figure 8.6. Sketch taken from lIlustration engraving. Warder and Dublin Weekly Mail, Saturday 24th August 1901, p11.

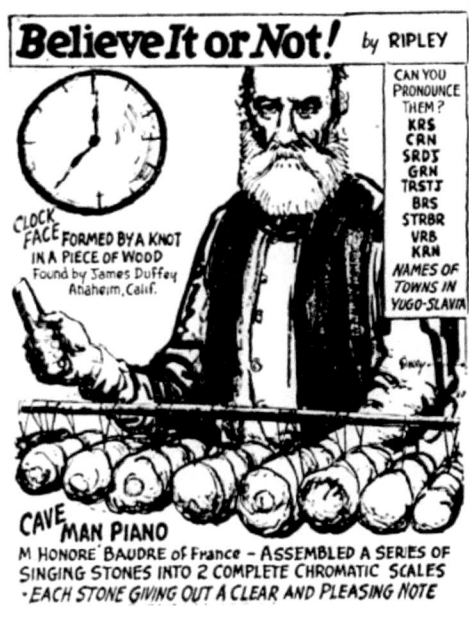

Figure 8.7. St Louis Post-Dispatch, Friday 2nd August 1946, p36.

---

[27] New York Daily Herald, Friday 17th October 1879, p11.
[28] L'Illustration, Saturday 13th July 1901. Includes French lyrics to the sonnet.

Figure 8.8. Possible photographic source for l'Illustration engraving. San Francisco Call and Post, Saturday 17th August 1901, p6.

state-of-the-art electric tramline.[29] Baudre's appearance there resulted in internationally syndicated newspaper articles about him, some of which took their content from a lengthy feature about Baudre in the noted Parisian weekly newspaper, *l'Illustration*. This particular article, published to coincide with the Brest exhibition was, at not far short of two thousand words, the longest one to be published about Baudre in his lifetime and included a specially commissioned engraving of him standing behind the geological piano (Figure 8.1). As far as it goes, the article gives a good account of the man, his interests and achievements, and while it doesn't reveal much more about the man than had been written earlier, the piece is conveyed by its author, Louis Forest, in a compelling style:

For more than thirty years of his life, he travelled wherever it was possible, among the rough flint embedded in chalk, to find the perfect sonorous flint. For more than thirty years he tested, day by day, one by one, thousands of stones. It was a complicated task. Each time it was necessary to suspend the flints at the centre of a string, strike them, and listen and appreciate the quality of the resultant sound. It really needed the added practised ear of a musician, one with angelic perseverance or, if you prefer, magnificent stubbornness. The patience of Job is not worthy of the name compared with the tireless dedication of M. Baudre.[30]

The engraving of Honoré Baudre used in the 1901 *Illustration* feature became widely circulated and used as the basis for various sketches used to accompany newspaper articles, including one from the same year (Fig. 8.6) and a much later American version which appeared in one of a syndicated series of odd-fact features called "Believe it or not!" in 1946 (Figure 8.7). Another engraving, by Louis Poyet (Figure 8.2) showed him playing the geological piano and remains the best visual indicator of what the instrument looks like. There seem to be no authenticated photographs of it but an image which appeared in at least one American paper in the same year as the *Illustration* article,1901, clearly relates to it and although the scanned newspaper quality make its hard to assess, it has the appearance of a photograph, possibly touched up, which suggests it may have been the source of the engraving itself (Figure 8.8).

Whether in Canada or France, Honoré Baudre did eventually find his low *do* note somewhere, but although one of the 1901 newspaper stories reported him saying there was a slight defect

---

[29] *Exposition Internationale* exhibition catalague.
[30] Translated from L'Illustration No.3046, 13 July 1901, p19.

which he hoped to remedy before his death, the missing high *do* appears to have remained elusive.[31] How long he lived beyond that time isn't known, but the article in *l'Illustration* does include one rare glimpse into the private life of Honoré Baudre:

> Today, very old, having lost a dear son, M. Honoré Baudre spends his time as a disillusioned old man, for whom life has become sad, making his stones sing. He plays his curious piano with skill, and, listening to the vibrations of the flint, he accompanies his regrets and his dreams.[32]

---

[31] Freeport Journal-Standard, Illinois, Thursday 10th October 1901, p6 (syndicated report).
[32] Translated from L'Illustration No.3046, 13 July 1901, p19.

# Chapter Nine

# The Abrahams

## Limelight in the Lakes

Following the success of two Keswick family rock bands, first the Richardsons then the Tills, it was almost inevitable that others would take the idea and try to run with it. The term "musical stones" began to be mentioned with some regularity in advertisements for entertainment venues around Britain, either as a separate item on a varied bill or as one element in a performer's act. Only a few, though, were prepared to go to the lengths of producing instruments on the scale of those first rock harmonicons. The two cousins with the name William Bowe have already been mentioned and also the Harrison Brothers, but there was another local family who also chose to continue what was starting to become something of a Keswick tradition. They were the Abrahams, whose name has already cropped up in their capacity as photographers, producing some of the early pictures of the Till family's Skiddaw Rock Band.

*Figure 9.1. George Perry Abraham's visiting card produced from his own photographic studio. Courtesy of Sue Steinberg.*

George Perry Abraham, born in 1846, was originally from Devizes in Wiltshire, first coming to Keswick in 1865 having served an apprenticeship with the London photographic studio Elliot & Fry. After a short period working for another photographer in Keswick, he decided to open his own shop and with an abundance of tourists now visiting the area found there was a reasonable living to be made from taking their photographs and selling the prints. (Figure 9.1) Two of Abraham's four children, George Dixon and Ashley, took up the interest and joined the business, which was later to move to new premises, a purpose-built studio in the middle of the town. George junior and Ashley also developed something of a passion for rock climbing, becoming pioneers of this new activity and combining these two pursuits they began to take their heavy plate cameras on climbing trips, first in the Cumbrian hills, then in Scotland and Wales and later in Italy, Austria and Switzerland. As a result they produced some remarkable photographs, some of the first of their

*Figure 9.2. George Perry Abraham with his his three sons, Ashley, Sydney and George. Courtesy of Sue Steinberg.*

kind, and these were used to illustrate numerous books they published, mainly on the subject of mountains and mountaineering.[1]

Quite how and when the Abrahams decided to build their own rock harmonicon is uncertain. It was certainly in use by 1890 and press reports from that year said that the instrument had taken twelve years to complete, which would indicate that they made a start on it around the time when the Till family were giving their first public performances and beginning to employ the photographic services of the Abrahams for their publicity material. Being in close proximity to the Till's rock harmonicon as they were taking photographs, capturing its grandeur for posterity with the father and his two sons standing behind it, may well have planted the seed of an idea to follow the same route. Whether they received encouragement and perhaps advice from the Tills in building their instrument isn't known, but once the Tills had departed for America in 1885 the Abrahams would have recognized that there was now a gap in the market to be exploited and this may have spurred them on to get the instrument finished. The Richardson and Till family bands had raised awareness of Keswick as a centre for musical stone through their extended touring around Britain and the Abrahams, though not in a position to work away from home for long periods with their business commitments, might have thought that a rock harmonicon could have commercial potential in Keswick itself.

---

[1] David Weeks  The Abraham Brothers in Foot and Howell Vol 2  p138

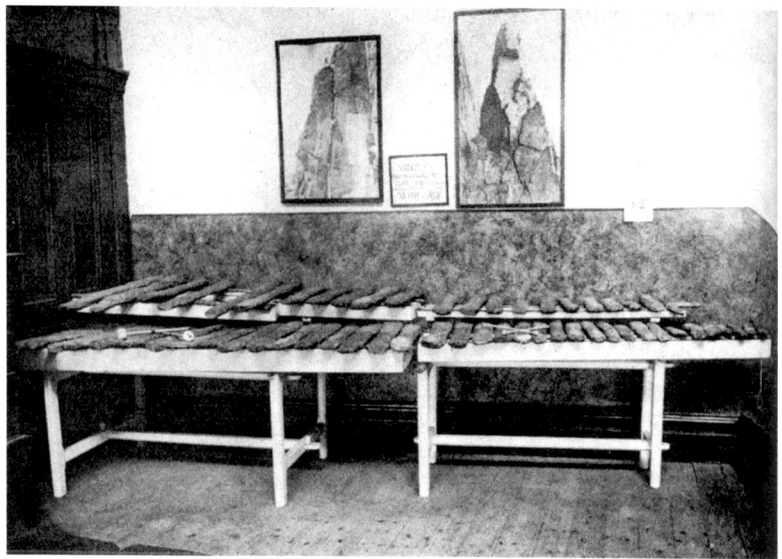

*Figure 9.3. The Abrahams' rock harmonicon.*

The template created by the Richardsons was now once again followed remarkably closely, this time by the Abraham family. As before, a father began collecting stones from the slopes around Skiddaw assisted by his two sons, which they then proceeded to assemble into an instrument of five octaves, to be played by the three of them side by side (Figure 9.3) If imitation is indeed the sincerest form of flattery then the Abraham's sincerity knew no bounds as they took their turn, this time retracing the steps of the Till family. Not only did they adopt the same band name as initially used by the Tills, billing themselves as the Skiddaw Rock Band, but they also plagiarised their promotional material. The letter from John Ruskin to William Till acknowledging receipt of a set of musical stones, which was to become "one of the proud possessions of the Till family"[2], was used in the Abraham's publicity, presenting it in such a way as to imply that Ruskin had in fact been writing about their instrument:

> Professor Ruskin, speaking of the Rock Harmonicon, said it had given him "a new insight into crystalline rock substance; also a new musical pleasure"[3]

Whether the passing of time and collective amnesia meant this kind of misleading appropriation tended to pass without notice, or that inaccurate and exaggerated claims in print were commonly taken with a generous pinch of salt, instances of this kind were common practice. Sometimes feathers were ruffled, as seen in John Fisher Crosthwaite's objection to Joseph Richardson's claim to have invented the rock harmonicon, but generally it seems that the rock bands, along with others in the entertainment business, got away with some colouring of the facts. The Tills, especially once they were in safely in the USA, regularly declared their stone instrument to be unique and the Abrahams' publicity continued in similar vein, declaring their

---

[2] From facsimile of article in Sunday Call, Newark NJ 10th March 1935 (Till archive, courtesy of Dr Michael Till)
[3] Aliffe p81

*Figure 9.4. An Abraham's hand-tinted postcard showing Keswick town centre.*

own rock harmonicon to be "certainly the only one of its kind in the world."[4] This kind of behaviour would seem to have been generally accepted as part of the general cut and thrust of business and there is no evidence that the Till Family took particular objection to the way the Abrahams went about things, the two families retaining a long friendship. Yet however much they borrowed from the original idea, George Abraham and his sons certainly had their own take on how they used their rock harmonicon, deciding to present it to the public as part of an innovative audio-visual experience.

Keswick residents had, since the era of Peter Crosthwaite and his contemporaries, been well aware of the commercial possibilities of meeting the needs of the now regular cohorts of tourists descending upon the town. The Abrahams were able to build up a successful business by offering the kind of photographic service which was to remain synonymous with holiday destinations until the arrival of the mobile phone, as well as selling postcard reproductions of their photographs, sometimes hand-tinted by George Perry Abraham (Figure 9.4). In addition, just as Crosthwaite had understood that a museum could provide refuge to visitors whose outdoor plans were dependably interrupted by outbreaks of rain, so the Abrahams realised that once the sun had disappeared for the day and mountain walking was no longer an option, these same visitors would welcome some indoor entertainment and they went about providing some.

## An Evening of Pictorial and Musical Entertainment

In 1890 the Abraham family began staging evening presentations which combined descriptive talks with photographic projections using three limelight lanterns, plus musical performances featuring their rock harmonicon. Richardson Henderson had tried something along similar

---

[4] Huddersfield Daily Chronicle  Monday 8th September 1890 p4 and elsewhere

Figure 9.5. Poster for the Limelight & Musical Entertainment. Courtesy of Andy Aliffe.

lines with his dioramas, but for those a light was projected onto painted landscapes. A "grand evening entertainment" with the Abrahams offered "a tour through the English Lakeland" with "over 200 limelight illustrations...with selections on the Musical Stones by the Skiddaw Rock Band"[5] and took place in their new premises, in a large upstairs room they called Victoria Hall. In what they advertised as "the only instrument of its kind extant"[6] (Figure 9.5), despite the fact there was at least one remarkably similar in the same town, the three men displayed their high quality photographs of the dramatic surrounding landscape, taken on full-plate cameras, and projected at a scale most of those attending would not have previously seen. According to their publicity the audience would be presented with an image 15 feet in diameter (4.57m).[7]

The addition of music would have undoubtedly enriched the evening experience, but its main function was to provide entertainment during breaks between each sequence of projections. These breaks were a practical necessity as the limelight triple projector (otherwise known as a trinopticon) was in danger of overheating and at regular intervals needed time to cool down. The rock harmonicon was of course the centre of attraction at this point in the proceedings, but for an added vocal element they were sometimes joined by a Miss Tangye, possibly related to William Tangye who around the same time was helping Richardson Henderson and his son in their attempt to revive interest in the Rock, Bell and Steel Band. From what is known of the Abrahams' musical repertoire it was not as ambitious as that of either the Richardsons or the Tills. Newspaper announcements referred to them playing "all the popular airs"[8] and elsewhere the singing of "glees, part songs, etc."[9] but with no mention of any classical favourites. But it all seemed to go down well enough:

> Mr. Abraham's very interesting entertainment was given before fairly large audiences on Tuesday and Friday evenings, with a change of programmes on the latter occasion. The entertainment makes a delightful evening, and nobody should miss the opportunity of seeing the presentment of the chief points of interest in the Lake

---

[5] English Lakes Visitor Saturday 22nd August 1891 p5
[6] Ibid
[7] Aliffe p79
[8] Dundee Courier Thursday 4th September 1890 p3
[9] Sunderland Daily Echo and Shipping Gazette Wednesday 15th November 1893 p2

*Figure 9.6. Ashley and George Abraham. Courtesy of Sue Steinberg.*

District under Mr. Abraham's guidance. Singing and performances on the musical stones (cleverly done by Messrs, Abraham and Sons) give agreeable variety to the programme."[10]

George Abraham and his two sons probably never intended to try and replicate the musical achievements of either the Richardsons or the Tills. George Dixon and Ashley were already making an impact with their climbing feats and their photography, setting the bar for what could be achieved when the two activities were combined. Although the Abrahams did travel to other parts of Britain, introducing others to the splendour of the Lake District through their photography and playing music on slabs of rock from the same landscape, their activities remained mostly centred in Keswick and the surrounding area. Their Lakeland presentations, which mainly took place during the weeks of August and September, were well publicised, gaining a good reputation, and continued for about a decade. After that the rock harmonicon remained on display in Victoria Building, their business premises in Lake Road, Keswick, free for anyone with an interest to have a go. There it stayed, long after its original protagonists had died, George Perry Abraham in 1923, his sons Ashley and George in 1951 and 1965 respectively. In the 1960s percussionist James Blades paid a visit to the photographic shop, by then managed by Ashley's son Geoffrey, and saw the instrument, still standing upstairs, in what had been turned into a museum. In his book *Percussion instruments and their history* Blades describes it as being "a fine specimen of workmanship."[11]

George Dixon Abraham and his wife Winifred had two daughters and one of them, Enid, later became known, as Enid J. Wilson, for her Lakeland contributions to The Guardian's *Country Diary* feature which she wrote regularly from 1950 until her death in 1988. As a young girl she would walk with her grandfather and father on the outskirts of Keswick watching them tap pieces of rock with a hammer and in one of her Guardian columns she described the contents of a "small pink four-plate leaflet" which she had in her possession, an example of the Abrahams' publicity material, making reference to the rock harmonicon:

> The leaflet [quotes] a national newspaper which said, "There is a strong fascination in listening to such sweet chords of music wrung from the dark and stern children of

---

[10] English Lake Visitor Saturday 23rd September 1893 p4
[11] Blades p84

MUSIC STONES

*Figure 9.7. Image from sleeve of "Wee" Jimmy Scott's Magical Memories LP. Courtesy of Dr. Michael Till.*

the mountains" - presumably a reference to the stones, not the players...Later on they had a fascination for me too, for this was my grandfather, always slightly flamboyant on such occasions, who sang local ballads in the intervals, accompanying himself on an ordinary piano. He also took the centre of the stones, my uncle [Ashley] played the difficult treble (small) stones and my father (less musical) was confined to firm "bongs" on the big low stones. The gas-lit room got hot, so did Uncle; grandfather's white mane got wilder and father's starched white "dicky" (a white starched front over an ordinary shirt) developed a tendency to pop out and up towards his nose.[12]

The current whereabouts of the Abraham's rock harmonicon are unknown, though before its disappearance it made a couple of TV appearances. The first of these was in 1966, on a regional BBC news programme, Look North, marking the centenary of the Abrahams' business and with Geoffery Abrahams playing it. Then in 1974, after the instrument had been sold to a musician called William Chamberlain, the British entertainer Roy Castle was to play it on the long-running children's TV programme *Blue Peter*. It seems to have then been retired from public attention apart from an appearance on a now elusive 1980 LP, *Magical Memories*, by a Scottish hammer dulcimer player "Wee" Jimmy Scott (Figure 9.7).

---

[12] Enid J. Wilson's A Country Diary  The Guardian Monday 21st August 1978  p10

# Chapter Ten

# A Yorkshire Dalesman and a Menorcan Don

## Neddy Dick and Don Antonio Roca y Várez

Keswick was unique in the story of musical stone in being a place where a repeating pattern emerged, similar sequences of events continuing to unfold, in which an individual became fascinated by the attractive ring of a certain type of rock, decided to act upon it and then managed to motivate others to also get involved. A succession of family bands were formed and the process sometimes took surprising turns; accoutrements were added, other instruments introduced and there were changes of personnel, but the sound of stone remained the key to it all, whether as the centre of attention or the catalyst.

Elsewhere things happened differently. For Honoré Baudre in France his engagement ringing rock remained pretty much an individual pursuit, becoming a mission for life for which he eventually earned a degree of recognition, even if the rest of the world had its mind on other things. But there were others too for whom the building of a lithophone and playing on it remained a more solitary, localised activity, their musical achievements rarely even catching the attention of the local press of the day. That we know about them at all today is sometimes purely the result of a few recollections which happen to have been passed on and documented somewhere and sometimes only now being rediscovered through online posts and archives. Two such people were Neddy Dick, a Yorkshire dalesman and a well-connected Menorcan, Don Antonio Roca y Várez.

**Neddy Dick**

High in England's Yorkshire Dales, in the sweeping, dramatic landscape of Swaledale sits the small village of Keld, where a musician called Neddy Dick was born in 1845. He spent his life there and it's where he died, in 1926 at the age of 81. His real name was Richard Alderson, but because it was a common surname and there were other Aldersons with the name Richard, it's thought that in keeping with local in that area tradition he became identified by his father's name, Edward, or Neddy. With the shortening of his first name he went on to be known as Neddy Dick.[1]

The two main sources of income in Keld had been sheep-farming and lead-mining, but towards the end of the nineteenth century both of these providers of employment were in decline, mainly due to competition from abroad. As a result many left the area to seek work elsewhere, a good number of them emigrating. Today, Keld no longer has a year-round shop, nor a pub, and while it once had three chapels, each of a different non-conformist denomination, it now has just one and even its future is uncertain. But Keld does have a campsite, providing accommodation for a steady flow of walkers and cyclists passing through, and it has a resource centre which includes a small but well-stocked museum, offering an insight into the close-knit

---

[1] Pegg, p45.

*Figure 10.1. Neddy Dick with his musical stones. Courtesy of Keld Resource Centre.*

*Figure 10.2. Keld today Photograph: Mike Adcock.*

*Figure 10.3. Inside Neddy Dick's cottage, with his musical stones to the left of the harmonium. Courtesy of Keld Resource Centre.*

community which has been established there for some two hundred years (Figure 10.2). On the walls of the museum, among the photographs of local notables from the past are some showing Neddy Dick, the man who became referred to as the musical genius of Keld.

Neddy Dick was born into a farming family, though his father had also worked as a lead-miner, but it was said that although he did farm, having inherited some land on which he kept a few cows and sheep, his real passion was music, which he chose to pursue in his own idiosyncratic way. Documentation about Neddy Dick is mostly limited to his later life, when he lived alone in his cottage in the centre of the village, occupying much of his time playing music. Initially this was on an old harmonium, which he customised by progressively adorning it with bells of different tunings. These were removed from domestic clocks he collected from travelling around the area. At first the bells were hung from a tree branch, nailed to the top of the organ, but photographs of the room show this to have been replaced at some point by an iron frame.

To begin with it was the chapels which provided the platform for much of the music-making in villages such as Keld, their so-called minstrel galleries being occupied by a number of instrumentalists playing fiddles, cellos, trumpets, clarinets and more besides. But as a rather more austere version of religious worship took hold, the solemn and awe-inspiring sound of the harmonium was considered better suited and these were installed in chapels and churches and the minstrel galleries removed.[2] In time things changed again and harmoniums fell out of favour, which may well have given Neddy Dick the opportunity to acquire one cheaply and give it a home in his cottage (Figure 10.3).

---

[2] Cooper, p91.

Sometime after Neddy Dick had acquired his harmonium he discovered that some of the rocks in the River Swale rang with different notes when struck and he decided to build himself a lithophone. He began gathering stones from the Swale and also from one of its tributaries, Arkle Beck, but according to one man, who as a child had helped him to harvest hay in a small field he owned, some stones were surreptitiously removed by Neddy Dick from dry-stone walls close to the village.[3] Once he had collected enough pieces of rock producing a sufficiently acceptable quality of sound and carried them back to his cottage, the process of tuning them began, determining their pitch with the aid of a tuning fork and chipping away at the rock just as the Keswick men had done years before. Whether Neddy Dick ever saw any of the Cumbrian rock harmonicons is not known but it is possible, Keswick not being much more than fifty miles from Keld. Either way it seems likely that he would have heard about them.

In order to tune the stones, Neddy Dick laid them on straw upon a specially erected bench in his living room, with the accidentals, or 'black notes', initially suspended by wire from the rafters. Once completed, the instrument comprised twenty-four stone slabs and was almost three metres long; the wooden mallets he used to play it he also made himself. For a while the lithophone stood inside the cottage, along with the harmonium and bells, but at times it was kept in his outhouse. Neddy Dick also adapted a cart to accommodate the musical stones, enabling him to transport them if requested to play somewhere away from home.

For most of the time Neddy Dick stayed where he was, choosing not to travel far from his cottage in Keld and giving few public performances. Nevertheless, he did become something of a legendary, almost mythical figure, his name continuing to be known locally over the decades which followed. This happened largely by word of mouth, through a shared social memory, and from time to time reminiscences would appear in print in local and regional newspapers, even though he was rarely written about during his lifetime. One time that did happen, however, was as early as 1900 in the lengthy account of a hill-walker, describing a ten-day tour of the north-west Yorkshire Dales. Neddy Dick would then have been in his mid-fifties and may not have yet begun to play his musical stones, as they are not mentioned.

> The Sabbath morn breaks clear and bright. We decide to visit Swinnergill, one of the many pretty and romantic ravines of the Upper Swale Valley. Leaving Cat Hole about ten o'clock and passing through Keld, our attention is arrested by strains of sweet melody breaking the stillness of the Sabbath. Turning into a little cottage, whence the sounds proceed, we find an old friend and one of the best dale residents, "Neddy Dick", welcoming the sunny morn with sweet notes from his set of musical bells, with harmonium accompaniment. We are not many minutes in his scrupulously clean cottage, when we are joined by a contingent of the Yorkshire Co-operative Holiday Association, who are at present in summer quarters in this part of the dale. They bring hymn books, or perhaps I should say song books, and we soon have a good choir.[4]

Once Neddy Dick had completed the assembly of his musical stones they too became a familiar sound in the neighbourhood, his doors being left open for the purpose. Sometimes people gathered outside his cottage to listen and on occasions he would be asked to play special requests. Neddy enlisted the help of a schoolboy, Lennox Crombie, son of the local Congregational

---

[3] Pegg, p45.
[4] Northern Echo, Tuesday 27th March 1900, p2.

*Figure 10.4. Neddy Dick playing his stones. Courtesy of Keld Resource Centre.*

Church minister, and taught him to play the stones so they could perform duets together. Lennox was at boarding school, but during school holidays he would be called upon if the need arose, earning himself some extra pocket money from contributions coming from appreciative audiences.[5] Lennox's mother would apparently chide Neddy Dick, already senior in years, when she saw him walk past her kitchen garden, returning from a long distance, carrying heavy stones. He would then laugh and tell her he was going to make a fortune if she would let her lad tour the country with him and that he was going to make a stand for that purpose, which he would fix on a donkey cart. This remained his dream and plans for a tour of some description had indeed begun to be put in place, but Neddy Dick died before this came to fruition.[6]

There are no press reviews of Neddy Dick's playing to be found in newspaper archives and most of what can be learned about his life must be gleaned from recollections published in letters and articles in local newspapers or from recordings made years later by some of those who remembered him. In 1930, a few years after his death, a book by J.Sutcliffe Smith was published entitled *Music of the Yorkshire Dales*. It was drawn from a series of letters written to a friend, Donald, with each chapter devoted to the culture of a particular dale. The first chapter, on Swaledale, describes how he travelled to Keld in the hope of seeing Neddy Dick, having heard about him and his stone instrument. Shortly before his bus arrived in Keld, Sutcliffe Smith enquired of a fellow passenger whether Neddy Dick still lived there, but was told he had died. Later, visiting a local inn, the Cat Hole, he learnt from the landlady that she had been left Neddy's harmonium, which now stood in the front room. The bells had apparently gone to a relative in Skipton but as for the musical stones, they seem to have come to a sorry end:

> The stones had, I was told, been removed to an outhouse after Neddy Dick became ill; and – pointing to a ruin – my informant said, "The outhouse was demolished and the stones lie mixed up with the rubbish."[7]

---

[5] The Dalesman *Readers Club* column, October 1955, p359. Article by Helen H. Shawcross, Lennox Crombie's older sister. From cutting in Keld Museum archive.
[6] Ibid.
[7] Sutcliffe Smith, pp19-20.

Sutcliffe Smith learnt more about Neddy Dick from other villagers he met, their uncredited accounts reported in his book, including the local dialect with which they were delivered.

> "He wer a queer un. He wer brought up to farming; but his mind was always running on music. He neglected himself badly; and though he had money he didn't know how to use it. Lots o' fowk came to hear him play on t'stones he had fished up out o' t'beck."[8]

There seems to have been general agreement that Neddy Dick had been an able musician and Sutcliffe Smith cited one man in particular who he met:

> I was able to gain a much better estimate of the man from a cultured musician who stayed in Keld during Neddy's lifetime. His account ran somewhat thus: "During my visits to Swaledale I was much impressed by Alderson's musical ability. On his stones – which had been selected with the utmost care, and tuned by chipping – he rapped out many melodies with facility.....I regard the man as one who possessed genius - musical and inventive"[9]

In the years following the publication of J.Sutcliffe Smith's book, though not necessarily prompted by it, correspondence began to appear intermittently in newspapers, sometimes uncredited, from those who remembered Neddy Dick and he was remembered fondly. Sometimes it is the same story being told, but with slight variations or additions. Together these recollections provide something of an insight into the man and, being only sketchy, the story they tell could be summarised fairly briefly, but that would fail to capture the sense of personal connection with the man which the recorded memories convey. In 1934 such a piece appeared in the *Yorkshire Evening Post*, the author only identified by the initials E.W.C.

> Once upon a time there lived in the fastnesses of Swaledale an old man called Neddy Dick. "Once upon a time" seems a hard phrase with which to start a story about this dalesman, for he died but a half-a-dozen years ago. Yet already in that valley they talk of Neddy Dick as though he died years ago - his romantic and peculiar personality has lent distance and an atmosphere of legendry to his days.
>
> I met Neddy Dick some years before his death, and recently when I went again to his native hamlet of Keld, I recalled the whisper I had heard about his death. Keld will never forget the old man, and there were memories of him in the hearts of many villagers and dalesmen. His real name was Richard Alderson. And he lived in a tiny grey cottage, set high on a windy hillside. There he spent his bachelorhood of 70 years. Baking his own bread, and living in a world of music and perfect contentment.
>
> He was, one supposes, an "eccentric" or "character" though both terms could only be applied if they meant a lovable individuality and a fine appreciation of the simple things surrounding him. The chief joy in Neddy Dick's life was an old and battered harmonium, from which he was wont to draw stirring melodies and dales tunes, just for his own satisfaction. Night after night, the sound of his music could be heard coming from the open door of his cottage,

---

[8] Ibid, p 20.
[9] Ibid, p21.

As the years went on, however, Neddy Dick felt he needed another mode of expression for his musical instruments, and a strange and delightful instrument made its appearance by the side of the harmonium. It consisted of a stand – a plain piece of wood – upon which were hung a score or more bells taken from grandfather clocks. The story of the acquisition of these bells would make fine reading in itself, if all the details were available. It is known that Neddy Dick made nightly pilgrimages into the dale, armed with clock bells, and made exchanges with the farmers and cottagers.

If Neddy had two bells of one note he would try and exchange one of them with a neighbour; and there are told in Swaledale many amusing tales of haggles and protests in the farm kitchens. Having assembled his bells with differing notes, Neddy Dick would arm himself with a short stick, and seated before his old friend the harmonium, proceeded to play and occasionally strike the bells, One who has seen this rugged dalesman sending the echoes flying around his cottage in this manner says it was a peculiar and inspiring spectacle.

But Neddy Dick did not rest content even with this combination of instruments. He began to search the brooks and streams of the dale in search of stones from which he might strike notes, and his range of musical stones became as famous as his bell instrument. I fancy that the old man's only regret was that he could not play all three pieces of apparatus at once."[10]

The following year E.W.C. mentioned Neddy Dick again briefly, in an article for the *Yorkshire Evening Post*, repeating some of the same information and referring to the stone instrument, "a rock band", as "the pride and wonder of Upper Swaledale". He concludes by saying "all that remains of Neddy Dick (whose census name was Richard Alderson) now lies beneath a limestone tablet in Muker churchyard."[11] The tombstone still stands but, covered in lichen, its inscription is hardly legible.

*Figure 10.5. Neddy Dick. Courtesy of Keld Resource Centre.*

---

[10] Yorkshire Evening Post, Friday 11th May 1934, p7.
[11] Yorkshire Evening Post, Wednesday 18th December 1935, p6.

In 1936 the same newspaper recorded the loss of another resident of Keld who had occupied the same cottage as Neddy Dick after the musician had died. The uncredited author of the piece recalled how a few months earlier he had sat with the man, Mr Harker, in the dining room of the cottage and talked about Neddy Dick and how he used to sit there testing his musical stones "before adding them to the array in an outhouse".

> With his passing a fund of anecdotes about Neddy Dick is lost, for Mr Harker knew him and his habits. He used to say Neddy Dick was "a droll'un" - and that, in Swaledale means more than you or I could say in a couple of paragraphs.[12]

A few months later a column in the *Yorkshire Post*, *"Diary of a Yorkshireman"* contained further memories of Neddy Dick and his musical stones, the writer recalling them being kept on a long table in an outhouse near his home, where "he would spend many hours, playing and singing to himself." With regard to Neddy Dick's aspiration to play all his instruments at the same time, there is a suggestion that this indeed came to pass, the diarist having been told that "he used to perform the feat of playing the stones, the bells and the harmonium all at once." As to what had happened to the stones after Neddy Dick died, there is a repeat of the general belief that they had been thrown away.[13]

A couple of weeks later, yet another unnamed correspondent wrote to the paper, hoping to shed further light on what had happened to Neddy Dick's musical stones:

> I have a clue to the fate of the musical stones that were the joy and pride of Neddy Dick, the musical genius of Keld, in Swaledale...On a visit to Keld last week I saw about half-a-dozen of the stones – built into a wall, and thus preserved for years to come. Mr Frank Metcalfe, of Keld put me on the trail. He said that when Neddy died the outhouse that was his music room was pulled down, and the stones were used to build a wall close at hand. "I built t'wall", said Mr Metcalfe, "and now I come to think on't, some o' them musical stones might have been used."
>
> An expedition of two at once left for the wall, and there Mr Metcalfe, after careful examination, identified a few of the stones as those that were played long ago by the quaint Neddy. Where the remainder of the stones are I do not know, but it is interesting to know that some of the relics are preserved in this unusual way. I hope that when that wall's day is done, someone will see to it that Keld still keeps these links with one of her most remarkable sons.[14]

This tale confirms some new information which J. Suttcliffe Smith adds in the final letter which ends his book. He writes of being informed that Neddy Dick's musical stones had been "extricated from the masonry under which they had long been hidden, and if I cared to pay Keld another visit I might see them".[15] This he proceeded to do and was shown a collection of

---

[12] Yorkshire Evening Post, Tuesday 3rd March 1936, p6
[13] Yorkshire Post and Leeds Intelligencer, Saturday 1st August 1936, *Diary of a Yorkshireman*, p8.
[14] Yorkshire Post and Leeds Intelligencer, Monday 17th August 1936 p6.
[15] Suttcliffe Smith, p246.

between fifty and sixty stones.[16] With some help, these stones were transferred to a workshop for further inspection.

> Our first results were only a series of dead, dull sounds. Next we placed the pieces of rock on parallel boards supported at the ends on boxes. Then we tapped them with a piece of hard wood, and were delighted not only to evoke musical notes, but fairly true intervals. From this it was not a difficult matter to conclude that all the stones contained the material for a chromatic scale of about five octaves.[17]

On this second visit to Keld, Sutcliffe Smith spoke to other people who had heard Neddy Dick perform on his musical stones, which interestingly he refers to as a Rock Band, the same term used by the Keswick players.

> They told how he delighted and astonished visitors to these high regions with his performances, some of which were quite brilliant; how he manipulated two hammers of wood at the same time, often playing independent parts; and how he turned his back on those who merely came to visit him for novelty.[18]

He ends on an optimistic note, with a conviction which was unfortunately not to come to pass..

> That the stones will be taken care of – if only to form a grotto to Alderson's memory - I feel convinced; and I fully believe that when this is done, and visitors enquire "What mean these stones?" the villagers will reply, "They are to the memory of Richard Alderson – a Lover of Sweet Sounds."[19]

More memories of Neddy Dick were to surface years later when in 1960 another resident of Keld, Laurie Rukin, who some still remember today, was recorded giving an interview in which he spoke of having known Neddy Dick and saying that he had, on occasion, heard him play. By then the musician would have been drawing to the end of his life and was apparently increasingly reticent about performing on his instruments, but could be persuaded.

> You had a job to get him to play then, you know, he would take a bit of 'ticing.. I used to take him a rabbit sometimes – he used to like one to eat… I took him once over one night and I said "Now you get this rabbit on conditions you play me a tune." "Oh, I can't play", he says, "Gramophones have done me", he says, "They've done me out of my business"…However, with a bit of 'ticing I got him to play me a tune. I says "If you don't, you don't get the rabbit. I'll take it to Ruth", who was an old lady just above ….so down he sat and he played. He played me the Hallelujah Chorus, which was a big favourite of his, and he played it very well. Otherwise, he was a man mostly on his own, he didn't have many friends particularly. He had a little bit of land. He had a field and a couple of cows and a few sheep and he used to look after them fairly well and made a living out of it. He was a man that would be fairly well off, fairly well-to-do. He had some property, he had some land as well. He would get the rent off that, you see. He would be able to

---
[16] Far in excess of the twenty-four stones are visible in existing photographs of Neddy Dick's lithophone, though they do show other pieces of rock, possibly rejected, set to one side.
[17] Sutcliffe Smith, p247.
[18] Ibid.
[19] Ibid.

live all right that way. Otherwise he was a very one-man band, he wouldn't join in with anybody else very much.[20]

Where Neddy Dick's musical stones are located today is not known. The reports that they were built into a wall have not been properly substantiated, and nor has the claim that the pieces of rock which J. Suttcliffe Smith tested and described at the end of his book were those used in the lithophone. The earlier part of Neddy Dick's life also remains shrouded in mystery. Had he always been a musician and if so what other instruments did he play? He certainly lived for his music and said himself that he heard music in the air.[21] Neddy Dick was clearly something of a recluse and one of the newspaper reminiscences refers to his seventy years of bachelorhood. But there is one account, written during his lifetime, which tells a different story, revealing details of an earlier period of his life, which if true, was certainly something he generally kept to himself.

The written piece referred to was published in the *Bridlington Free Press* in 1907, delivered rather in the style of a children's bedtime story of the period, and is about a man referred to as Neddy Dick.[22] It describes him, in a way which seems completely consistent with the way others were later to remember Neddy Dick, as "a puzzle to his neighbours" who "lived by himself, his conversation seldom extending beyond a 'good morning' in response to the salute of some passing villager." It then goes on to tell that there was one person, a little girl called Mary Anderson, who delivered his milk every morning, with whom he was prepared to say rather more than merely passing the time of day. We learn that their friendship grew when the young girl showed affection for Neddy's dog, particularly when it was unwell. A time came when Mary Anderson was due to give a recitation at the local Sunday School anniversary event. Initially Neddy Dick told her he would be unable to go, but when she told him firmly that if he didn't, then that would be the end of their friendship, he relented and turned up on the appointed day, though he had not attended a place of worship for twenty years. The subject of Mary's recitation was "Heaven" and it moved Neddy Dick deeply, bringing him to tears. After the service, Mary caught up with him as he was walking slowly home and he explained to her why he was upset. Her recitation, which was entitled "Mother gone before", had brought to mind memories of Lucy, the one woman who had loved him, and also of their three children, all of whom had died long before. He explained to Mary that God had taken them from him and from that time on he had never attended chapel again. The story ends with Mary telling Neddy Dick, the next time she sees him, of a dream she had had in which she had seen his lost family in heaven, and then persuading Neddy to go with her to chapel the coming Sunday. He agrees to do so and while there he receives a revelatory vision, just as in Mary's dream, of Lucy and his three children, all now angels.

How much of this somewhat maudlin, sentimental story, is factually true is impossible to say, but it does fly in the face of other published memories of Neddy Dick, which make no reference to him ever being anything but alone in his adult life. Being published in a newspaper from Bridlington, a coastal town some distance from Keld, it may not have become an episode generally known to the residents of his village. With little else to go on, it perhaps provides at

---

[20] Transcript of radio interview. From SWAAG website *https://swaag.org/*
[21] Pegg, p45.
[22] Bridlington Free Press, Friday 18th October 1907, p6.

*Figure 10.6. The cottage in Keld where Neddy Dick lived, as it is today. Photograph: Mike Adcock.*

least a clue to the back story of the musical man of Keld, with his harmonium, bells and musical stones, who people knew as Neddy Dick.

### Antonio Roca y Várez

Far from the Yorkshire dales, on the Balearic island of Menorca, Antonio Roca y Várez was already becoming a man of many interests by the time he decided to build himself a lithophone in his late twenties. He was born in 1866, into a family of some importance, his father being an eminent doctor and an authority on matters of health, while his mother's family owned land and property in the centre of the island. Roca read philosophy and literature at the University of Barcelona before going on to take his doctorate in Madrid. On returning to Menorca he worked for a few years as a school teacher and it was during this time, in 1893, that he constructed his stone instrument. Whether or not he knew of precedents elsewhere in Europe isn't known, but the story goes, and it's becoming a familiar one, that he chanced to discover that some of the flat pieces of rock on his family's land rang when struck with a stick. Having collected a number of pieces he began to tune them there *in situ*, to the notes of a major scale. Alongside his academic achievements Roca had considerable musical ability and also had perfect pitch, which would have proved useful in the tuning process. He had decided on an instrument which would would span two and a half octaves and once it was finished he decided to add the accidentals, making it fully chromatic. It being impossible to construct such an instrument in silence, it soon attracted the interest of others in the area and a local newspaper published an article about the lithophone, telling how it could be heard from a distance of two kilometres:

*Figure 10.7. Antonio Roca playing his lithophone. Courtesy of Carles Garcia-Roca.*

> Groups of musicians and enthusiasts leave the town for Torrealta, prompted by curiosity to see and hear such an instrument for the first time in their lives...Let us applaud Sr. Roca for his original invention, much deserved by the way, for such admirable work.[23]

Encouraged by this interest, Roca applied himself to becoming proficient on his new lithophone and began making plans to stage an outdoor public concert to display its qualities (Figure 10.7). Roca's playing on the lithophone was to be accompanied by a pianist and a guitarist, with another band playing in support. It was decided that the concert should take place on the 9th August 1896 in Llumena Nou, the same area where he had collected the pieces of stone. Moving a stone instrument far would alone have presented something of a logistical challenge, transporting a piano across an uneven terrain probably presented an even greater one. An impressively large audience of around 1200 people attended, some arriving on foot, others by cart. The programme for the concert was ambitious, particularly if it was only to be for a single performance. It included items from Rossini's *Barber of Seville* and Verdi's *Il Trovatore* plus other pieces whose names have not stood the test of time so well, but mainly classical in style. There may have also been some original pieces included: *Alayor Masurca*, which opened the trio's second set, uses an alternative spelling of Alaior, the region where the stones were collected and in which the performance took place.

The summer concert was a great success and a noted local musician and composer, Ignacio Gatiérrez later wrote about it:

> The lithophone meets the requirements for performing all kinds of musical devices including even trills. We must mention the great agility, precision and phrasing with

---

[23] Translated from El Bien Público, Wednesday 8th November 1893. From archive of Carles Garcia-Roca.

*Figure 10.8. Gold medal inscribed "Antonio Roca y Várez, Mahon 1901". Courtesy of Carles Garcia-Roca.*

*Figure 10.9. Don Antonio Roca y Várez.. Courtesy of Carles Garcia-Roca.*

which Sr. Roca performed the pieces in the programme, which were accompanied by guitar and piano. Alaior can boast of having been the first town in Menorca to have heard the lithophone.[24]

Whether Antonio Roca y Várez gave any other concerts on the island is undocumented, but five years later he was invited to take his lithophone to Naples to an exhibition, the *Esposizione Partenopea Permanente*, where he was awarded their gold medal (Figure 10.8). It was at just the same time that Honoré Baudre was exhibiting his flint lithophone at the large exhibition in Brest and, while this concurrence was completely coincidental, it does provide another indication of how the emergence of new musical instruments at the time was attracting a wide interest within the scientific community as well as in the arts. Lithophones continued to be the subject of widespread curiosity beyond just their musical potential.

Although teaching became the profession of Antonio Roca, he never felt it to be his true vocation and left it to pursue other interests, though those continued to include the subject of education, as well as medicine and science. In 1900 he had been appointed as Portugal's vice-consul on the island of Menorca, it having been a *de facto* hereditary position, with his father, grandfather and great-grandfather having held the post before him. It would appear not to have occupied a great deal of Roca's time as he also held the role of vice-consul of Denmark, but the Portuguese appointment came to a premature end when he was dismissed

---

[24] Translation. From archive of Carles Garcia-Roca.

for writing a newspaper article on the subject of royalty which offended the Portuguese government. However, as a result of his diplomatic and academic work, and also having set up a private library at his home in Mahón, he was given an honorary title, becoming Don Antonio Roca y Várez.

Yet despite being awarded this honour, Don Antonio Roca y Várez found himself unable to wear the mantle of establishment figure comfortably. While he seems to have had a benevolent nature, wishing to do something for the social good, there was something of the bohemian in him, averse to playing by the rules. He enjoyed presenting himself in different personas and would sometimes sign off pieces he had written with the name "Ótón Navarro y Cieza", an anagram of his actual name. Having no real financial concerns, thanks to the assets accumulated on his mother's side of the family, Roca could afford to spend much of his time as he pleased and one way he chose to occupy himself was pursuing his love of photography. He took photographs of the surrounding landscape and others depicting different aspects of life Menorca. An added point of interest was that many of these photographs were taken with a stereoscopic camera, 3D photography being in vogue at the time for those who could afford it. The photographs, which were to become a unique record of Menorca at that time, were featured in an exhibition in Mahón, Menorca in 2017 and later in different galleries around the island.

In 1904 the small island of Colom, close to Menorca, came up for auction. It was considered of little value for agricultural use and although there had been a lead mine there, it was no longer operational. Antonio Roca was nevertheless attracted by the idea of owning an island, managed to put in a winning bid and got it for a knock-down price, against the better judgement of his wife, Magdalena Bofill, who considered it a fanciful project which they could ill-afford. Roca did for a while try to grow crops and rear some livestock but it was not successful and neither were his attempts to resurrect the use of a quarry and the lead-mine. Instead the island became a summer residence for the family.

With all this going on in his life it seems hardly surprising that Antonio Roca was unable to throw himself wholeheartedly into his undoubted love of music. Years later his grandson was to recall his considerable music ability, telling of a time when his grandfather had attended an opera in Mahón (which has the oldest opera house in Spain) and when he arrived home sat at the piano and played the melodies he had heard from memory, just as Mozart had done with Allegri's *Miserere*.

There is no known record of the Menorca lithophone being played in public again from the time the award was presented in Naples in 1901 until Roca's death in 1925, or since. Neither is it known what happened to the instrument. Compared with some, the lithophone had a rather crude appearance, but it may well have had an impressive sound. A few years ago the picture showing Roca playing his instrument, probably on the piece of land where he built it, began to appear for the first time online and documentation about its creator began to appear, the story of iRoca and his lithophone having been hitherto virtually unknown or forgotten. That it can be told now is almost solely due to the interest shown by a family member, Carles Garcia-Roca, who believed it was time for some wider recognition of the musical achievement of his great-

great-grandfather, Don Antonio Roca y Várez. Carles works as a hospital paediatrician, having taken up a career in medicine, as his father and grandfather had, along with generations of the family before before them. All except for Don Antonio Roca y Várez who followed his own path.[25]

---

[25] Personal correspondence with Carles Garcia-Roca, great-great-grandson of Don Antonio Roca y Várez.

# Chapter Eleven

# Circuses, music halls and musical pavements
## Arthur Nelson, the Pavanellas and the Bozza Troupe

With the face of public entertainment continuing to change throughout the nineteenth century, the music halls in Britain were playing an increasingly central role, providing a rich and varied fare, affordable and appealing to both the urban working class and the different strata of the expanding middle-class. Building on their increasing popularity, new music halls continued to open, particularly in the large cities, offering a dizzy mix of song, dance, comedy, escapology and acrobatics, along with a selection of novelty acts defying description and both high-brow and low-brow music. Another, already established form of popular entertainment was provided by circuses, some travelling, some static and they were enjoying a welcome revival. While music halls and circuses each had their own particular and distinctive characteristics there was also overlap, with performers who moved from working in one to the other. Musical stones began to make regular appearances at the music hall as they also did at the circus, though there there was a distinct likelihood of them being played by a juggling clown riding bareback on a horse.

### Arthur Nelson and the circus

Circus epitomised the notion of variety entertainment with its combination of clowning, music and the appeal of possible jeopardy through the inclusion of both high-wire acts and potentially dangerous animals. A clown by the name of Arthur Nelson was one of a number of circus performers who, as early as the 1840s, began playing musical stones and other unusual instruments along with, in his case, performing various stunts and acrobatic feats. Starting off professionally as an actor he went on to work with a number of circuses before working as a freelance performer, becoming known particularly for his version of a rock harmonicon.

In 1845, Arthur Nelson, then aged thirty-four, was appearing with Cooke's Royal Circus in Great Yarmouth in Norfolk when he chose to present a particular stunt which he had undertaken before. The stunt in question involved him sitting in a wooden washtub, dressed as a clown, and sailing up the River Yare into the conjoining River Bure, the washtub being towed by four geese. (Figure 11.1) What ensued was a catastrophe on a tragically large scale. A crowd of close to 400 people were bunched together on one side of a bridge watching Arthur Nelson from above as he moved down the river. Suddenly the bridge collapsed under the weight and the onlookers were cast into the water, with the result that seventy-nine people lost their lives. In the aftermath, although Nelson was not held directly responsible he was devastated by what had happened and was never to get over the feeling that he was to blame. Shortly after that he decided to leave the country, travelling to America and residing for a while in New York.

While he was in the USA Arthur Nelson sought ways to continue his performing career. He had taken with him his rock harmonicon and other instruments and making use of contacts there was able to generate some work, being added to the bill of various vaudeville shows.

# Circuses, Music Halls and Musical Pavements

Figure 11.1. Poster for Arthur Nelson's stunt in Great Yarmouth. Courtesy of Andy Aliffe.

The rock harmonicon he took with him had forty notes, so at three and a half octaves was smaller than others coming out of Keswick, but was, like them, constructed using Skiddaw stone. Par for the course, he promoted the instrument as being unique and of his own invention, but did augment it with his musical pine sticks and what he called an ancient dulcimer, modelled, he claimed, on the lyre David played to Saul. During his stay in New York Nelson met up with the great showman, P.T. Barnum, though this was many years before he set up his famous circus with James Bailey. Barnum was, however, running the hugely successful Barnum's American Museum and booked Nelson to play there.

By 1851 Arthur Nelson was back in England, appearing at Welch & McCollum's Circus at Drury Lane Theatre in London, and then at the large National Standard Theatre in Shoreditch. Two years later Nelson joined the company run by the famed equestrian performer Pablo Fanque (Figure 11.2) for a series of shows in Edinburgh (Figure 11.3) In an era when white performers were making careers out of blacking up their faces to present stereotypical versions of black people, Pablo Fanque had achieved the unusual feat of being a black man who owned a circus, a predominantly white form of entertainment.

> Pablo Fanque's Amphitheatre has a very strong company, and is doing excellent business every evening, as well as at the morning performance last Monday, which went off with great satisfaction. The Brothers Hutchinson are very clever, and Madame Franconi is a most graceful and daring rider. Mr Arthur Nelson, with his rock harmonicon and antics as a clown, is also a favourite.[1]

Many years later Pablo Fanque was to be immortalised by the Beatles in the song *For the benefit of Mr Kite*, though there were possibly few who bought the Sergeant Pepper album who knew quite who Pablo Fanque had been.

---

[1] The Era, London, Sunday 16th January 1853, p10.

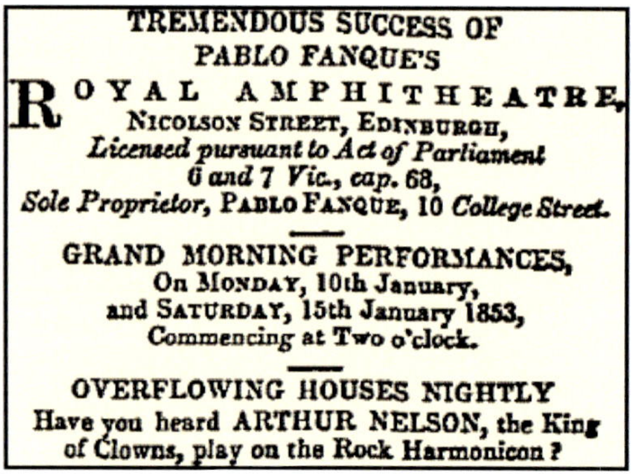

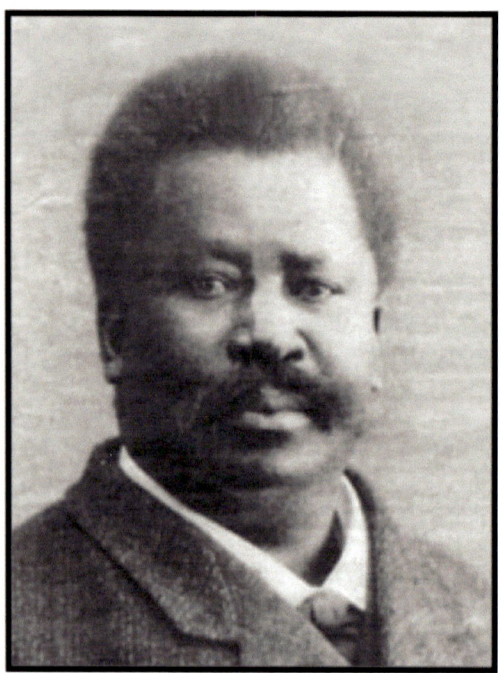

*Figure 11.2. Pablo Fanque. Courtesy of Andy Aliffe.*

TREMENDOUS SUCCESS OF
PABLO FANQUE'S
ROYAL AMPHITHEATRE,
NICOLSON STREET, EDINBURGH,
*Licensed pursuant to Act of Parliament*
*6 and 7 Vic., cap. 68,*
*Sole Proprietor*, PABLO FANQUE, 10 *College Street.*

GRAND MORNING PERFORMANCES,
On MONDAY, 10th January,
and SATURDAY, 15th January 1853,
Commencing at Two o'clock.

OVERFLOWING HOUSES NIGHTLY
Have you heard ARTHUR NELSON, the King of Clowns, play on the Rock Harmonicon?

*Figure 11.3. Publicity for Pablo Fanque's Edinburgh show featuring Arthur Nelson. Courtesy of Andy Aliffe.*

In addition to his abilities as a musician, Arthur Nelson was evidently a natural performer and entertainer in a way which may not have come so easily to all members of the family rock bands of that era, however well their musical performances were received. Nelson's playing was indeed complimented, but he seems to have been first and foremost a clown.

He was happy to collaborate with others and while he may not himself have chosen to perform on horseback he had been closely associated with equestrian performance and was involved in creating, arranging and directing the sequences being presented.

Nelson's humour as a clown was not purely slapstick, with some later promotional material, referring to his verbal wit as well as his musical prowess:

Engagement for six nights only MR ARTHUR NELSON, the Celebrated Jester and Musical Momus, whose Lively Wit, Satirical Puns and inexhaustible Fund of Anecdote and Raillery have gained for him the appellation of CLOWN KING: who will at each performance introduce his MUSICAL PINE STCKS and from rough pieces of stone form a ROCK HARMONICON from whence will issue such sweet and dulcet sounds, that the listener may imagine he is in a happy Dream of Fairy Land.[2]

The implication in the press announcement is that Nelson's rock harmonicon was not presented on stage as a finished item but that he assembled the instrument as part of the performance, bringing yet another twist to the genre.

Before long Arthur Nelson was travelling again, this time across the world to Australia, where he arrived early 1855. He was based in Melbourne, and although he publicised his availability

[2] Caledonian Mercury, Wednesday 18th January 1860, p1.

for bookings[3] there is no evidence of him making much of an impact and he was soon making his way back to the old country and had returned to Britain by March 1856. Arthur Nelson continued to perform solo, usually sharing the bill with other performers, sometimes as part of a circus show. In 1857 he appeared at different venues around the north of England, his publicity now including a reference to him as the Jester to the Court of Nepaul.[4] The following year, when he was back working in the south of the country, appearing in March at Emidy's Continental Cirque in Ipswich, the press coverage threw a little more light on the Nepalese connection.

> ....His excellency Prince Jung Bahadoor, Ambassador of Nepaul, presented Mr. Nelson with a splendid gold medal, as a token of admiration of his wonder on the Rock Harmonica [sic], musical pine sticks, clay tiles, glasses, bells, and steel bars, at Vauxhall Royal Gardens, June 4, 1851. Mr N. being the only individual who has had the honor of performing at three such establishments during their entire seasons, viz.:- The Theatre Royal, Drury Lane; Mr Julien's Orchestra, Surrey Zoological Gardens; and the Royal Property, Vauxhall Gardens.[5]

The reference to Louis Jullien is a rare example of a specific connection being made between the aforementioned celebrated French conductor and a performer on a rock harmonicon. Arthur Nelson was showing an ability to bring what he had to offer to a range of entertainment platforms, from the theatre and circus world where he started, to the popular but prestigious London locations such as the Surrey Zoological Gardens and the numerous music halls.

In 1858 Nelson began performing in a bizarre touring show called "The Aztec Lilliputians". Five years earlier an exhibition had been staged around Britain which was to develop into an odd and decidedly dubious combination of anthropology, music and freak-show entertainment. Two children, known as Maximo and Bartolan, who were said to be from Mexico, had been previously brought to New York and exhibited as examples of a hitherto unknown race of people. They were described as being Aztecs, though later research concluded that they had probably originated in El Salvador. Having created a considerable amount of interest in America, the two children were brought over to Britain where they toured extensively and were welcomed by the great and good of British society, including a visit to Buckingham Palace, where they were taken along by Royal Command "and examined with curiosity by the Queen and Royal family".[6] The exhibition of what were deemed to be peculiar human specimens was later expanded to include two people from South Africa, known as Earthmen (because they were said to live underground) in what was presented as a kind of grotesque tableau. To accompany these human exhibits from the other side of the world, music was provided from closer to home, by some Highland bell-ringers, a pianist called Miss E. Butler, Mr W.Morris on the Crystal Ophonic and Mr. Arthur Nelson, now being described as a rock and wood melodist.[7]

Arthur Nelson continued to work around Britain for the next couple of years, visiting Ireland in the summer of 1859 with the Aztec Lilliputians, performing at the Alhambra Palace

---

[3] Aliffe, p47.
[4] Liverpool Albion, Monday 22nd June 1857, p1.
[5] Suffolk Chronicle, Saturday 13th March 1858, p2.
[6] New York Times, Saturday 23rd July 1853, p2.
[7] Winchester Journal, Saturday 18th September 1858, p5

Circus in Birmingham in November, working with Ginnett's Circus in Sheffield in December and travelling up to Edinburgh in the new year to perform in Sangers' Monstre Circus and Hippodrome. But that was to be the end of his performing career. His last public appearance was at the Alhambra Palace in April 1860, introducing a young female horse-tamer giving a display of her skills and in August that year he died, at the age of thirty-nine.

In the years following Arthur Nelson's death the use of musical stones continued to be a regular part of the musical entertainment in circuses. Two generations of the Orford family began to make a name for themselves in the 1860s, possibly modelling themselves on the example set by Nelson, combining clownery, music and other skills. One of them, always billed only has W. Orford combined this with his considerable skills as a horseman, raising the bar of what was possible when it came to displays of versatility on a lithophone.

> There are now some clever feats by Mr W Orford, who in a performance on musical stones and a horseback juggling act, displays ability of a high order. A new clown is added, and a pretty set of quadrilles is gone through on highly trained horses.[8]

## Music hall stones

Circus continued to be popular in Britain, but the rising stars of performance venues were the music halls and musical stones regularly appeared among the multifarious acts on offer. A classic novelty music act which became very popular in the 1880s on the music hall circuit and who also worked in circus were The Four Jees, sometimes billed as the Jee Brothers (Figure 11.4). Multi-instrumentalists who delighted in subverting the use of established instruments while trampling down the boundaries of what might be defined as musical, they too included a rock harmonicon in their performances:

> The Four Jees displayed really marvellous musical versatility and skill. They rattled welcome melody from the xylophone, or wood or rock "harmonicon" and the tallest of the company proved an admirable player of the piano, cornet and trombone. The two first-named instruments he played at the same time. Another of the party extracted music from a broomstick with the assistance of a dusting-brush, and two of them with bells on their heads and bells on their toes served out harmony in pleasant but very abnormal fashion.[9]

There was an aspect of music hall which was rather paternal and worthy, a way of introducing high culture to ordinary people and so it was that operatic arias were sung and classical favourites performed, but it was undoubtedly the comic and frequently risqué songs which proved to be the most popular musical fare. With novelty again being paramount there was plenty of scope for fresh takes on musical virtuosity and the use of musical stones fitted the bill perfectly. The stones used were smaller than those of the Keswick rock harmonicons and would commonly be played in conjunction with other instruments, in the manner of The Four Jees, or appear as one musical ingredient of a varied act. Musical stones began to be listed with some regularity in publicity for music halls, sometimes with the name of the player but not in all cases, the instrument itself being promoted as the attraction. With so many delights on

---

[8] Birmingham Post, Thursday 12th March 1885, From a review of Newsome's Circus at Curzon Hall, Birmingham.
[9] The Era, Saturday 25th October 1884, p10.

# CIRCUSES, MUSIC HALLS AND MUSICAL PAVEMENTS

*Figure 11.4. Poster of the Jee Brothers.*

offer however, musical stones, once they had started to become common-place, might only receive a passing mention in the press, for example:

> There is an excellent company this week, including the reappearance of the Brothers Wills, the original black clowns, who are very clever on the bells, musical stones etc., and have met with a very hearty reception.[10]

---

[10] London and Provincial Entr'acte, Saturday 24th June 1871, p7. From review of a show at London's Oxford Music Hall.

The Brothers Wills, described as "original black clowns" were not originally black at all, but a blackface act combining clowning with playing musical stones and other items. They seem to have enjoyed some success and a review from another appearance, this time at another London music hall, the London Pavilion, gives a further impression of what was on offer:

> The Brothers Wills gave a novel and agreeable entertainment. They presented themselves to view grotesquely dressed as Clowns. One of them played on musical stones, the pair performed together on steel bars, and one of the twain played prettily on bells, while his companion, with a rueful countenance sat reflecting on the past. Clever hat spinning and nimble dancing followed.[11]

## The Pavanellas

The most original and successful music hall performers to explore the musical use of stone were probably the Pavanellas, a five-piece group who were also associated with the circus. They approached things in a different, decidedly more theatrical way than those considered so far. Presenting themselves in the role of Parisian paviors occupied with repairing or replacing paving stones, they produced music from their stone slabs and the various tools they carried with them. The Pavanellas began to make a name for themselves in Britain from late1883, but before that had been playing in France and according to their agent's publicity had spent a six-month period in Paris, during which time they played at the Folies Bergère and at the Cirque d'Été in the Champs Élysées. There was some ambiguity about their nationality, possibly deliberate, and they were often referred to as being French musicians but at least three of them, brothers with the surname Pavanelli, were actually Italian.

In November 1883, having recently arrived in England, the performers appeared for some weeks at the recently opened Grand Circus in Manchester, billed as the Pavanelli Bozza Troupe and a few weeks later they moved to London, where they remained for a while. Carl Bozza was another Italian musician and clown with some surprisingly innovative ideas about musical performance, but the association with Bozza appears to have ended around this time and reviews began referring to them as the Pavanellas. with the Bozza Troupe continuing as a separate act, maintaining the musical pavior idea, but as part of a wider repertoire. Most of the Pavanellas' work was in and and around the capital and they were soon to be found playing in the leading venues for music hall and popular entertainment, including the Canterbury Theatre of Varieties in Lambeth, Lusby's in the Mile End Road and the Royal Aquarium in Westminster. This was a large centre for exhibitions, concerts and plays, opened in 1876 and constructed using iron and glass as well as stone. Despite its name, it had never successfully contained fish in its large glass tanks but for a while was an important centre for entertainment. And the entertainment was varied, to say the least. An account of a daytime performance given there in late December 1883 describes a bill which included a recital on the grand organ, a lecture on memory, acrobatic displays, juggling and a blackface comedy act, in addition to the Pavanellas, who were praised in the press for their novel act which was described in London's *Morning Post*:

> The scene presented was one only too well known to the denizens of the metropolis. The roadway was supposed to be in need of repairs or repaving, and a party of paviors

---

[11] The Era, Sunday 18th January 1874, p4.

# CIRCUSES, MUSIC HALLS AND MUSICAL PAVEMENTS

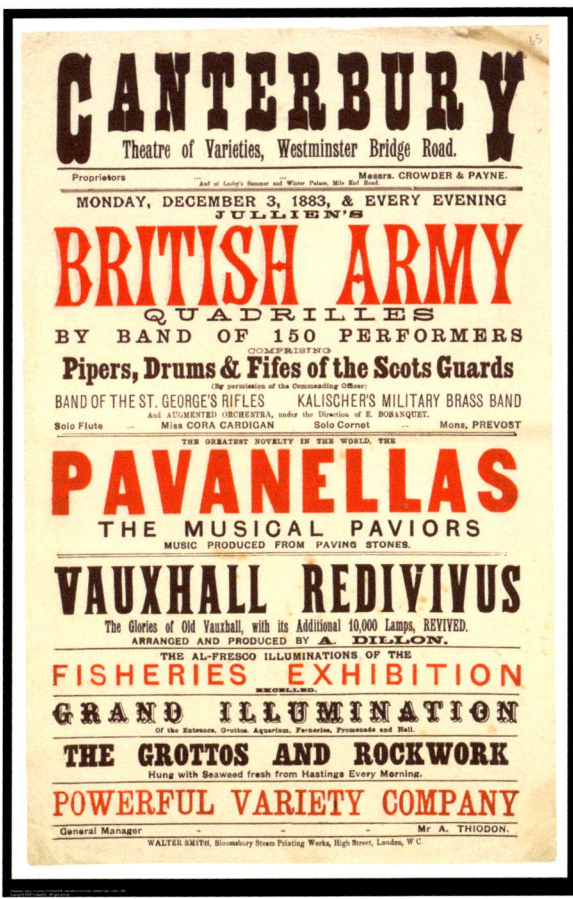

Figure 11.5. Poster for Canterbury Theatre of Varieties featuring the Pavanellas. Courtesy of Andy Aliffe.

had been told off to carry out the work. Attired in blouses and other appropriate costumes and equipped with the instruments of their calling, they entered wheeling barrows filled with sand and stones. Having placed the latter in position, and adjusted them with "picks", in the orthodox fashion, the workmen proceeded to extract the most melodious music from the apparently ordinary paving stones. The novel instrumental concert was further supplemented by an equally wonderful performance on the well-known tools that, in the vernacular of the craft, are denominated "rammers." How it was done remained, of course, a secret to the audience, but that enhanced the interest that was universally excited. As a wonderful feat it will doubtless attract numerous visitors during the holidays.[12]

How it was done is a moot point. It appears that things were not quite what they seemed in the skills displayed by these musical paviors and that the theatricality of their performance did indeed require a suspension of disbelief. A later American newspaper article on novelty musical acts claimed that although musical paviors appeared to be producing sound from stone paving slabs, the different musical notes were actually produced by tuned steel bars within the so-called "rammers" used to strike the slabs.[13] So it may be that they were not truly producing their music from stone just as they were neither paviors nor French. The Pavanellas may indeed have found their way into these pages by false pretences, but illusory or not their contribution remains, on some level, part of the story of musical stone.

Although working with agents was the best way of getting a steady stream of bookings, another good tactic was to become attached to performance troupes with an already established reputation. The Pavanellas managed to do this, initially by appearing alongside the Court Minstrels, a successful blackface minstrel act led by Horace Livermore, who went on to become

---

[12] The Morning Post, Thursday 27th December 1883, p5.
[13] The San Francisco Examiner, Wednesday 11th April 1894, p14.

a theatre and music hall entrepreneur. While the Pavanellas were passing themselves off as French workers, the Court Minstrels in their act were taking mimicry to a different level, depending as it did on a heavy application of burnt cork.

The Pavanellas' appearances, particularly in London, almost always took place alongside music hall acts displaying a miscellaneous range of skills: another event at the Royal Aquarium, in January 1884, was advertised as featuring Tyrolean singers, contortionists, a ventriloquist, performing goats and a troupe of gladiators; the world of music hall was by no means limited to music. That year the Pavanellas travelled to the north of England for a series of engagements in April and May, performing in Liverpool at the New Star Music Hall, later to become the Liverpool Playhouse, where the entertainment they provided was described as being not only a novelty "but a real musical treat".[14] They also performed for several nights at Harmstone's Circus in South Shields, where the publicity confidently described them as "the most novel speciality ever witnessed" and recommended they "should be seen by all lovers of classical music". For indeed the Pavanellas, like the family rock bands before them, found a successful formula in mixing popular songs with classical favourites, blending crowd-pleasing novelty with something rather more refined. In August they crossed the Irish Sea, playing for a few days in Dublin at Dan Lowrey's Star of Erin Music Hall, where those thinking of attending were promised the opportunity of hearing "Madame Angot Quadrilles beautifully performed on common paving stones."[15]

Over the following two years, as well as appearing regularly in London venues the Pavanellas continued to perform across Britain, including visits to Wales and Scotland, but in the the summer of 1886 they were to cross the Atlantic where they set up base in New York. There they began working with the Wilson & Rankin Minstrels, another blackface troupe, often featuring around twenty performers. The Pavanellas quickly made an impression, their act regularly reported as having received multiple encores. A theatrical novelty they may have been, but their considerable musical abilities were also acknowledged:

> The Pavanellas, the musical paviors of Paris, now with the Wilson & Rankin minstrels, is the strongest musical feature on the American stage. Last night they played a pot pourri from Offenbach's comic opera "Orpheus aux Enfers", upon ordinary stone, or granite blocks, using the regular pavers' hammers, and from the street rammers played a number from Auber's "Fra Diavolo". From spades,picks and brooms they played Handel's march for trumpets, "For a hero", and in their mouths an instrument closely resembling the tones of a flute, but in shape very like a conch shell, the beautiful aria "L'esprit du Francais" to a full organ accompaniment was wailed out in beautiful harmonies.[16]

At least one newspaper review questioned why the Pavanellas, along with some gymnasts, should have been with a minstrel show.[17] One reason is probably that by the 1880s the blackface minstrel genre, which had proved extremely popular and promoted as the first truly American

---

[14] Liverpool Daily Post, Tuesday 15th April 1884, p8.
[15] Freeman's Journal, Dublin, Thursday 21st August 1884, p4.
[16] Vincennes Sun-Commercial, Indiana, Monday 8th November 1886, p4. Citing review previously appearing in Cincinnati Enquirer.
[17] Vicksburg Herald, Tuesday 28th September 1886, p4.

form of theatre, was in decline and it was deemed necessary to offer a greater variety of entertainment to ensure sizeable audiences. However, for the Pavanellas the association with Wilson & Rankin was to last for less than a year. In April 1887 they let it be known through the press that they were owed up to $3800 in unpaid salaries and it was reported that they would be returning to Paris "sadder but wiser men".[18] A few months earlier this financial situation had played a part in a tragic turn of events for the Pavanellas. The eldest of the three Pavanelli brothers was accompanied during their stay in New York by his wife, who was possibly also one of the performers, and somewhere along the line a relationship had developed between her and one of the younger brothers. In an attempt to avoid a creditor to whom he owed money, her husband had travelled to Boston and in his absence the two lovers plotted to have him arrested, enabling them, in his absence, to elope together. The husband subsequently returned to New York before the arrest took place and at this point his wife changed her mind and decided to stay with him after all.[19] According to one of the press reports on the matter, the younger brother, Tarquinio Pavanelli, then declared that his life was not worth living without her and proceeded to commit suicide by shooting himself.[20]

Despite this devastating set-back, the Pavanellas continued to perform with the Wilson & Rankin for a further few months, presumably with a replacement as they continued to be described as a five-piece group. The minstrel troupe was by that time considered to be past its best, a review of an April concert in Indianapolis expressing the view that the Pavanellas alone "relieved the olio of utter dreariness".[21] Audience numbers at some concerts were low, probably an indication of the poor financial state of the troupe, which had played its part in the earlier tragedy. Along with the personal drama which had beset the group it was clearly time to move on. The newspaper which had ran the story cited above, telling of the money owed to the group, concluded the piece with a generous tribute:

> The Pavanellas, it will be remembered, appeared here twice during the past season, and each time gave a very finished and novel musical act – the paviors of Paris who found music in everything.[22]

The Pavanellas continued to perform in the USA independently of the Wilson & Rankin minstrel troupe for a while, but following a series of performances in New Haven Connecticut in January 1888 the surviving members of the original group made their way back to London. They were soon playing regularly at the Queen's Palace of Varieties in Poplar, one of the leading music-halls and in March were on the bill in a concert celebrating an anniversary of the venue's opening. Among those playing alongside them that night was Harry Champion, later to become one of the best-known of all music-hall entertainers. It was certainly well attended:

> Every part of the building was crowded, and many of those who had paid the highest prices for admission found that they could get no nearer to the stage than the saloon,

---

[18] The Wheeling Daily Intelligencer, Saturday 4th June 1887, p6.
[19] Aberdeen Journal, Saturday 1st January 1887, p7.
[20] The Post-Star, New York, Monday 20th December 1886, p4.
[21] Indianapolis Journal, Tuesday 12th April 1887, p8.
[22] Ibid.

and had to trust rather to their ears and their mouths than to their eyes for their evening's entertainment.[23]

After that the Pavanellas' name disappeared from listings and they seem to have called it a day. Already, while they were away in America, others had seen an opportunity to fill a gap in the market and this continued once they had disbanded. Just as previously there had been those who quickly picked up on the idea of a rock harmonicon being a winning formula, so others began to try their luck as musical paviors and advertisements from agencies began to appear seeking engagements for such artists on their books. So the Troupe Fielitz, who seem to have been based in Amsterdam, but were nevertheless referred to as "funny musical pavers of Paris", were offered to promoters as "having appeared in all European countries and America".[24] It seems to have achieved some results as the following year a similar advertisement noted that they had "just returned from a very successful tourné in the République Argentina, Uruguay and the Empire of Brazil."[25]

## The Bozza Troupe

The Bozza Troupe, formerly allied with the Pavanellis, continued to perform, offering to the public their "eccentric, musical and electric entertainment".[26] They had separated their act into three components: "The Musical Kitchen", "The Musical Knife-grinders" and "The Musical Paviors". The Musical Kitchen involved the players conjuring music from a variety of culinary items, as implied in the name, a gift to music critics who relished the chance of reviewing something out of the ordinary. Melodies were played on plates, along with "harmonies being supplied from stewpots and frying-pans, while a beer barrel at the back is played as a drum" and including "a nutmeg-grater obligato."[27]

While the exploration of the musical possibilities of kitchen utensils seems feasible enough, the musical knife-grinder act, in the view of the San Francisco newspaper article, was, like that of musical paviors, a deception. On the other hand, the electrical element of the Bozza Troupe's entertainment does seem to have been a quite remarkable innovation. Carl Bozza had developed what he called his Electodynaphone, which was being played publicly as early as 1882, at the Cirque d'Été in Paris. A visiting American journalist who witnessed it described it later in an article for the New York Times:

> Five clowns [played] on sixteen horns, hautboys, accordions, clarionets, kettle-drums, bass-drums, cymbals and pistols hung upon the sixteen pillars supporting the roof of [the] establishment, each of which instrument is connected with a wire connected in its turn with a keyboard, which is in communication with a galvanized battery in the basement of the building.[28]

The development of this particular invention seems to have become increasingly important to Carl Bozza and by 1885 he was able to operate the whole thing himself from a keyboard

---

[23] The Era, Saturday 3rd March 1888, p15.
[24] The Era, Saturday 20th August 1887, p19
[25] The Era, Saturday 28th January 1888, p22
[26] The Era, Saturday 1st November 1884, p17.
[27] The Era, Saturday 15th November 1884, p10.
[28] New York Times, Sunday 15th October 1882, p3.

on stage, with all the instruments "suspended in mid-air".[29] Meanwhile the Bozza troupe's tripartite performance, comprising paving stone, knife-grinders and kitchen items continued successfully for the remainder of the century, appearing across Britain and in Europe, earning a plaudit in *The Era* which offered high praise indeed: "The Bozza Troupe of instrumentalists extract music from almost anything."[30]

---

[29] Irish Times, Tuesday 1st January 1885, p5
[30] The Era, Saturday 10th December 1887, p17

# Chapter Twelve

# The Twentieth Century

## A chronological miscellany of musical stone

As the new century was getting under way, the era of the rock harmonicon was drawing to a close. The second generation of the Till Family Rock Band continued playing until 1918 but with much less frequency than before and the Abrahams were putting their energies into photography and and their numerous books on rock-climbing. There was to be no more lithophone activity on the scale of the Richardsons in the 1840s or the Tills in the 1880s, extensive travelling and filling concert halls now being a thing of the past for the exponents of musical stone. Nevertheless, new names were soon to discover its possibilities, some revisiting earlier approaches, others coming to it afresh, finding different paths along which to develop the idea. The novelty value of stone being put to musical use, whether on an amateur or professional level, continued to be newsworthy even if the attention span for such things rarely lasted beyond a few days or possibly weeks. In parts of the world where stone had continued to play a part in musical culture there was a decline in its use, old traditions becoming eroded as western influence increased. But in Vietnam, the rediscovery of musical stones from the ancient past, from 1949 onwards, inspired a revival of lithophone playing which continues to unfold, though there have been winners and losers along the way. That story will be the subject of Chapter 13.

### Albert Coates

One of those whose interest in musical stone came and went with little consequence but who is worthy of a mention if only for his admirable ambition, is the once well-known conductor and composer Albert Coates (Figure 12.1). In 1928 an item appeared in a number of British newspapers picking up on a comment from Coates, saying that he'd like to form a stone orchestra. This was taking lithophone thinking to a new level and had he fulfilled his dream it would have perhaps created something even more remarkable than the five-octave rock harmonicons of Joseph Richardson and those who came after him. Unfortunately it never came to that.

Born in St Petersburg, his mother being Russian, Coates had settled in England in 1919 having fled the Bolshevik revolution. For a while he was employed by the London Symphony Orchestra, regularly conducting Wagner at the Royal Opera House, but later worked abroad and eventually settled in South Africa. The newspaper stories vary in the details they chose to highlight, but it seems that Albert Coates had been in discussions about writing an opera to be called *Ashurbanipal*, based on the life of the Assyrian king, and to be premiered in Dresden. Coates told that having seen a lithophone on a trip to America, it had occurred to him that it might be fitting for a production with such a historical theme to employ stone instruments.

"This is not so mad as it sounds…In a New York museum there are ancient stones used as musical instruments, and in Keswick Museum, I am told, they have the complete scale in stones."[1]

It seems likely that the instrument Albert Coated had seen in New York was the one the museum had received from William Till and, like the ones he mentions in Keswick, not ancient at all.

A report, in Cardiff's *Western Mail*, under the headline "The vision of a famous conductor" quoted Albert Coates expanding on his idea:

"During my travels I have come across colossal musical stones, which give a most heavenly tone when struck. I should just love an orchestra of stones. Imagine Chaliapin singing a note and then, bang, wallop - some stones are struck and there is a perfect orchestral accompaniment. I think it would cause quite a sensation at Queen's Hall," he said laughingly, "and I would just love to see the violinists and other players sitting among vast rocks on the platform playing their novel instruments"[2]

*Figure 12.1. Conductor and composer Albert Coates.*

Another paper had Coates describing his idea as "ultra-modern".[3] Whether or not this was said in irony, it nicely reflects the paradox of this ancient form of music-making being rediscovered and presented once more, as it had been with each generation over the previous century, as something new, literally a novelty. Unfortunately neither Albert Coates' opera *Ashurbanipal*, nor his stone orchestra, saw the light of day, but a few years after Albert Coates' brief flirtation with the idea of using stone in his music there was something of a revival of interest back in Keswick itself, the three stone instruments by then housed in the town museum once more attracting attention.

## William Davey

The curator of Keswick Museum in the 1930s was a man called William Davey. He was a proficient musician who became adept at playing the lithophones in the museum's collection, allegedly capable of playing on them "anything from opera to jazz"[4] (Figure 12.2). In 1936

---
[1] Daily Record, Glasgow, Saturday 20th October 1928, p9.
[2] Western Mail, Cardiff, Friday 19th October 1928, p8.
[3] Yorkshire Post and Leeds Intelligencer, Friday 19th October 1928, p11.
[4] Daily Telegraph, Saturday 15th August, p16.

*Figure 12.2. William Davey, then curator of Keswick Museum playing the Richardson instrument in the 1930s. Courtesy of Keswick Museum and Art Gallery.*

he featured in a short film for Pathé in which he played firstly on Peter Crosthwaite's Music Stones (*D'ye ken John Peel*) then on the Richardson Rock, Bell and Steel Band (*Men of Harlech*). As a result of this appearance, which would have been screened widely in cinemas, offers began to come in. An unnamed London businessman with interests in theatre offered Davey what was described as "a large sum" if he would produce another such instrument which could be transported further afield. There was also interest from German and American syndicates, with one promoter promising him he would earn a fortune if he would agree to undertake an American tour.[5] Davey declined all these approaches, giving his reasons to the *Penrith Observer*:

> "In the first place, the musical stones were bequeathed to the museum by the descendants of the late Joseph Richardson. He spent a lifetime in chipping and carving the large pieces of Skiddaw slate from which the stones are made. Mr Richardson and his three sons gave three Command performances [sic] before Queen Victoria, and also visited virtually every royal palace in Europe to give request performances. It was only on these occasions that the stones left Lakeland, but they will never leave again."[6]

William Davey also received a request from the BBC to perform on the Richardson instrument for a special programme to be broadcast from Lake Windermere, but again he would have none of it due to the twenty-mile trip it would entail. Almost a century earlier Joseph Richardson, facing far greater logistical challenges, had been much less squeamish about travelling with the

---

[5] Ibid.
[6] *Penrith Observer*, Tuesday 4th August 1936, p10.

instrument almost constantly, the length and breadth of the country and beyond. Years later, in 1959, when William Davey was still curator at the Keswick Museum after more than thirty years in the job, an article about him by Peter Cragg was published in the *Cumbria Magazine*. Among the items discussed with Davey in Cragg's interview with him was Joseph Richardson's Rock, Bell and Steel Band:

> On the day of my visit Mr Davey strummed it with his fingers and produced a delightful tune. Sometimes he used mallets, but students of music who persuade him to play the instrument prefer him to use his fingers[7]

It seems that he did eventually play for a BBC broadcast, as William Davey disclosed in the interview that his largest audiences had been when playing for the Corporation.[8]

Another resident of Keswick in the 1930s, hearing of Davey's decision to decline the offers of fame and fortune that had been made to him, saw an opportunity. Norman Byers was a piano-tuner living in Applethwaite, close to Keswick and the same village in which the Richardson family had lived. For six years he had also worked as a pianist in the local cinema, during which time he had constructed his own set of musical stones, spanning up to three octaves and again using the local Skiddaw hornfels rock (Figure 12.3). He did this in the belief that it might bring him the possibility of a new career, his skills as an accompanist to silent films being less often required as the "talkies" began to dominate cinema programmes, while the advent of the gramophone and radio had reduced the demand for live music. Byers declared that he was "willing to go anywhere for a job with his musical stones".[9] An accomplished musician on a number of instruments, Byers played entirely by ear and was able to hear a tune once or twice and then "play it throughout without hesitation or error".[10] His musical inventiveness apparently went even further:

> In fact he can get music out of almost anything that will ring, and played a tune on his wife's silver forks and spoons. When working at Gretna during the war he rigged up a temporary pipe band made out of old discarded pieces of pipe. He has also experimented with glasses. He has also made a one-string harp and played a tune on it, and is making a one-string violin.[11]

As others in Keswick had done years before, Norman Byers decided to form a family rock band, teaching his wife and sixteen-year old son to play. They received a mention in a local newspaper when they presented a musical selection at an event at which, in addition, "Miss Siddle's dancing pupils gave a display",[12] but there is no evidence of it having led to great success. However, it seems that, like William Davey, Norman Byers too got to perform on his set of musical stones for the BBC and a shellac recording has survived as testament to that.[13]

---

[7] Peter Cragg writing in the Cumbria Magazine, November 1959, pp 233-4.
[8] Ibid.
[9] Penrith Observer, Tuesday 27th October 1936, p15.
[10] Ibid.
[11] Ibid.
[12] Penrith Observer, Tuesday 1st December 1936 p11
[13] Personal correspondence with John Phillips, February 2025.

# Music Stones

*Figure 12.3. Norman Byers' set of musical stones. Courtesy of Andy Aliffe.*

The era of the rock harmonicon in Cumbria had apparently passed, for the time being at least. As well as having considerable musical skills, Norman Byers was also an adept water-colourist and during the summer period he sat by Derwentwater, painting and selling his original postcards, along with wooden toys he had carved during the winter months, to passing tourists. It would seem that this was now proving to be a more rewarding vocation than playing musical stones.

It was not until just into the present century that Joseph Richardson's rock harmonicon was to be taken out of the museum for further public performances. In 2005 Jamie Barnes, then Duty Officer at Keswick Museum, initiated a concert on the bank of Coniston Water, close to John Ruskin's former home, Brantwood. It came about as a result of a collaboration with New York composer Brian Dewan, resulting in a seven movement piece with only the lower row of bars of the Richardson instrument being used, supported on a newly constructed frame and soundbox. The performance was amplified across the lake and into Coniston village, whose Ruskin Museum housed what was left of Ruskin's own lithophone. The following year further performances took place, in Leeds and Liverpool.[14]

## Helen Cumpson

In the USA, in February 1937, an item in the New York paper the *Buffalo News* began as follows:

> What is reported to be the only collection of musical stones in Buffalo, and one of the few in the United States, is owned by Miss Helen Cumpson of 100 Lancaster Avenue. Her collection consists of ten granite stones of different sizes, all scaled in the key of F.[15]

Helen Cumpson worked at the time in the Catalog Department of Buffalo Library but during her vacation, while spending time with her sister's four children in Brattleboro, Vermont she began collecting pieces of ringing granite she found there. Returning to collect more stones, they took with them a child's metallophone to check the tuning and managed to collect enough for a major scale. Cumpson began thinking of ways the stones could be used educationally, not only within her family but more broadly, having worked as a teacher and also as a musical supervisor in kindergartens. She subsequently demonstrated the granite stones in schools,

---

[14] Foot & Howell, Vol.1 p39. Essay by Jamie Barnes: *Joseph Richardson & Sons and the Famous Muscal Stones of Skiddaw.*
[15] Buffalo News, Buffalo New York, Friday 26th February 1937, p5.

showing the similarity between the sound they made and that of Alpine bells and spoke about her ideas.

> "Children find music in everything. The stones are one way of capturing their interest and having them to learn how to create melody. Stones, wood, old iron – any of them may be similarly used."[16]

The *Buffalo News* article went on to say that on a trip Pittsburgh Helen Cumpson heard of a man who had visited Yellowstone Park and collected enough ringing stones to assemble a sixteen-note scale. It sometimes seems that everybody is just a step away from meeting somebody who's had an encounter with musical stone.

## Edward Troxell

Four years after the article about Helen Cumpson appeared in the *Buffalo News* another story hit American papers, this time the subject was a geologist, Dr Edward Leffingwell Troxell, living not so far away in Hartford, Connecticut. Since 1925 Troxell had held a full-time professorship at Trinity College in Hartford, became director of the Connecticut Geological and Natural History Survey, and was for a time president of the Association of American State Geologists. He wrote extensively, publishing over a hundred academic papers and in addition to his work as a geologist his particular expertise was in the field of vertebrate palaeontology, studying the early evolution of horses. But it was stone not bone which caused him to become a headline story in 1941.

On a visit to Shenandoah Caverns in Virginia, Trexell was surprised and impressed when one of the guides struck a stalactite to demonstrate its fine ringing tone. It began him thinking that he could extend his geological interest even further by constructing a musical instrument from rock.

> "This gave me the idea that possibly other types of stone have resonance. Upon my return to Connecticut I examined the lava forms on Summit Street near the College and chipped off some long pieces of the rock and found that they produced tones when struck with a hammer."[17]

It was a few years later, on a field trip with students to show them the columnar structure of the same kind of volcanic rock, a type of basalt also known as trap rock, that he returned to the idea. He began collecting longer pieces, up to three feet long, and set about the task in hand, as recounted later in the same newspaper article:

> He brought these home and armed with a 10-cent pitch pipe, proceeded to arrange them according to pitch. Since then he has been busy searching for rocks to fill in the gaps. To date he has collected about 100 columns, out of which he has made a scale of more than three octaves ranging above and below middle C. He has not attempted to

---

[16] Ibid.
[17] Hartford Courant, Connecticut, Saturday 29th March 1941, p3.

*Figure 12.4. Newspaper photograph of Edward Troxell playing his petrophone.*

> supply the half-tones as yet. The instrument as it is now is tuned to standard pitch and is practically perfect, the professor claims.[18]

The instrument was similar in appearance to nineteenth century lithophones, the stone slabs resting on sponge rubber strips running along two planks of wood, supported by two trestles. Even if Trexell was not aware of previous examples, it would by that time have been natural to base the instrument on the construction of a xylophone, by then a well-established and familiar instrument. Once it was completed, Troxell set about thinking up a suitable name for his invention, which he, like others before him, thought was the first of its kind. The Trinity College president suggested "lithophone" but eventually the professor opted for "petrophone", derived from the Greek word *petra*, meaning rock, which he considered was "more euphonious".[19]

> Unfortunately the professor's knowledge of Greek and Latin has proved of no use in naming the individual stones. His best inspiration up to the present is tone-stones, but any other suggestion would be welcome.[20]

News about the professor's musical instrument soon spread across the Trinity College campus with students apparently queuing at his door to witness the product of his labours in order to write about it in college magazines. This in turn led to attention from local media, resulting in a number of newspaper articles (Figure 12.4) and radio interviews. For a while it changed the

---

[18] Ibid.
[19] *Springfield Daily Republican*, Massachusetts, Saturday 19th October 1941, p52
[20] Ibid.

life of this already successful professional in a way he had neither envisaged nor intended. He became inundated with letters, all of which he endeavoured to honour with a reply, meaning, he claimed, "that he had been forced to abandon practice of intricate scores and hardly found time to occasionally play 'Chopsticks'."[21] Nevertheless it was also pointed out that "he received more enjoyment from his fan-mail than from his stone-age Steinway" and that he "perused each letter carefully, in the hope of making some interesting new acquaintances."[22] The correspondence he received was not, however, limited only to enquiries about his petrophone.

> Requests for radio interviews and for material for featured articles have also poured in on the professor. In these connections he has been asked the colour of his eyes, and his hair, what his age is and whether he can read and write.[23]

Other letters, more pertinent to the subject, were sent to inform Troxell of similar instruments the writers had seen or been told about. Some clearly referred to known examples such as the Till family's rockophone, but one letter in particular told of another, apparently unheralded example, produced by the correspondent's father.

> "Back in the 1880 when my father was a boy living in the hills of New Hampshire, he heard the ring of rocks as they were released from what they called up there a 'dump cart.' Father spent about 17 years collecting musical rocks from the stone walls of New Hampshire and Maine. His method of raising and lowering the tones was the same as yours…When my brother and I were at home and in school, the three of us played what he had named a rockophone. The largest bass note was approximately 36 inches and at its widest part about 13 inches."[24]

Edward Troxell was by all accounts a mild-mannered man with a good sense of humour, and seems to have taken the building of his petrophone seriously enough to make a good job of it, while recognizing that his true and more significant work lay elsewhere. He had no pretensions about his own musical skills, though admitted to having "dabbled on a French horn at one time"[25] and did have ambitions for the instrument.

> He is on the lookout for a xylophonist of ability who can do full justice to his instrument. "We might even have a concert at the Bushnell [Hartford's concert-hall] someday", he said, with a far-away look in his twinkling eyes."[26]

Nevertheless, Troxell himself was proficient enough on his petrophone to play his interpretation of the slow movement from Dvorak's New World Symphony as his party piece, but when asked about his musical ambitions he was gently teasing.

> "I'm waiting to be asked to chime in with an orchestra" Professor Troxell wistfully stated recently and admitted that he has not even been invited to join in a college musical.[27]

---

[21] Hartford Courant, Monday 13th October 1941, p3.
[22] Ibid.
[23] Springfield Daily Republican, Saturday 19th October 1941, p52.
[24] Hartford Courant, Monday 13th October 1941, p3.
[25] Greensburg Daily News, Pennsylvania, Friday 23rd May 1941, p20.
[26] Hartford Courant, Saturday 29th March 1941, p3.
[27] Springfield Daily Republican Saturday 19th October 1941 p52

*Figure 12.5. Edward Troxell teaching at Trinity College, Hartford, Connecticut, 1950s.*

Troxell also recognized the impracticability of his petrophone.

"Even if it were possible to create a variety of tunes, it would take a boxcar to move the instrument from place to place. I'm playing it only for my own amusement and the amusement of my guests and I'm having a lot of fun with it."[28]

Once the story of Edward Troxell's petraphone had run its course it seemed to receive no further mention in print, and apart from playing the instrument for his own and his friends' enjoyment he continued to be engaged in his professional career until his retirement from Trinity College in 1954. Troxell's final interview about the petraphone appeared in the Springfield Daily Republican a mere six months after the first bout of news stories about the instrument. In it he seemed keen to set the record straight on one matter, once more with tongue firmly in cheek.

"I don't mind talking about my petrophone. In fact I feel like a mother talking about her baby. But," he added sadly, "when the accounts appeared they stated that I used a 10-cent pitch pipe to tune the stones. I didn't. I used the best pitch pipe I could buy."[29]

## The Great Stalacpipe Organ

The Luray Caverns are to be found in Virginia and contain one of the world's finest displays of stalactites and stalagmites. Discovered in 1878, the caverns became a popular tourist attraction from around the turn of the century, and later the largest of the caves, 260 feet below the surface, was used for dances, becoming known as The Ballroom. But from the late 1950s it began to draw visitors for a quite different reason. In 1954, just a few years after geologist Edward Troxell had built his lithophone, motivated by watching a guide strike a stalactite in Shenandoah Caverns, an electronics engineer and mathematician called Leland W. Sprinkle had a similar experience just a half hour's drive away in Luray Caverns, which inspired him to create a lithophone like no other.

Accounts vary as to quite how this all came about, but there seems to be agreement that it started with Sprinkle taking his son Robert to the Luray Caverns for a birthday treat. Some

---

[28] Greensburg Daily News, Friday 23rd May 1941, p20.
[29] Springfield Daily Republican, Saturday 19th October 1941, p52.

*Figure 12.6. The Great Stalacpipe Organ in the Luray Caverns, Virginia. Courtesy of Luray Caverns, VA, USA.*

newspapers at the time claimed that five-year old Robert accidentally hit his head on one of the calcite stalactites and his father, notwithstanding any concerns for his son's well-being, was impressed by the sound. Other versions, perhaps taking less poetic licence, say that it was one of the guides demonstrating the ringing sound of a stalactites which got Sprinkle's creative mind working, just as it had Troxell's. In an interview years later. Robert, by then an adult, recalled a guide demonstrating the musicality of the stalactites by performing a rendition of *Mary had a little lamb*. But whatever the specific details of the initial encounter, the net result was that Leland W. Sprinkle began to envisage the possibility of creating a wondrous instrument in this vast subterranean chamber. He spoke about his idea to the then owner of the caves, who was supportive, and the eventual result was the Great Stalacpipe Organ (Figure 12.6).

Working as a computer technician in the basement of the Pentagon during the early years of the Cold War, Leland W. Sprinkle had already shown considerable ingenuity, having patented several inventions[30] and alongside his electronic engineering work had found time to study organ at the Peabody Institute in Baltimore, to a high enough standard to be giving radio recitals.[31] Sprinkle was therefore well qualified to take on the task he had set himself and, like others before him, became bitten by the lithophone bug, to the extent that it soon began to take precedence, once he was away from his day job. By that time he had left the Pentagon and after a period spent teaching mathematics he began working for the National Park Service,

---

[30] Plus one invention possibly not patented, for an electronic spanking machine which anticipated child naughtiness before the event, described by him in a satirical letter to Washington's Evening Star newspaper, Friday 15th October 1954 p18.
[31] WCFM (Washington Cooperative FM radio station). Recital listed in Evening Star, Sunday 15th February 1954, p99.

*Figure 12.7. One of the rubber mallets used to strike each stalactite, triggered by a solenoid connected by cable to the organ console. Courtesy of Luray Caverns, VA, USA.*

where he remained until he retired. But, according to his son Robert, during that time he had a dual identity, spending his evenings at home working on parts of the organ. Weekends too were regularly spent in the caves, sometimes accompanied by his family who lent a hand when required.

The first thing Leyland Sprinkle had to do was to determine which stalactites produced a sufficiently musical tone to be considered. This process, according to one estimate, resulted in only one in a hundred of those tested being chosen, with allegedly the most beautiful formations likely to be duds.[32] Suitable candidates would then be tested for pitch, with the help of thirteen tuning-forks, with any necessary tuning being carried out using an aluminium oxide sanding wheel. With this it was also possible, through grinding, to improve the tone of the stalactite, eliminating any unwanted harmonics. A mounted rubber mallet (Figure 12.7) was attached to a neighbouring piece of rock, leaving the sounding stalactite free to resonate, and when a note was played on the organ manual an electronic signal would travel along hundreds of feet of cable to a solenoid, which in turn triggered the striking of the stalactite by the mallet.

---

[32] Information sheet from archive. Courtesy of Luray Caverns.

*Figure 12.8. Organ console, Luray Caverns. Courtesy of Luray Caverns, VA, USA.*

Because of the distance the signals had to travel to the stalactites there was a significant delay in the sound coming back to the player, an effect exacerbated by the natural acoustics of the caves. This made the organ difficult to play and particularly unsuitable for anything at fast tempo. So Sprinkle designed the organ to be played automatically as well as manually from the keyboard, devising a system similar to that used in player pianos and some other mechanically operated instruments. This he made using a metal drum covered with a thin outer layer of plastic, perforated with holes corresponding to the notes and chords in the musical arrangement. Metal brushes would then make contact, through the perforations, with power transistors, sending a signal via cabling to the solenoid, again causing the rubber mallet to strike the stalactite, but this time the order coming from a mechanism not the fingers of a human hand. Sprinkle made the musical transcriptions himself, which he then transferred to the "piano rolls".

It took Leland Sprinkle three years to build the Great Stalacpipe Organ and he did so with the help and support of a nearby organ manufacturer, Klann's, who were also able to supply the required components. The name given to the instrument was apparently suggested by the Washington Post music editor at the time, Paul Hume, disregarding the fact that it was, of course, not a pipe organ but an elaborate percussion instrument. The first performance was given on 29th July 1956, and after some refinements had been carried out the organ was officially presented to the public the following year. There was a considerable degree of press interest in the occasion which, along with the Luray Caverns own advertising campaign, ensured high attendance figures. Newspaper reports varied in the amount of information they chose to convey about the Stalacpipe Organ. One in particular, syndicated to newspapers across several states, made a creditable attempt at describing the background and workings of the instrument, though less helpful when reporting the musical result, characterising it as "the stalactite goes boom, bong or beep, according to the natural pitch."[33]

The organ soon proved to be a popular tourist attraction and was also made available for social occasions, with 140 weddings taking place to the sound of this remarkable instrument during

---

[33] Miami Herald, Florida, Sunday 5th October 1958, p106 (syndicated report0.

*Figure 12.9. Advertisement for The Great Stalacpipe Organ. Richmond Times-Dispatch Sunday 13th April 1958.*

the first year of opening. This would certainly have met with the approval of those in the community whose views on the cavern were reflected in one newspaper report:

> In the old days public dances were held in the Ballroom, and lowdown affairs they were. The construction of the organ during the last years has given way to loftier thoughts however.[34]

As part of the rebranding process, and perhaps with the intention of underlining the respectability of the new venture, The Ballroom now became known as The Cathedral. As an environment for housing such an instrument it presented considerable challenges.

The caverns are subject to almost 100% humidity with a steady temperature of around 12º C (54º F) and although the stalactites were in their natural surroundings, the other component parts

---

[34] News Journal, Wilmington, Delaware, Wednesday 1st October 1958, p15 (syndicated report).

were not and therefore needed to be protected. So the organ console itself was positioned on a heated platform, with further heaters inside, while the control room containing the power source was covered with heat lamps. The musical stalactites, however, remained relatively maintenance free and being in a relatively dry part of the caves would not, according to Leland Sprinkle, require tuning for around a thousand years.[35] Years later his son recalled one of the ways Sprinkle had dealt with the problem of amplifying the sound of the stalactites:

> "When [my father] began discovering rocks that were too far away [to be heard acoustically], he needed to figure out a way to amplify something that was constantly being dripped on…We had a hot plate and an aluminum pot at home and we took very large chunks of beeswax and melted the beeswax, then dipped these magnetic pickups in the beeswax. It didn't interfere with the magnetic field at all, but it kept the wiring from getting corroded."[36]

Thirty-seven stalactites were used for the Great Stalacpipe Organ, spread across an area of three and a half acres (approximately 1.5 hectares) and connected to the instrument with thousands of feet of cable. This explains why it is classified by the Guinness Book of Records as being the world's largest musical instrument. The organ console itself was fitted with four manuals but only one of these, with a span of three and a half octaves, was used. It came to light in recent years, when Robert Sprinkle was going through some of his father's old paperwork, that the original intention was to eventually use all four manuals of the organ, with far more stalactites being used across a much larger area. The total area of the Luray Caverns was 64 acres, so the space taken up by the organ was modest by comparison. These additional stalactites would have provided duplicate notes, but different in volume and tone, broadening the sound quality of the organ and providing a more immersive, surround-sound experience. The initial idea was that the instrument should rely on the pure sound of the stalactites reverberating within the natural acoustics of the cave, but once a decision was made to amplify the sound electronically some of the more ambitious plans were abandoned. Leland Sprinkle's mechanism for automatic playing of the organ is no longer used, having been replaced by a MIDI file player to send signals to the stalactites, though the original has been preserved to use as a backup.[37]

Leland Sprinkle was a quite singular man, remembered as somebody with a brilliant mind and a generous spirit, always ready to help those in need. A man of many achievements, it was nevertheless the Great Stalacpipe Organ which seemed to be the one he felt to be of greatest importance and of which he was most proud. Robert Harnsberger, who had been the manager of the Luray Caverns, with whom Sprinkle had first discussed the idea, remembered, like his son Robert, his dedication to the project:

> "Sprinkle worked all day and night sometimes on the organ. It was never too late to work…If it hadn't been for his perseverance, we would not have gotten the organ completed. He had a willingness so stay with it. It was the only kind in the world, and he was determined to get it in working order, and he did."[38]

---

[35] 2015 interview with Robert Sprinkle for Sonic Scoop https://sonicscoop.com/inside-great-stalacpipe-organ-worlds-largest-instrument/
[36] Ibid.
[37] Personal correspondence with Bill Huffman, Director of Marketing and PR at Luray Caverns.
[38] From *A light within the cavern*, Pentagram Sunday 13th August 2000 article about Leonard Sprinkle by Nancy Nichols Jagelka Courtesy of Luray Caverns archive.

Leland W.Sprinkle died in 1990 at the age of 82 knowing that he had not managed to fully realise his ambitions for the organ, but also that it would never have been possible. Larry Moyers, who as a teenager was employed as a guide at the Caverns and had helped Sprinkle work on the organ later worked as an engineer on the instrument. In later years he recalled Sprinkle telling him that the organ would never be finished because it had so much potential.[39] Robert Sprinkle believed his father saw the Great Stalacpipe Organ as his legacy which others could continue:

> "He thought that he could make an instrument out of an ancient *thing*—something that had existed for millions of years, that had a mellifluous potential that he could unlock. There was just the notion that there was something in there that he could liberate. To him, it wasn't a sideshow. To him it was a mission and he didn't want it to die with him. He wanted it to be maintainable, usable—he wanted other people to be able to use it."[40]

## Carl Orff and Klaus Becker-Ehmck

The German composer Carl Orff (1895-1982) is best know for his contribution to musical education and for his composition *Carmina Burana*, but is also notable for being one of the few orchestral composers in the twentieth century to specify the use of a lithophone, which he did in some of his later works. The first of these, a choral work entitled *Antigonae*, had its premiere in 1949 and took Orff's interest in the use of percussion instruments to a new level with a percussion ensemble at the centre of the proceedings, providing the main accompaniment to the singing. One of the instruments of the ensemble was a lithophone, specially designed and built in collaboration with a young mechanical engineering student, Klaus Becker-Ehmck, and which they called a steinspiel (Figure 12.10).

*Figure 12.10. Klaus Becker-Ehmck's Steinspiel Courtesy of Bernd Becker-Ehmck, Studio 49.*

*Carmina Burana* had had its first performance in 1937, the composition soon becoming popular internationally, as it remains. Yet despite this, or perhaps in part because of it, Orff's other work has not been paid the attention that might have been expected. A reason might be that his subsequent compositions lacked the immediate appeal of *Carmina Burana*, and while his music certainly had modernist

---
[39] Ibid.
[40] Interview with Robert Sprinkle. (see footnote 30)

Figure 12.11. *Carl Orff 1953. Photograph © Schott Promotion.*

credentials (Debussy and Stravinsky were significant influences) the path he chose failed to tally with the main concerns and priorities of contemporary music during his lifetime, with *Carmina Burana* causing him to be largely dismissed by the serious music critics as a populist. That he was held in low regard is indicated by the way his unique contribution was overlooked in accounts of that era: two of the most widely read books on twentieth century concert music, both published towards the end of that century, make no mention of Carl Orff at all.[41]

Another reason for Orff being sidelined may be the cloud which hung over his career arising from his decision to remain in Germany after the Nazis came to power in 1933, when many of his friends and associates chose to leave. This has been the subject of a good deal of debate over the years but while Orff did benefit from a degree of success during that period, investigations made after the war showed him not to have supported the doctrines of the regime. Carl Orff himself had Jewish ancestry and, ironically, while *Carmina Burana* was the most widely successful musical work to be produced in Germany during the Third Reich, it was also criticised by some on racial grounds as being too eclectic, influenced as it was by music from different cultures.

Carl Orff was undoubtedly an innovator, in both his composition and his education work, in the importance he placed on percussion instruments. His biographer Andreas Liess noted that "even in his earliest work his preference for percussion and for the piano as a percussion instrument was evident."[42] Three of Orff's works for the stage employ an ensemble composed entirely of percussion instruments and James Blades points out that although Orff never became a percussionist himself, his ambition at school had been to study the timpani. Blades clearly had a high regard for Orff, calling his contribution unique and the compliment feels in no way backhanded when he says of Orff's scoring for percussion that "in all cases the writing is that of a composer with the gift of producing rhythmic and tonal intensity without complexity."[43]

Carl Orff had developed his ideas on music education in the 1920s working with musician and teacher Gunild Keetman. Together they developed an approach to music learning to which

---

[41] HH Stuckenschmidt, Twentieth Century Music 1969 and Paul Griffiths, Modern Music 1978.
[42] Liess, p45
[43] Blades, p432

they gave the name "Schulwerk" which, in seeking to stimulate children's musical imagination, stressed the importance of play, making music accessible in the early stages through the use of rhythm (hence the importance of percussion) and pentatonic scales.

*Antigonae* was the first of what was to become a trilogy of works based on translations of plays from Ancient Greece, the other two each produced a decade after its predecessor, *Oedipus der Tyrann* in 1959 and *Prometheus Bound* in 1968. In all three works, which were choral stage pieces rather than operas, Orff developed the use of percussion ensembles first introduced in *Carmina Burana*, giving them an even more prominent role. In the arrangements of the three later works Orff reversed the roles of the orchestral groupings, with most of the accompaniment to the vocal and choral parts being provided by the percussion ensemble, while the melodic instruments, conventionally at the forefront of proceedings, were employed purely to add colour and reinforcement at certain points. Starting with *Antigonae*, Orff had particular ideas in mind regarding the nature of the percussion to be used, reaching beyond conventional orchestral percussion and exploring the possibility of devising new instruments for the purpose, one of which was to be a lithophone. This was when he started to draw on the knowledge of mechanical engineering student, Klaus Becker-Ehmck.

Becker-Ehmck had a strong interest in music, having had aspirations to be a singer, and already had a high regard for the work of Carl Orff. The two men soon established a good relationship, Orff deciding the nature of the sounds and tones he required from the percussion instruments he chose to use, with Becker-Ehmck rising to the challenge of finding solutions. Sometimes this involved constructing versions of existing instruments to a more exacting standard, but between them they also devised two newly-designed instruments. One was a cradle-shaped, so-called "trough xylophone", its wooden bars supported in a gentle inverted arc, rising from the centre in each direction. The other was a soprano lithophone to which they gave the name "steinspiel".

It being so early in his career, Klaus Becker-Ehmck had no workshop or studio to develop and build instruments, so instead he used his parents' garage. In the absence of power tools he turned to the family washing-machine, removed the motor and adapted it accordingly, on the promise of briefly re-instating it weekly when washday came around. This was the start of the small company he founded which became known as Studio 49 (named after the year of its inception) and which still operates today, with Klaus Becker-Ehmck's son Bernd Becker-Ehmck as CEO. Around the same time as Orff was working on *Antigonae* there was a revival of interest in Carl Orff's ideas on music education with his Schulwerk approach forming the centre of a successful radio series, presented by Gunild Keetman. Orff and Becker-Ehmck were thus able to combine their work on the instrumentation for the stage production with the production of percussion instruments suitable for use in teaching.

The instrumentation for *Antigonae* was unlike anything previously seen in a concert hall. In addition to ten of the newly designed trough xylophones (soprano, tenor and bass) and the soprano steinspiel, the large percussion ensemble comprised the following: seven or eight timpani, one small drum, one large African slit-drum, two high bells, three glockenspiel, four pairs of antique cymbals, three suspended cymbals, three pairs of crash cymbals, a small anvil, three triangles, two bass drums, six tambourines, six pairs of castanets and ten differently pitched Javanese gongs. Other instrumentalists enlisted from the ranks of a conventional

*Figure 12.12. Gathering for 25th anniversary of foundation of Studio 49, 1974. Photograph shows Gunild Keetman, Klaus Becker-Ehmck, Carl Orff and behind him his wife, Liselotte Orff. Courtesy of Bernd Becker-Ehmck, Studio 49.*

orchestra were taken on to provide the playing of six flutes, six oboes, three cors anglais, six trumpets, four harps, nine double basses and, almost unbelievably, six grand pianos with two players seated at each instrument.[44]

The soprano steinspiel, with a range of one and a quarter octaves and having its own distinct tone, would have sounded sufficiently different from the other instruments, to ensure that even standing alone its voice would be heard. As can be seen in the photograph (Figure 12.10), its notes were arranged in a completely different way from lithophones such as gamelan, balafon, xylophone or rock harmonicon with their bars lying horizontally from left to right. The steinspiel's fifteen stone discs hung suspended at different points on a tubular steel frame, itself just under a metre in height.

*Antigone* was first performed at the Saltzburg Festival in August 1949, the other two works of the trilogy having their premiere performances in Stuttgart, all three of them featuring the steinspiel within the percussion ensemble. None of the three works have been regularly performed however and as a result there was a drop in demand for the steinspiel. Studio 49 included it their catalogue from 1972 until 1996, but soon after that production ceased, though the company have retained two instruments for rental use.[45]

---

[44] According to orchestration published by Schott Music.
[45] Personal correspondence with Bernd Becker-Ehmck, Studio 49.

## Tom Wasinger

A recurring feature in these accounts of ringing rock discoveries has been the progression from surprise and delight in the initial find, to an absorbing preoccupation in collecting more pieces of rock in order to bring it to a usable state, and then a fresh surprise expressed by those who were later witness to the musical result. Two centuries after Peter Crosthwaite had collected his Music Stones on the outskirts of Keswick in the north of England in 1785, the pattern was once more repeated, this time in the USA when a syndicated story made headlines in newspapers from California in the west to Maine in the east and from Alaska in the north to Texas in the south. It was sparked by the release in 1989 of an album called *Rock Music* by a young musician from Colorado, Tom Wasinger. With the story appearing in newspapers in 1990 not 1840, the sub-editor's headlines inevitably had a new twist: "Musician Rocks Out", "Colorado musician rocks with some stones", "Real old-fashioned rock" and "The sound that is literally rock music"

Wasinger had released his first album four years earlier, *Paradox Found*, a collection of his own songs, but *Rock Music* was a quite different matter. Completely instrumental, it was produced using recorded samples of different examples of ringing rock he had been collecting. Tom Wasinger's first encounter with musical stone had been some years before when composer and sound artist Bruce Odland, then living in Denver, had recorded the sound of what he had identified as a pre-Columbian obsidian gong in Denver's Natural History Museum. Having sampled the sound of the stone gong, Odland had then used it in a studio recording he was undertaking at the time. Wasinger, who had been brought in to play guitar on the session, was impressed by the sound of the stone and began a search for his own musical stones, beginning with a visit to shop and museum in the vicinity selling unusual rocks and minerals, some of which he was able to take away and take sound samples. But he also took trips into the hills, seeking out suitable rocks himself:

*Figure 12.13. Tom Wasinger's Stone Marimba. Courtesy of Tom Wasinger.*

"Once I got on a roll it was impossible to take a hike without banging on every everything in sight. Where I live there's this whole mountain of andesite, which is very musical. But many of the pieces were too big to move, so we did some recording on location. My father has a farm in Kansas and I found some stone from a riverbank there that sounds really great. Even the flagstone sidewalks you walk on in Boulder

*Figure 12.14. Tom Wasinger's Stone Slit-drums . Courtesy of Tom Wasinger.*

sound really good, if you get the right piece - although it doesn't ring, it sounds like bamboo or wood."[46]

The area in Colorado where Tom Wasinger lived is rich in the variety of rock available, even the name of the city in which he lived, Boulder, providing a geological reference. Among the rock types he collected, according to the newspaper story, were jade, sandstone, bassanite, flagstone, andesite and agate. Once he had made sound samples of the different pieces of rock he edited them together to produce the eight tracks which make up the *Rock Music* album. Rock music in its twentieth-century usage it wasn't. Tom Wasinger had recently visited Indonesia and listened to Balinese gamelan music and the influence that had on him is evident in the pieces on the album, characterised as they are by repeated melodic motifs, sometimes overlaid with improvisation. As well as the newspaper story, Tom Wasinger and his *Rock Music* album were picked up on by National Public radio, who interviewed him for their show *All Things Considered* and by the Cable News Network.

Initially Wasinger was unable to tie in the release of the *Rock Music* album with any live performances, it being a completely studio based project. But soon afterwards, in collaboration with a musician friend Mark McCoin, who had studied Indonesian gamelan, he began to build up a collection of instruments made from different types of rock. Attracted by the distinctive sound of gamelan which employ different tunings depending on which part of Indonesia that tradition is from, they decided not to tune the stones to the western tempered scale but to create one of their own.

---

[46] The Philadelphia Inquirer, Monday 26th February 1990, p12.

*Figure 12.15. The Lost Angel Stone Ensemble. Courtesy of Tom Wasinger.*

"I had Dick at the rock museum cut thin slabs of a glassy stone called basanite on his diamond saw, which we tuned to our scale and suspended over resonators like some gamelan instruments, or like the western vibraphone. We used resonant slate to create hanging stone gongs, vertical stone marimbas, as well as the tops of slit drums with stone tongues (also known as tongue drums.) One of these was built to stand vertically so it could be played with a bass drum pedal. We discovered that Sugarloaf mountain overlooking my house was covered with scree fields of resonant andesite. We brought back slabs of this in tune with our scale which we laid flat on the floor and played with our feet with small pieces of sandstone glued with epoxy to the underside of Tai Chi shoes. We used tiny basanite scraps to make horizontal hanging chimes."[47]

With a selection of new tuned percussion instruments (Figures 12.13 an 12.14), each of them featuring the sound of stone, they were ready to perform live with what they decided to call The Lost Angel Stone Ensemble. They also acquired three stone flutes, one a copy of a jade ocarina tuned to their invented scale, the other two Chinese side-flutes which they bought on eBay. When they arrived in the post Wasinger discovered they were already tuned to the same key and scale that they had randomly come up with years before. Their first gig with this set-up was playing on a syndicated public radio show E-town. This was followed up with some touring mainly in Colorado and the Pacific Northwest.

When he was in his thirties, having been a professional musician since he was in his teens, Tom Wasinger decided to focus his attention on music production. One of his first projects was to record a collection of lullabies from different cultures around the world, resulting in the album *The World Sings Goodnight* released in 1993. He then became increasingly involved in the recording of Native American music, resulting in three Grammy awards, two for albums by Mary Youngblood, the other a compilation, as well as numerous other awards for other recordings of Native American artists. Tom Wasinger still plays occasionally with The Lost Angel Stone Ensemble, latterly with multi-instrumentalist Jesse Manno, while continuing to produce a range of music from different cultures.

---

[47] Personal correspondence with Tom Wasinger 2023.

### Lunar music

Perhaps the most remarkable story about twentieth-century lithophones may be only apocryphal but we can hope that it was true. It tells that after the 1969 moon landing President Richard Nixon was persuaded by his friend William F Ludwig (CEO of the drum manufacturer) to let him have some samples of the moon rock brought back by the astronauts. He then proceeded to make a lunar lithophone out of them. Unfortunately there is no record of where it is now, if it ever existed.[48]

---

[48] Ibid.

# Chapter Thirteen

# Vietnam

## The rediscovery of lithophones in South East Asia

1949, the year in which Klaus Becker-Ehmck designed his steinspiel for Carl Orff, also proved to be a significant one for the lithophone in Vietnam. It was then that a discovery was made in its Central Highlands which resulted in Vietnam becoming the country most strongly identified with the use of musical stone in modern times. Eleven slabs of stone were unearthed which were thought to have been some kind of ancient musical instrument and it became a big story in Vietnam and also internationally, certainly within the archaeological community. The subject of prehistoric lithophones has been outside the remit of this book, but the significance of this find is that it has led to an unparalleled revival of interest in playing the lithophone in Vietnam, albeit with a twenty-first century take on it.

It was in the February of 1949 that a group of road-builders working close to the village of Ndut Lien Krak discovered the eleven stone slabs which were buried upright in the ground. When the men returned to their village and told others what they had found, it aroused the curiosity of a Frenchman, Georges Condominas, who was living there at the time. He asked if they would show him the stones, which they proceeded to do the following day and Condominas was amazed by what he saw. The slabs, ranging in length from 65 to 110 cm, had all been chiselled to shape and it was clear that they had served some particular purpose. There were no other artefacts alongside which might have provided a clue as to the nature of the stone slabs, but according to one report Condominas accidentally struck one of the stones and it rang out, which led to him think that the set of slabs might have been some kind of musical instrument.[1]

The people of Ndut Lien Krak belong to a tribe known as the M'nông Gar, a sub-group of the M'nông, one of the fifty-four ethnic groups which make up Vietnam's population. Georges Condominas, an ethnologist working for the French government, the colonial power then ruling the country, had been living alongside the M'nông Gar, observing and documenting their daily lives along with their customs and rituals. Despite this seemingly paternalist relationship, the villagers had a high regard for Condominas, while he felt a strong attachment to them and had learned to speak their language. He himself had Vietnamese ancestry on his mother's side. Believing that the stone slabs were not only a form of musical instrument but possibly one that dated back to ancient times, Condominas asked if he could have them sent back to Paris for further examination. There was some initial reluctance from the villagers whose animistic beliefs led them to think that the stones might possess special powers, but it was decided that because nobody had so far dreamt about the stones, that meant, according to their belief, that they were not yet of special significance to the tribe. So with the villagers' consent the stones were sent to Paris and, having examined them, the view of the archaeologists and a musicologist, André Schaeffner, was that it was indeed an ancient musical instrument. The tuning of the stones was thought to correspond to early examples of Indonesian gamelan,

---

[1] New Scientist, January 1957 No.10, *The Stones of Ndut Lien Krak*.

# Vietnam

*Figure 13.1. Ancient musical stones in the Vietnamese Institute of Musicology, Hanoi. Photograph: Mike Adcock.*

which would tally with the ethnic background of some of the groups living in that area. The set of stones were not, however, returned to the Central Highlands of Vietnam and they remain in Paris, in the Musée de l'Homme, to this day.

The vast majority of the population of Vietnam, around 86%, belong to the Kinh ethnic group. The remaining 14% is made up of fifty-three other groups, who are referred to collectively as 'minority people'. Of these a small number have at some time used ringing stones in their traditional rituals and ceremonies, including the M'nông Rlăm who continue to play stone, though the tradition is disappearing. Their playing is usually in groups of three players, each playing a large stone, suspended like a chime. The Ma people were also known to have used musical stone and it's thought that another group, the Raglai, may have done so at one time. When the Ndut Lien Krak stones were discovered the local villagers were of the opinion that they had been left there by yet another, relatively large ethnic group, the Cham. The music of all these groups tends to be modal, employing few notes and based on cyclical rhythm patterns. Played on a range of instruments including metallic gongs and both wind and percussion instruments made from bamboo, it has a very different sound from the music of the Kinh people, reflecting the different geographical and social backgrounds from which they originated.

The large number of ethnic groupings in Vietnam is the result of immigration which took place over a timescale of up to a few thousand years. In the north, many people, including the Kinh, came from China and Thailand, while further south immigration was largely from regions now located in Malaysia and Indonesia. The Kinh became the dominant culture and has remained so. Since what is referred to in Vietnam as "the American war" there has been a drive to unite the country whilst at the same time publicly celebrating, some would say paying

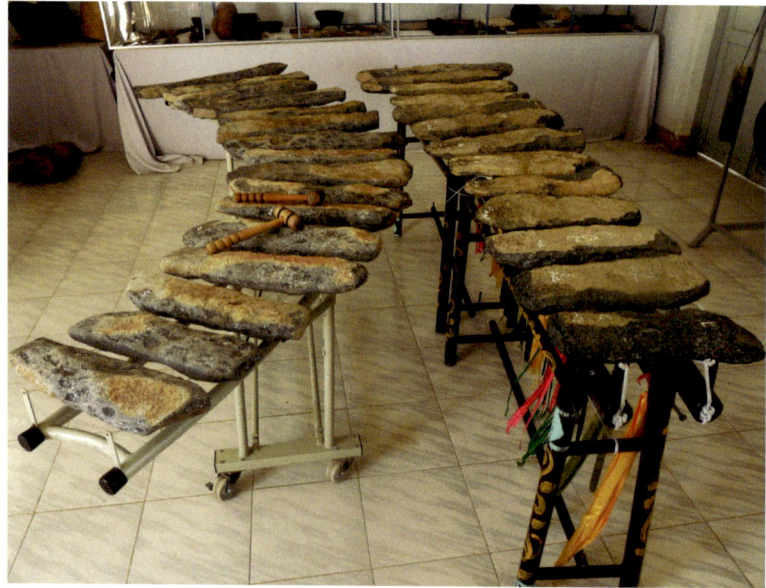

*Figure 13.2. Lithophones in Raglai Centre, Khanh Son. Photograph: Mike Adcock.*

lip-service to, the richly diverse cultural mix in its make-up. This has played a significant part in the way in which the lithophone has come back into use.

As awareness of the Ndut Lien Krak discovery spread, other such stones began to be found in Vietnam (Figure 13.1). A remarkable story emerged of a set of resonant stone slabs having been unearthed seven years earlier than those in Ndut Lien Krak. A man from the Raglai people, living in the province of Khánh Hòa, had been digging for yams with his son in 1942 when they came across some large slabs of stone. They went about removing them from the ground until they had unearthed a total of twelve, plus two smaller cucumber-shaped stones. Once they had surmised that the larger ones might have had a musical purpose, they made a plausible guess that the two smaller stones could have been used as beaters.

While there is no evidence of the Raglai having played stone in the past, there remains a belief among some of their people that they might have once done so. One thing which is certain is that in Vietnam there has been a widespread use of ringing stone for the purpose of crop protection. Methods vary: sometimes stones are suspended in a bamboo frame, the device operating like a wind chime, a kind of aural scarecrow to deter would-be foragers, whether birds or animals. Another common method is that a stone is suspended above a stream, again in a frame, and another stone, activated by the water current, strikes the hanging one. This method was used in Raglai culture and once the father and son had brought the stones they had found back to their home in Khánh Son, it was decided to use some of them in the time-honoured manner, as crop protectors. Some years later, after the war started in 1955, being aware of the stones cultural value, the family hid them away to protect them. Once the hostilities had ceased, Bo Ren, who as a boy had discovered the stones with his father around two decades earlier, retrieved them and they were handed over in the late 1970s to the Khánh

*Figure 13.3. Khánh Son stones being played in 1980 Courtesy of Khánh Hòa Museum, Nha Trang.*

Hòa museum in Nha Trang. There the stones stayed for a while before being sent to Hanoi to be included in an exhibition, after which, unbelievably, they seem to have been mislaid for many years.

In 2023 I visited the village of Khánh Son, where there is a small centre dedicated to Raglai culture, with, among other things, a number of traditional musical instruments on display. There is a strong local awareness of the musical stones discovered in 1942 and alongside other instruments are two lithophones taking up a good deal of space in a fairly small room (Figure 13.2). One of these was constructed quite recently, the other one is older and apparently includes stones which were part of the original discovery. The set which went missing for years, known as the Khánh Son stones, had finally been located shortly before my visit, not in Hanoi but in Ho Chi Minh City. It was due to be returned either to the museum in Nha Trang or possibly to the Raglai centre in Khánh Son, which was the local preference. The two sets of stones already on display in the centre can be played by visitors and are sometimes used in performance, by a new generation, inspired by discoveries from the past, having decided to initiate a revival of what are thought to have been former practices. The stones which went missing for a few years must have still been there in 1980 as the Khánh Hòa museum in Nha Trang, when I visited it, was displaying a photograph from that year of some Raglai people playing them (Figure 13.3).

It is certainly feasible that in earlier times the Raglai use of stone crop protectors led them to use the sound ritualistically and that as with the aforementioned M'nông Rlăm people it took on a musical form. This may not have survived in modern Raglai culture, but during my visit to During my visit to Khánh Son I learned something else about the crop protectors, hearing it from two separate sources. The sound of the crop protector came to have another use, though not necessarily formalised into a ritual. It has become part of the Raglai collective memory that in former times if someone was feeling in distress, they would go and sit by a stream where there was a crop-protection device operating in order to be calmed by the sound it produced. Sometimes it is not such a big step from the purely functional to the musical.

As Vietnam began to get back on its feet after the war, so arts and culture came to be seen as more important, not just as a way of bringing the country together but also through the role it was to play in one of the main developing industries, tourism. Performances embracing music, dance, puppetry and theatre were devised and tailored to cater for both the rising number of foreign visitors and an increase in leisure travel within the country, at least for those who could afford it. The stylized performances reflected the rich mix of Vietnam's artistic life, packaged into a format which was self-evidently non-western in origin and style but adapted and sanitized to avoid testing the patience of casual attendees on vacation. Whilst it's common throughout the world to find bland distillations of local music being pumped out in bars and gift shops, providing a sense of local flavour without challenging any musical predilections, in Vietnam it seems to have been done with a rigour which goes beyond that, producing, in effect, a new genre. Musician and composer Philip Blackburn spent an extended period of time in Vietnam in 1993 and has described the phenomenon:

> The Traditional Music Department at the Hanoi Conservatory has had an enormous influence on the direction of musical culture. While professing to preserve the tradition for future generations it has succeeded already in altering it beyond recognition. By adopting the Soviet techniques of appropriating melodies and arranging them into simple forms as vehicles for instrumental virtuosity the original purpose of the music (such as being a work song, for boating, harvest, or courting) has been lost. The music that used to be passed down orally within families has been notated in the Western method and is now fixed as a repertory piece with a standard interpretation. This Modernized Folk Music is now the official version of traditional music and can be heard on recordings, TV and radio and in hotel lobbies throughout the country. A friend visiting Ban Me Thuot asked the local musicians how they felt about their music being lifted. At first they replied what an honor it was for their music to be considered by city people, but in private they are quite angry at the disrespect.[2]

Thirty years on, my own experience suggested that not much has changed. While the majority of those taking place in such elaborate showcases are Kinh people, the different cultures of the minority people are represented, but there is a sense that this is included more to enrich the visual effect, through borrowed traditional styles of dress and a range of exotic looking musical instruments, than to properly reflect the broad range of Vietnamese music. Tending to mix slow poignant melodies with briskly played folk tunes, this generic folk music conforms to a safe expectation of what Vietnamese music might broadly be supposed to sound like. Added to this, there has also been a long-standing influence of western music in the Vietnamese musical establishment, going back to the French colonial period and earlier, which has also served to make this official tourist music reassuringly accessible to visiting audiences. The result is that a very selective version of Vietnamese music continues to be presented, technically impressive but somewhat anodyne.

---

[2] Philip Blackburn, *Voices of Vietnam* (Roots World).

*Figure 13.4. Dinh Linh & Truy Mai, Ho Chi Minh City. Photograph: Ingrid Lund.*

The instruments from the minority people used in these concerts include flutes, reed pipes, tuned and untuned percussion, plus extraordinary hybrids such as a bowed mouth-fiddle, the *dan k'ni*, but lithophones have increasingly made an appearance (Figure 13.4). Initially these took a rustic form but in time redesigned versions were introduced, closely resembling a xylophone and tuned to the western twelve-note scale. One sad consequence of westernisation in relation to Vietnamese music, seemingly reinforced with each generation, is the conviction of so many in the country, even among music scholars, that the western tempered scale is objectively correct and thus superior to vernacular traditions. So while there is undoubtedly a revival of interest in the lithophone in Vietnam and a pride in its historical importance, when it comes to tuning newly assembled instruments they are almost invariably made to conform to the notes of a piano.

The massive global influence of western music, to the detriment of much local music, has had many repercussions. For Vietnam, with its burgeoning tourist industry, adjusting the tuning of instruments from the different ethnic cultures to an international standard certainly makes it easier on the tourist ear. It also makes them more compatible with the popular and ubiquitous western instruments, particularly guitars and keyboards with which they are often combined, but in the process it has engendered a sadly prevalent view that when it comes to tuning, west is best. For Vietnam's minority people this has meant that their musical traditions have been affected two-fold: from the predominance of the majority Kinh music and from westernisation, leading to it remaining marginalised and increasingly so even within their own communities. This has meant that the notion of a lithophone has been radically reinterpreted in a way which makes the modern version bear little resemblance to the stone instruments traditionally used and likewise the music played on them.

*Figure 13.5. Undated lithophone in Hanoi music shop, 2008. Photograph: Mike Adcock.*

*Figure 13.6. Three ringing stones, until relatively recently played by the M'nong people in the Central Highlands of Vietnam. Photograph: Mike Adcock.*

On my first visit to Vietnam in 2008 it was not too difficult, with the help of a Hanoi travel company and a bit of good luck, to see, hear and play a good number of lithophones even though I was only in the country for two weeks. As well as a couple of sets in the Vietnamese Institute of Musicology in Hanoi, one ancient, one modern, I also stumbled upon what could well have been an ancient lithophone on display in a nearby regular music shop (Figure 13.5). There were a couple of beaters provided too, so anybody could have a go. I assumed it wasn't

*Figure 13.7. Phan Tri Dung playing his chromatic lithophone in his company office in Ho Chi Minh City, 2008. Photograph: Mike Adcock.*

*Figure 13.8. Lithophone built by Nguyen Minh Ngiệp being played in Tuy Hòa Photograph: Mike Adcock.*

for sale and that wasn't the point: in a music shop on the manically bustling streets of the capital the ancient past was coming alive and everyone was invited to get a taste.

On the same trip I visited a historian, Dieu Bang, in Buon Ma Thuot in the Central Highlands, who I had been told had a set of stones formerly used by a M'nông tribe. In 1993 he had bought three *goong lú* (musical stones) from M'nông Rlăm people living in a small village in the province of Dak Rlap. According to information he had, the three stones (Figure 13.6) were estimated by ethnologists and musicologists to have been first used more than two thousand years ago. It was from what these people had told Dieu Bang that I learned that ringing stones were used by their ancestors as crop-protectors long before they were played musically. Sadly, despite them being in one sense priceless, the *goong lú* clearly did have a monetary value and the custodians of the stones, had chosen or felt forced, to sell them.

In Ho Chi Minh City, on my 2008 trip, I visited a company director and inventor called Phan Tri Dung, who had designed Vietnam's first smart toilet and had also built his own large lithophone, inspired by the various ancient lithophones he knew to have been discovered in his country in the preceding years (Figure 13.7). His belief, not supported by any serious academic research, was that ancient Vietnamese lithophones were not merely pentatonic or heptatonic but sometimes dodecatonic, producing a twelve-note scale similar to that used in western music and therefore more sophisticated than scholars had hitherto supposed.

The construction of his instrument was carried out with the hope that it would support his case. I was treated to a demonstration of the instrument in Phan Tri Dung's office, with a performance by three specially enlisted, skilled musicians. The instrument was set up in the round with the player in the centre and the large stone slabs arranged chromatically in the manner of a piano keyboard, spanning a little over an octave. The premise upon which it was constructed might have been contentious, but its significance is that it represents another example of how the ancient musical past, certainly in Vietnam, can continue to influence the present.

On the same trip I visited two successful musical families, firstly in Hanoi, then in Ho Chi Minh City and each time I heard an impressive, professional performance on a range of Vietnamese instruments. Most of these originated from the cultures of minority people and each performance included a recital on a modern, home-made, xylophone-style lithophone. The music, mostly fast and furious, was executed with skill and panache. But these musical stones looked nothing like the ancient stones I'd seen at the Institute of Musicology, or the three hefty slabs lying on the floor in Dieu Bang's house and they didn't sound the same either. Neither did they look or sound like the tiny lithophone I bought in a tourist shop in Hanoi, with its shiny, machine cut granite slabs about a centimetre wide. I began to wonder what all these versions of musical stone actually had in common. What seemed to unite them was really just a concept, an idea of an instrument, a token representation of Vietnam's musical past.

On my trip to Vietnam in 2023, as well as seeing more fine examples of ancient lithophones behind glass in museums, I also found modern lithophones being played. In Tuy Hòa, a small coastal city in the province of Phú Yên, I came across, purely by chance, a lithophone being played to passers-by in a park (Figure 13.8). Two young women took it in turns to play a modern lithophone to a pre-recorded accompaniment. It transpired that the instrument had been built by a man called Nguyen Minh Ngiệp who ran a stall in the park selling gifts and refreshments. I met him later and the following day he drove me to see his Ancient Soul Centre, a cultural heritage centre he had opened some years earlier. Some distance away from the city, it was an extraordinary place, displaying a host of no longer used domestic artefacts Nguyen Minh Nghiep had collected as well as a range of musical instruments, including several lithophones

*Figure 13.9. Stone instruments at the Ancient Soul Centre. Photograph: Mike Adcock.*

*Figure 13.10. Playing of lithophones at the Ancient Soul Centre. Photograph: Mike Adcock.*

he had built (Figure 13.9). These were played while we were there, again with a pre-recorded backing but sometimes with or three people playing lithophones in arrangements of popular Vietnamese melodies and songs (Figure 13.10). Again, the instruments had been to tuned to the western scale, but they were functional in appearance and felt somehow closer in spirit to Vietnam's past than other modern lithophones I had seen. Nguyen Minh Ngiệp has been considering developing his ideas, recognizing the need to acknowledge the importance of the very different musical heritage of stone instruments as played by Vietnam's minority cultures. He is one of those contributing a statement about his involvement with musical stone in Chapter 16.

# Chapter Fourteen

# Experimental Music Stones
## Investigations in geological indeterminacy

In the 1950s, around seventy years after Honoré Baudre's 1881 presentation in New York had been promoted as "experimental music", this term began to find favour as a way to describe not so much a new style of music, but a fresh approach to it. A group of mainly young musicians and composers, initially in the USA, began to reject what they saw as the elitism of modern composed music, dominated as it was by the use of atonal twelve-tone serialism. Instead, they chose to pull the rug from under what they saw as a stiflingly doctrinaire approach to music by questioning the very nature of creativity itself.

The central figure in this group was the composer John Cage who began to base his musical decisions not on aesthetic choices but on the use of chance, which he preferred to refer to as indeterminacy. As the word "experimental" started to be used in relation to some of the composers around Cage, he expressed the view that it was an appropriate term to use "providing it is understood not as descriptive of an act to be later judged in terms of success and failure, but simply as of an act the outcome of which is unknown."[1] The liberating effect this had on the group helped lead to a change in assumptions previously made about the nature of a musical performance, and one of these was in the field of instrumentation. Even earlier, in the 1940s, Cage was writing pieces for prepared piano, which included instructions on how the sound of the piano should be changed by inserting bolts and small screws and other objects between the strings, with the player sometimes required to pluck the strings instead of using the keyboard. The natural development of this idea, particularly embraced by those associated with the Fluxus group, was that the objects used to perform music need not be limited by prescribed ideas of what constituted a musical instrument. A piece of stone was certainly fair game and possibly of particular interest precisely because, unlike wood or metal, it was not a material conventionally associated with music-making. While it's hard to find experimental musicians who chose to put stone at the centre of their work, it did feature from time to time.

### Cornelius Cardew

Possibly the first of the experimental composers to call for the use of stone in a work was the British composer Cornelius Cardew (Figure 14.1). Born in 1936, the educational path taken by Cardew would have made him ideally placed for a successful career in the established world of music, having been a boy chorister at Canterbury Cathedral before going on to study composition, piano and cello at the Royal Academy of Music. However, he soon began to deviate from the mainstream, taking an interest in electronic music and, after winning a scholarship to study in Cologne, worked for three years as an assistant to composer Karlheinz Stockhausen. Invaluable an experience as this must have been, once he began to learn of the ideas coming out of New York from John Cage and fellow composers who shared his interest in

---
[1] Cage, p13.

*Figure 14.1. Cornelius Cardew 1970 Photograph © John Walmsley.*

indeterminacy, Cardew decided to choose that as a more fruitful path to take. The time spent in Cologne had already shown him that traditional music notation was longer adequate for representing the wider palette of sounds being explored in contemporary music and instead began to produce graphic scores for his own compositions.

Beyond its practical shortcomings, conventional notation was also seen as an unwelcome impediment by composers wishing their music to be more inclusive and not only accessible to players who'd attained the highest grades on their instrument or a university degree in music. So as well as offering an alternative to a system of notation which had become stretched to its limits, graphic scores offered a solution, giving a diagrammatic indication of what should be played and when. Cardew and others began to use these, combining symbols, letters and numbers, as well as some notational elements taken from the old way of doing things. The problem which emerged with this, however, was that one set of difficulties was being replaced by another, it requiring everybody involved to learn a new visual vocabulary, indeed new languages which might change from a score by one composer to that of another. So what followed was at least a partial shift to the use of written instructions, telling players verbally what they were required to do. It was this combined approach which Cardew chose to take in *The Great Learning*, one of his major works and the one which included an instruction to play stone pebbles.

*The Great Learning* evolved between 1968 and 1971 and arose from a period in which Cardew had become interested in aspects of Chinese philosophy, particularly Confucianism. The text was a

# EXPERIMENTAL MUSIC STONES

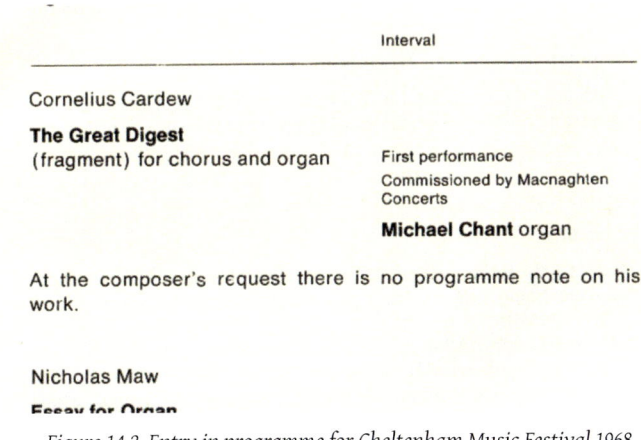

Figure 14.2. Entry in programme for Cheltenham Music Festival 1968. Courtesy of Chris Cundy.

translation by Ezra Pound of the first chapter of four books of the Confucian religion and was said to have been written by Confucius himself. This chapter, whose title was translated as *The Great Learning*, was made up of seven paragraphs, a structure which Cardew also adopted. Much of Cardew's setting of *The Great Learning* is purely vocal with some simple instrumentation and the score, while at times exacting in its requirements, left a good deal open to interpretation. In the first paragraph, which received its premiere at the Cheltenham Music Festival in 1968 under the working title of *The Great Digest*, Cardew specifies the use of stones. The festival programme indicated that the composer requested that there should be no programme notes for his work (Figure 14.2).

In his biography of Cornelius Cardew, *A Life Unfinished*, pianist John Tilbury wrote about the piece:

> The opening of Paragraph 1 is a master-stroke; no characteristic motif, no orthodox presentation of a tone-row, no *Klang Zauberei* to bewitch and impress the listener's ear; simply a minor third on the organ, p possibly, accompanied by a clatter of stones: a compelling evocation of pre-history. Within a matter of seconds of the commencement of this seven-hour work Cardew encapsulates the ethical purity of the Confucian text by the simplest of means, and the immediacy of communication is quite remarkable.[2]

The initial performance of what was to become known as Paragraph 1 of *The Great Learning*, was the result of a commission by Macnaghten Concerts and featured an assortment of musicians and a chorus, though it was not required to sing. Increasingly, Cardew was to favour inviting untrained musicians to perform his pieces, feeling that their individual traits would become absorbed within the whole, enriching the outcome "as if from a higher sphere".[3] But for the premiere of *The Great Digest*, which took place in Cheltenham's Town Hall, a professional chorus was engaged, the Louis Halsey Singers, and it was they who were charged with playing the stones:

---

[2] Tilbury, p480.
[3] Nyman, p122.

> CHORUS All members of the chorus provide themselves with two stones. The phrases at the beginning are to be played with these stones, each member interpreting the notation as he or she sees fit. Each phrase may begin at any time after the conductor's beat and may overlap into the next beat, but not further. The sounds should be produced by the two stones together, not by bringing the stones into contact with other objects.[4]

In addition, the chorus spoke the text and was at times required to play whistles while an organ part was played, at this first performance by Michael Chant. The Cheltenham concert was recorded and later broadcast by the BBC and, as can clearly be heard in this recording, the reception from the audience for the Cardew piece was, to say the least, mixed. The sound of boisterous boos and slow handclapping augment the spoken text and its accompaniment of stones being clacked and whistles blown, rather sadly ironic in the circumstances, given the text's advocacy of a sense of harmonious well-being, both individual and social:

> The Great Learning takes root in clarifying the way wherein the intelligence increases through the process of looking straight into one's heart and acting on the results; it is rooted in watching with affection the way people grow; it is rooted in coming to rest. Being at ease in perfect equity.[5]

The performance of *The Great Digest* received mixed reviews in the press. In the *Times* the following day, published under the headline "Ill-mannered display greets novelty", music critic William Mann was far from dismissive, but was troubled by the reception it received:

> Tonight there was an ugly element of hooliganism in the Town Hall, and the last five minutes or so of Cornelius Cardew's *The Great Digest* were rendered almost inaudible by foot-stamping and slow hand-claps. At the end there were bravos as well as boos for Mr. Cardew....Hypnosis is surely the intention, [the] last section, which I found totally compelling until the audience participation became noisy, should be listened to in private or with a few friends, not in a public place where the effect can be, and was, ruined by a bunch of unimaginative yobs."[6]

E.M.Webster, writing in the magazine *Musical Opinion,* was less generous, being of the view that *The Great Digest* should have been named *The Great Leg-Pull*, though his credibility as a witness was somewhat undermined by getting Cornelius Cardew's name wrong.[7]

When the BBC recording of the concert was later broadcast, Cardew gave a spoken introduction in which he was not critical of the dissenters, who he regarded as perfectly exemplifying the message of "looking straight into one's heart and acting on the results..."

> "....Well this is what the audience seem to do in this performance. I find it encouraging. They don't politely wait until the ordeal is over and then discuss it over a mug of beer. And the other faction, those who wanted just to listen to the music peacefully, they got up too and called loudly for quiet. Altogether there was an exhilarating lack of

---
[4] *The Great Learning Paragraph 1* Cornelius Cardew, Experimental Music Catalogue 1971.
[5] Ibid.
[6] The Times, Wednesday 10th July 1968. From Victor Schonfield's archive of press-cuttings, courtesy of University of Huddersfield Library.
[7] He refers to him as Nicholas Cardew. Musical Opinion, September 1968. Ibid.

politeness, and I mean a lack of that bad kind of politeness which consists of sparing people's feelings as opposed to engaging their feelings"[8]

Responses to the broadcast, which has been transmitted subsequently, have varied among other composers with a background in experimental music. Gavin Bryars described the performance as " a total disaster", though his sardonic criticism was not so much of the audience behaviour as that of the hired chorus:

> "The chorus behaved like hooligans – they didn't have a clue on how to click stones together, which seems astonishing for a chorus..."[9]

Michael Parsons, who, along with Cardew and Howard Skempton was one of the founder members of the Scratch Orchestra, which was created to perform *The Great Learning* following the 1968 prototype, takes a different view. His memory of hearing the broadcast recording of the Cheltenham concert, was of being "much impressed by the stone tapping, which sounded fresh and surprising in the context of a formal concert."[10]

John Tilbury recalls what he describes as a "possibly apocryphal anecdote" from the concert which he thinks was recounted to him by the composer Tim Souster:

> After the Cheltenham performance an elderly gentleman who looked like a retired colonel pushed through the crowd in the artists' room to confront the composer. He grabbed Cardew's hand and said, "Thank you Mr Cardew, what a relief to hear your music after all this horrible modern stuff." It is the unpredictability of Cardew's music which so often produces unpredictable responses. [11]

When *The Great Digest* was performed for a second time, in October 1968 at London's Wigmore Hall, the piece was better received by the audience, though Ronald Crichton, writing in the *Financial Times*, was perhaps inadvertently damming with faint praise in stating that "To me, after a long and busy day, it was undemanding and refreshing."

Cornelius Cardew's decision to use stones in *Paragraph 1* seems to have been at least in part because of their lack of sophistication, the most basic of materials being put in combination with the primary source of human sound, the voice, plus blown whistles and an organ. Stone and air. But there is also a link with Confucianism. In ancient Chinese philosophy, long before the time of Confucius, there was seen to be a harmonic relationship between different aspects of the universe, whether that be points of the compass, the seasons, weather or physical matter; essentially a connection between the spiritual and the physical. Social harmony too depended on this balance being maintained and music was seen to be of great value in being able to express that interrelationship. The material from which a musical instrument was made was itself of importance and stone was placed at the highest level in the order of things, in harmony with heaven itself. This is why Chinese ceremonial chimes were made from stone, initially usually limestone or marble, but eventually from the finest stone, jade. For Confucius,

---

[8] BBC Archive.
[9] From interval feature in BBC Radio 3 broadcast from Huddersfield Contemporary Music Festival November 2006.
[10] Personal correspondence with Michael Parsons, October 2024.
[11] Tilbury, p515, footnote 71.

music of the highest quality was especially important, embodying as it did the value of virtue and there is documentation, in the writing of one of his pupils, of him playing a stone chime, the *qing*:

> "The master was playing one day on a musical stone in Wei, when a man carrying a straw basket passed the door of the house where Confucius was and said 'This heart is full, that so beats the musical stone'"[12]

It seems highly likely that Cardew, in using a text from Confucius, would have been aware of the significance of using stone in this context. But there is another, unconnected way in which Cornelius Cardew may have given consideration to the sound of stone earlier in his life and that dates back to the time his parents lived in west Africa. His father, Michael Cardew, was a successful and respected potter, having set up what was to become Winchcombe Pottery in Gloucestershire and in 1951 he took up a government post in Nigeria to build and develop a pottery training centre in the country. During the years he and his wife Mariel were there they became close friends with another British couple, Bernard and Catherine Fagg. Bernard Fagg was also working in Nigeria, employed by the British Colonial Service. A qualified archaeologist, he came to hear about some rock gongs within a few hours travelling distance from where they were living which captured his interest and he began a study of them.

Rock gongs are large outcrops of stone which ring out when struck, in some cases very loudly. Bernard Fagg discovered that they had been traditionally used ceremonially and in some places this tradition continued. Fagg sought out more rock gongs, engaging with local people to learn about them and wrote a paper on the subject for an archaeology journal.[13] This was to trigger a wider interest in rock gongs for a while with further papers being written by other archaeologists as well as more by Fagg himself. It seems certain that Michael Cardew would have known of Bernard Fagg's interest and, given his son's involvement in music, probably told Cornelius about the rock gongs and Fagg's developing interest in musical stones in general. During that period, when Cornelius Cardew was studying back in England, he may have visited his parents in Nigeria and possibly seen rock gongs at first hand but there is no known evidence for that.[14]

*The Great Learning* soon began to expand to include further paragraphs and in 1969, in order to perform the work more widely, Cornelius Cardew, along with Michael Parsons and Howard Skempton, formed the Scratch Orchestra. It was made up of musicians and composers from different backgrounds, both trained and untrained, and over the next few years they toured around a variety of venues performing selected paragraphs from *The Great Learning*, which once completed would be too long to perform in its entirety in normal circumstances. The Orchestra's repertoire was to feature other pieces using sounds from unconventional sources, including one which called upon the players to "tune a river by moving the stones in it"[15] As suitable and willing venues were sought out, British art schools often proved to be receptive

---

[12] Sachs, p168.
[13] Man 23, 1956.
[14] From conversations with Angela Rackham, daughter of Bernard Fagg. Following the family's return to England Fagg was appointed as Director of the Pitt Rivers Museum in Oxford. His interest in musical stone continued and following his retirement he began writing a book on the subject. After his death in 1987 this was completed by his wife M.Catherine Fagg and published in 1997 as *Rock Music* by the Pitt Rivers Museum.
[15] Personal correspondence with Michael Chant, December 2024.

*Figure 14.3. The Scratch Orchestra. Photograph by Raha Tavallali. Courtesy of Cornelius Cardew Concert Trust.*

hosts, with both students and staff prepared to participate in performances. These institutions were always more receptive to the ideas of John Cage and his followers than university music departments and continued to provide an important platform for experimental composers and musicians to present their work.

The Scratch Orchestra was not to continue for long. Cornelius Cardew was soon to completely renounce many of his musical and spiritual ideas on political grounds, becoming instrumental in forming the Revolutionary Communist Party of England (Marxist-Leninist). Even the Scratch Orchestra, founded on democratic, inclusive principles was, in Cardew's view, still too elitist and bourgeois in its taste and values and the orchestra itself became torn apart through ideological differences. Cardew attempted to change the text of *The Great Learning*, reinterpreting the words of Confucius (who he now rejected as a reactionary comparable to Mussolini) to reflect a Maoist agenda and dismissing his original version of *The Great Learning* as "a piece of inflated rubbish".[16] Whether Cornelius Cardew would have later re-evaluated his position yet again with regard to *The Great Learning* we will never know as he was tragically killed in a hit-and-run accident in 1981 at the age of forty-five.

Once the Scratch Orchestra had disbanded there were no further performances at that time, though in 1982, following Cardew's death, a memorial performance of Paragraph 1 was given at the Queen Elizabeth Hall in London. The piece continues to be performed from time to time, under the direction of both Howard Skempton, Michael Parsons and others. Skempton

---

[16] Cardew, p101.

retains an affection for the piece, having conducted it in the 1980s.[17] Parsons has subsequently incorporated the playing of stones in a choral piece called *Nevrazumitelny*, (2013) where they were used in a prologue to the main body of the work. The use of stones in the composition, a setting of a poem by Wendy Mulford, reflects aspects of the poem which dealt with rocks and mining, but was also intended as a homage to Cornelius Cardew and his score for *Paragraph 1*.[18]

## Christian Wolff

Working alongside John Cage in New York in the 1950s were three other composers, Morton Feldman, Earle Brown and Christian Wolff (Figure 14.4). Born in 1934, Wolff was the youngest and the only one not to have had a formal music education. Sharing the others' interest in indeterminacy, his early compositions involved musical problem solving with most of the pieces limited to only three or four different notes. Through a combination of notation, graphic symbols, numbers and letters, the scores indicated which notes were to be played within a given time frame (sometimes impossibly short) with the unpredictable outcome being the result of the player's best endeavour to play what was given. In time Wolff, like Cornelius Cardew, started to question the validity of writing pieces which could only be played by those who, if not necessarily musically accomplished, were at least in the know. This led to him also using written instructions in his compositions, which sometimes allowing a degree of improvisation. In 1968 Christian Wolff began to write a series of pieces which became known collectively as *Prose Collection* and relied on purely verbal notation which, said Wolff, "leaves a lot of room for the player to use his discretion....I'm trying to see how little I can indicate and yet come up with a piece that still has a life of its own,".[19]

Two early companion pieces in *Prose Collection* were *Stones* and *Sticks*. In this case, the fact that the titles of both refer purely to the material to be played indicates that Wolff distinguishes between objects chosen to be used for a musical purpose and a bespoke musical instrument, a point he makes in the contribution he has made to this book (Chapter 16). Both pieces certainly feel like an invitation to improvise but as Michael Nyman states, they should not be approached thoughtlessly:

*Figure 14.4. Christian Wolff.*

Any performance naturally takes on the qualities unique to these materials (in a way a performance is 'about' the properties of stones and sticks) yet the clear but subtle language with which Wolff expresses his proposals gives a crucially important guide to the spirit of the interpretation.[20]

---

[17] Personal correspondence with Howard Skempton, November 2024.
[18] Conversation with Michael Parsons, October 2024.
[19] Nyman, p113.
[20] Ibid, p114.

*Stones* by Christian Wolff:

> Make sounds with stones, draw sounds out of stones, discreetly; using a number of sizes and kinds (and colours); for the most part discreetly; sometimes in rapid sequences. For the most part striking stones with stones, but also stones on other surfaces (inside the open head of a drum, for instance) or other than struck (bowed, for instance or amplified). Do not break anything.[21]

## Pauline Oliveros

In hindsight, the special case made for experimental music being something distinct from other twentieth-century avant-garde music might seem, especially to an outsider, as pernickety and confusing, given a general tendency for it all to be lumped together as "difficult music". There are undoubtedly overlaps and internal contradictions but these musical labels can nevertheless help illuminate some some significant differences in intent, particularly in identifying a distinction between two different values, one placed on process, the other on producing a finished result, usually with a predetermined outcome. In the work of composer and musician Pauline Oliveros (Figure 14.4), the emphasis is very much on the former, bound up with the value she placed on listening. The reason for her appearance here is because she wrote two pieces for stones.

Born in 1932, so of the same generation as Cornelius Cardew and Christian Wolff, Pauline Oliveros grew up in Houston Texas and began playing what was to remain her main instrument of choice, the accordion, at the age of nine. But her choice of listening was, from the start, idiosyncratic. Her grandfather had made a crystal set radio and she found the sounds made by turning its tuning dial of greater interest than what was being broadcast, whether that was music or speech. Later she was to find the strange noises emanating from her father's short-wave radio even more compelling. The sounds surrounding her home also left an impression.

*Figure 14.5. Pauline Oliveros. Picture taken at Deep Listening retreat in Norway, June 2015. Photograph © Will Dibrell.*

"I was hearing all the insects and birds and animals that were sounding in the Houston, Texas environment. It was very dense – it was almost like a rainforest…and I liked the cicadas."[22]

When she got her first tape recorder as a twenty-first birthday present, Oliveros noticed, after recording some environmental sounds and then playing it back, that there were things on there

---

[21] Nyman, p114. Included with the agreement of the composer.
[22] Interview on Red Bull Music Theatre 2016: https://www.youtube.com/watch?v=xMo5j3ebJw0]

she hadn't noticed at the time of recording, something she was to remember as a light bulb moment in her musical development. From then on she made listening a priority in her life, highlighting the important distinction between the passive experience of hearing and the active one of listening. Her personal and often repeated dictum became "my practice is to listen to everything all the time and remind myself when I am not listening."[23]

Pauline Oliveros studied music at the San Francisco Academy, where she was in the same class as Terry Riley and Morton Subotnick. She soon began experimenting with the electronic processing of sounds, investigating the use of tape delays and oscillators and co-founded the San Francisco Tape Center. Yet despite being a pioneer in this field it was always the experiential aspect of music, taking listening as the starting point which was of greatest importance to her. Always conscious of environmental sounds (in particular the sound of frogs in the pond outside her window at the Tape Center), Oliveros was incorporating those from the start into her hybrid, electroacoustic pieces. At different times these included found objects, voice, her accordion and other acoustic instruments and allowed for a strong element of improvisation.

*Rock Piece*, the first of the two pieces Pauline Oliveros composed for stone, dates from 1979 and takes the form of a written instruction. Each participant of the group has a pair of resonant rocks and the piece begins with a period of listening out for any environmental pulses before establishing an independent steady pulse striking the two stones together. The object is to maintain that independence, so that if a player finds themselves in time with another they must stop, listen and find another independent pulse. The piece also calls on the players to move around the space "listening to each other and for echoes".[24]

*Rock Piece*, which in two paragraphs refers three times to the requirement to listen, anticipates what was to become the phrase Pauline Oliveros became most associated with, "deep listening". This was to originate from a recording she made, along with Stuart Dempster and Panaiotis, in an underground cistern in Port Townsend, Washington State in October 1988. The primary reason for recording there was the extraordinary acoustic, offering an unusually smooth natural acoustic and a delay of around 45 seconds. The recording was released as a CD the following year under the title *Deep* Listening, which was simultaneously profound, in terms of its musical demands, and literal, given its subterranean location. Following on from that Pauline Oliveros set up her Deep Listening Foundation, which has continued to this day, offering workshops, courses, training, retreats and various projects.

The second Oliveros stone piece was *Pebble Music* from 1992. This was rather more specific than *Rock Piece*, both in the type of pebbles to be used (small, smooth, flat-shaped and rounded, about 3/4 to 1 inch in size) and in its structural detail. Firstly, different playing techniques are established, based on five main suggestions (rubbing pebbles together, clicking them together, shaking with the hands or within a container, dropping onto a surface from varying distances and rolling or spinning across varying surfaces). The score itself then comprises a grid of sixteen squares, each representing approximately a minute in time and four sounds to be heard together. These are taken from the selection of specified pebble-playing techniques, the use of voice and different musical instruments, taken from what is available at the time of playing. In *Pebble Music* voices and instruments are instructed to follow the rhythms from

---
[23] Various, including Ted Talk, 2016: https://www.youtube.com/watch?v=_QHfOuRrJB8
[24] From *Rock Piece* by Pauline Oliveros 1979: https://sensatejournal.com/pauline-oliveros-rock-piece/

the pebbles and while the nature of playing is not indicated, there is an intention that the aim should be to keep together, so possibly with a musical pulse, rather than be independent of one another.[25]

## Frog Peak Music

The Pauline Oliveros piece *Pebble Music* features in the *Frog Peak Rock Music Book*, which also includes Christian Wolff's *Stones* instruction piece. This compendium of pieces was published in 1995 by Frog Peak Music, a USA-based composers' collective devoted to the production and publication of experimental music. True to its title (in the literal meaning of rock) it contains thirty-three scores for pieces incorporating the sound of stone, contributed by seventeen composers, including two joint compositions. The introduction to the book, written by Daniel Goode, himself one of the contributors, is given the title "Rock Music Redefined" and provides an overview of what to expect, along with some background.

> Twentieth century rock music may be both a rebellion against and an evolution of modernist ideas....Stones as instruments mock industrial civilization and the precisionism of orchestral and electronic instruments. They are often complex noise bands or mixtures of pitches even within one stone. And too, these composers are more respectful of their found sounds and found intonation than any historical tuning system. Henry Cowell might welcome inclusion in this collection. Probably, Arnold Schoenberg would not.[26]

The pieces included in the book, none of which use traditional music notation, are varied but share a similar general approach. Most are intended for group performances, requiring a commitment to the realisation of the pieces but not necessarily a high level of musical ability. Some have a feeling of ritual about them, in others the instructions read more like the rules of a game, with one composition by Jon Gibson actually given the title *Rock Game*. Divided into eight sections, his piece begins simply enough with everyone invited to click four quavers with their own pair of rocks, repeating that until somebody gives a cue to move on to the second section, which has a quaver rest between each played quaver, again repeated until a further sign is given. As the piece progresses the gaps increase in length until the final section,

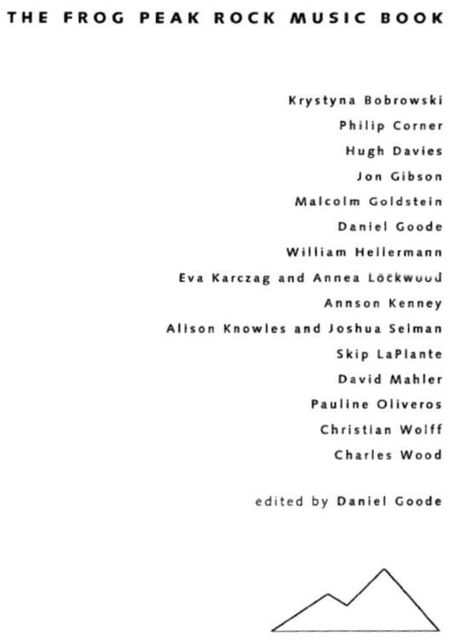
THE FROG PEAK ROCK MUSIC BOOK

Krystyna Bobrowski
Philip Corner
Hugh Davies
Jon Gibson
Malcolm Goldstein
Daniel Goode
William Hellermann
Eva Karczag and Annea Lockwood
Annson Kenney
Alison Knowles and Joshua Selman
Skip LaPlante
David Mahler
Pauline Oliveros
Christian Wolff
Charles Wood

edited by Daniel Goode

*Figure 14.6. Title page of Frog Peak Rock Music Book. Courtesy of Frog Peak Music.*

[25] Goode, p75.
[26] The Frog Peak Rock Music Book, pp4-5.

## Rock Game

For two or more performers sitting or standing — perhaps in a circle.

Each performer has a pair of rocks to click together.

Performers as well as members of the audience are blindfolded (or otherwise have eyes closed).

The piece begins at figure 1 with performers playing the pulse tutti in unison. The tempo is 1/8th note = ca. 240 or rather brisk.

Each figure can be repeated any number of times until a verbal cue to go to the next figure is given by an assigned person saying the number of the upcoming figure or possibly something else.

The performers maintain the pulse on their own, using no external cue (e.g. counting out loud) other than listening and trying to play together with the others.

With each new figure, the clicks are twice as far apart so that staying together will become increasingly difficult, if not impossible to do, and the audience perception of the descrepancies along with a sense of space and anticipation that should occur in the later figures is basically what the piece is about. Consequently, even if the clicks get way "off", the performers should continue playing and trying to stay together.

After initially using rocks, other sound-making devices can be explored in subsequent playings. Also, other numerical sequences can be explored.

*Figure 14.7. Instructions for Jon Gibson's Rock Game Courtesy of Frog Peak Music.*

24  The Frog Peak Rock Music Book

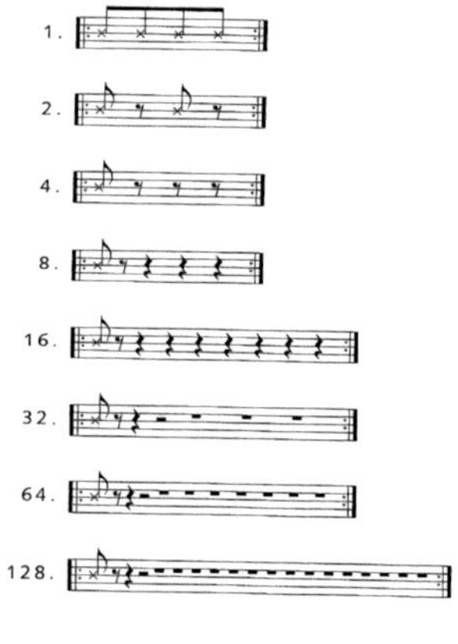

*Figure 14.8. Score for Rock Game. Courtesy of Frog Peak Music.*

25  Jon Gibson

which has a gaping 127 quaver rest between each note. The object is for players to try to keep together, counting internally without any external guide, a difficult if not impossible task (Figures 14.7 and 14.8).

> The audience perception of the discrepancies along with a sense of space and anticipation that should occur in the later figures is basically what the piece is about.[27]

Other pieces in the book are site specific. One, *Music for Snowlake #2* by Skip La Plante, is for a location in a national wilderness site in Oregon and instructions are given on how to get there. The piece requires pieces of broken slate to be thrown down at a slate wall from which they will bounce into the lake.

> Melodies are produced as thrown stones bounce down the hill. Most rocks struck by a thrown stone produce a clear pitch. Rocks striking the water produce various sounds depending on the size of the stone, the depth of the water where the stone lands, the spin of the stone as it enters the water and whether the stone hits the water flat or on the edge….Each thrown rock results in a unique melody.[28]

Alison Knowles and Joshua Selman's joint piece *A Variety of Rocks* begins with a written question "What is immutable in rocks", then specifies how small rocks should be combined with other objects, which becomes the basis for the score:

> Select a group of objects. Suggestions: Sheet of blank, colored tissue paper and rocks. Pebbles in capped glass jar. Two rocks one for each hand. Rock and sandpaper. Stemware glass of colored water and handful of pebbles. A nail, a chopstick and a rock. A text about rocks. One rock and something of your choice. Trace these objects. Mark the tracings for time. With the above collection of objects play the tracing as a score.

Directions for Performance

> A group gathers and selects from the collection of objects. The duration of the piece is decided by the group. The performance starts on a signal from the leader. Space is proportional to time.[29]

The pieces brought together in *The Frog Peak Rock Music Book*, hard to define though they are, sit comfortably beneath the generous umbrella category of experimental music, while at the same time sharing aspects of land art, conceptual art and performance art. With regard to their use of stone, what sets the pieces apart from most of the examples written about in my book is that they make use of stone in its natural form. The stone used in the compositions presented in *The Frog Peak Rock Music Book* has not been worked, not tuned, not transformed in the way that lithophones generally have been. Whereas the nineteenth century rock harmonicon players were taking on the music establishment at its own game, playing operatic arias and popular favourites on the most unlikely of instruments, the *Frog Peak Rock Music Book* compositions take stone as stone, sometimes in its own back yard, music played on its home ground, offering a variety of different, original ways of exploring what anybody can do with it.

---

[27] Ibid, p24.
[28] Ibid, p68.
[29] Ibid, p58.

# Chapter Fifteen

# The gift of sound and vision
## Sculptural music and musical sculpture

It may come as no surprise to learn that some of those who have chosen to explore the musical potential of stone came to it from a background in stone-carving or stone sculpture. For anyone spending their days working with stone, whether extracting it from a quarry, employed as a stonemason or making sculpture, the sound of stone will be an intrinsic part of the process, a factor in gaining an understanding of the material and how to work it. The sound made when a piece of rock is struck will reveal something about its quality and will be a consideration when deciding to choose one section of rock over another. In Welsh slate quarries, for example, if the slate rang sweetly it was a sign of good quality and that it would be suitable for roof tiles.[1] Conversely, when quarrying for aggregate, stone which rings may be rejected as being unsuitable, its resonance signifying it as being too hard.

The sound produced during the process of stone-carving changes according to the way the chisel is applied to the stone, and this informs the technique: Lida Kindersley, renowned stone-

Figure 15.1. Lida Kindersley. Courtesy of Cardozo Kindersley Workshop.

---

[1] Conversation with retired quarry worker at Llanberis Slate Museum, 2011.

carver and letter cutter (Figure 15.1), says that when she hears apprentices working in the next room she can tell by the tone whether they are holding the chisel correctly, perhaps holding it too tightly, which will affect the flow of the cut.[2] From gaining a heightened awareness of the quality of tone of certain types of rock it can be but a small step further to thinking about the possibilities of using it musically, and there are other ways too in which connections can be made between stone-carving and music.

In addition to tone, there are three other properties of a sound which help us define it: pitch, volume and duration, and these four properties are the fundamental building blocks of music. So far, tone and pitch have been the key factors referred to in relation to building a lithophone: whether the stone has an attractive sound and whether it emits a definable note, the usual preference being that the note can be changed by tuning. Volume is also an important consideration and this will vary depending on the type of stone and its internal structure. To enable dynamic expression in the playing there will need to be an audible difference in volume depending on the force at which the stone is struck and this too will vary from one piece of stone to another. The volume and tone of a lithophone, like other tuned percussion instruments, will also depends on the choice of beaters, whether the tips are soft or hard and what material they are made from.

The fourth property of a sound, duration, brings us to another another aspect of stone-carving. Duration is considered by some to be the most important characteristic of sound in relation to music.[3] Whatever the tonal or melodic nature of a piece of music, however quiet or loud it is, music is essentially a time-based art. The entirety of a painting can be seen at a glance, but to hear the whole of a piece of music we need to stay until the end. The duration of a sound and the division of consecutive sounds, equally or unequally, creates rhythm and rhythm is generally recognized as playing a crucial role in the technique of stone-carving. Rhythm in music is something which relates directly to a physical movement in time as an instrument is being played (though not necessarily in electronic or computer-based music) and that is also central to the technique of stone-carving. By entering into a rhythmic flow in the use of the stone-carving tool the practitioner is able to fully engage in the process and this has more in common with a musical performance than might be thought.

When Joseph Richardson was working as a stonemason in the 1830s, the repetitive sound of stone being fashioned was part of his daily life, long before he'd decided to build a rock harmonicon. But as a man who had entertained musical ideas since he was a child it's hard to think that he made no musical connection as he heard the rhythmic sound of his hammer and chisel all day in the stone-yard. As well as being been attuned to listening to the changing tonal properties of stone as he worked, the rhythmic pace of striking the stone would also be part of his skill set. Indeed, the experience he would have gained, of the interaction between hand and stone might well have proved to be of benefit, as he changed career, possibly allowing him to translate his skills as a stonemason to becoming a respected musician on an unlikely percussion instrument. While there is no record of Richardson himself making an association between the two activities, in later years the connections between stone-carving and music-making were being openly discussed.

---

[2] Conversation with Lida Kindersley, October 2024.
[3] John Cage, in describing music as being fundamentally concerned with the interplay between sound and silence, pointed out that duration was the only thing the two had in common. Cage p13.

The twentieth century brought with it an increased interest in interdisciplinary approaches in the arts. This happened partly because it was a time when some of the basic assumptions underlying different art forms were being challenged (the requirement of painting and sculpture to represent objects from the physical world, the need for music to conform to western tonality, etc.) So while the technical issues facing stone sculptors in the twentieth century were not so very different from those faced by the sculptors of ancient Greece or Rome, or Donatello and Michelangelo in Renaissance Italy, questions were being asked, certainly within the avant garde, about the nature of making art. In testing these ideas, comparisons were being made by looking to other cultures and to other ways of being creative. Arnold Schoenberg, a figurative painter as well being a composer, and Wassily Kandinsky, a painter who also played the violin, found mutual inspiration as they both pushed the boundaries in their chosen vocations. Dadaists and surrealists began to blur the boundaries between visual art, poetry, performance and music, switching from one to another within a single live event. Later, the improvisatory paintings of American abstract expressionist painters were inspired by the bebop jazz of the time, Jackson Pollock having himself filmed in the process of creating his art: painting as performance. It's perhaps surprising then, to find no real evidence of early to mid twentieth-century stone sculptors choosing to produce music with their chisels, but things were certainly beginning to go that way.

## Constantin Brancusi

*Figure 15.2. Constantin Brancusi.*

In an essay about the seminal Romanian sculptor Constantin Brancusi (Figure 15.2), the American critic Dore Ashton found significance in his love of music, writing at some length about it. Noting his friendship with Erik Satie, she finds in Brancusi's work parallels with the way the composer structured his musical pieces, referring to "the musical properties or the rhythms implicit in his life's work."[4] Whilst this is partly a matter of finding visual equivalents of a musical idea, Ashton also refers to the physical activity of carving, whether it be in wood, plaster or stone:

I have no doubt that Brancusi hearkened to an inner rhythm as he worked, as fundamental as the fact that each person walks in an idiosyncratic rhythm, and that folk dances, which Brancusi was said to have relished performing, spring from organic responses as simple as the beat of the heart. This difficult issue of rhythm has to do with Brancusi's work techniques

---

[4] Ashton, p34.

and with his idealism. When he was working on his wood version of the *Endless Column*, the box frame saw was thrust back and forth in a definite rhythm; otherwise, it would not have functioned well for him.[5]

Ashton cites a visit British sculptor Barbara Hepworth made to Brancusi's studio in Paris in 1933[6], after which she wrote: "I think Brancusi's understanding of these timeless elements in sculpture is very close to Stravinsky's understanding of rhythm."[7] In using this quote, Ashton thinks Hepworth was particularly referring to the music of *The Right of Spring*, and that she had probably attended its 1913 premiere.[8]

## Barbara Hepworth

Barbara Hepworth (Figure 15.3) had always had a passionate interest in music and dancing and the rhythm she found in Brancusi's work was something she brought to her own practice as a sculptor. Writing of the time when she first saw his sculptures, she later noted how this was already finding its way into her own work:

Carving became increasingly rhythmic, and I was aware of the special pleasure that sculptors can have through carving, that of a complete unity of physical and mental rhythm.[9]

Hepworth continued to refer to this rhythmic aspect of her own work, not metaphorically, but in relation to the actual process of carving:

"I have always loved the joy of carving and the rhythm of movement that grows in the sculpture itself just as I like dancing or skating. I like the relaxation of sound and movement.

*Figure 15.3. Barbara Hepworth carving Head, 1930. Photograph © Bowness*

---

[5] Ibid.
[6] Ashton dates this visit as 1932, but archive material has since shown this to have taken place the following year (personal communication with Sophie Bowness, Trustee of the Hepworth Estate, January 2025.)
[7] Ashton, p36.
[8] Ibid.
[9] Hepworth, p39.

Figure 15.4. Priaulx Rainier. Photograph © Schott Promotion

Figure 15.5. Barbara Hepworth with The Cosdon Head 1949. Photograph by Hans Wild, © Bowness

When I am carving, or when I am listening to somebody else carving I know what is happening not by what I see but what I hear."[10]

In 1953 a short film was made about Barbara Hepworth's work entitled *Figures in a Landscape*.[11] Directed by Dudley Shaw Ashton, its soundtrack was composed by Ivy Priaulx Rainier, who had become a close friend of Hepworth. Priaulx Rainier (Figure 15.4) was born in South Africa but had moved to Britain in her teens, though much of her music continued to be influenced by that of her homeland. Her soundtrack for the film featured a small wind ensemble led by French horn-player Dennis Brain plus percussionist James Blades who can be heard playing a set of untuned rocks. With Priaulx Rainier dividing her time between London and St Ives where Hepworth was living, each of the women found inspiration in the other's work. Three years before the film, Priaulx Rainier spent time in the St Ives studio listening to the sounds she heard coming from the hammering of Hepworth and her assistants, "notating the rhythm of hands and tools as they struck Irish Blue Limestone."[12] She then developed this into a short piece she called *Rhythms of the Stones*. A modernist composer, though not a serialist, Priaulx Rainier's compositions continued to be informed by the African music she had heard in her childhood. Meanwhile, Hepworth found herself captivated by her music and its strongly rhythmic character.

---

[10] From 1961 BBC TV documentary *Barbara Hepworth*, BBC Archive.
[11] Available on British Film Institute (BFI) website.
[12] Oliver Soden online essay about Priaulx-Rainier.

In interviews and in her writing Barbara Hepworth would refer both to the rhythmic nature of her stone-carving and to the sound it produced. In a letter to Priaulx Rainier in the 1950s she made a comment similar to the observation of stone-carver Lida Kindersley cited earlier: hearing the sound of her assistants working outside in her garden, Hepworth wrote to her friend "I must go, the hammers are not rhythmical."[13] Later, in her 1970 book *A Pictorial Autobiography* she wrote that "The sound of a mallet or hammer is music to my ears, when either is used rhythmically, and I can tell by the sound alone what is going on."[14]

Paying attention to this rhythmic aspect of the carving process was to become accepted practice for stone sculptors. In his 1965 book *The Technique of Sculpture* John Mills stressed its importance:

> "The striking of the hammer is important, the angle of impact upon the end of the chisel, point or claw, and the rhythm of striking. The rhythm is important because to be able to carve for long periods (and it must be realised that the carving is not the quickest process), you must sustain your energy and use it in such a way that the stone does not dissipate this strength and quickly exhaust you. A steady rhythm also enables you to think in the speed of the material."[15]

This is essentially practical advice, given to help produce satisfactory results, but the sensibilities it calls for are ones shared with those of musicians; although the objectives are different the processes have much in common. Consciously or not, the sculptor chipping away at a lump of stone might also be seen to be creating a piece of music, perhaps an improvisation, by listening to the subtle changes in sound coming from the chisel, feeling the sense of time, the rhythm throughout their body; producing something which, unlike the stone sculpture, will disappear as soon as it is heard, sound leaving no residue. As if illustrating the point, towards the end of the 1961 BBC documentary *Barbara Hepworth* there is a half-minute section, devoid of commentary, showing her standing outside her studio, carving a large piece of particularly resonant stone, with the regular rhythmic sound of the chisel ringing out above the drone of a plane flying far above, this time the sound of the sculptural performance preserved for posterity in the filming process.

## Henry Moore

Barbara Hepworth's friend and fellow sculptor Henry Moore, who she met when they were both studying at Leeds School of Art, also famously worked with stone, but there is no record of him making any connections between the process of carving and music. He appears to have shown no particular interest in music and when asked about his musical taste his stock answer was to say he liked Bach and Beethoven, though in a French TV interview in 1977 he did add Handel to the two whose music he enjoyed most.[16]

There is, however, an anecdote which indicates that Moore was certainly aware of the sound produced by his stone-carving and put it to some use. Moore would spend hours carving in his

---

[13] Peter Sheppard Skjaerved, online essay about Priaulx-Rainier
[14] Hepworth, p49.
[15] Mills, p33.
[16] Personal correspondence with Alexander Davis, Moore's bibliographer.

studio next to his house in Perry Green, Hertfordshire. Sometimes he would take a break from his labours and choose to sit for a while, perhaps reading his newspaper, smoking a pipe. If his wife Irina was in the house at the time and he wished her to be under the impression that he was still working away, he would tap the table loudly and regularly to imitate the sound of his chisel. Another account, unsubstantiated, tells of him constructing a mechanical device to create the sound, possibly involving a chisel striking the block of stone, which he could then operate by foot, for the same purpose.[17]

As this story shows, when sound is an intrinsic part of the stone-carver's daily life its significance can be functional as well as profound. Stone sculptor Ann-Margreth Bohl, who has long been fascinated by the "cacophony of sounds which are released as the chisels move, scrape and remove parts of the stone", adds that it has also at times helped her to locate workshops when visiting stonemasons or sculptors.[18] Just as the crop-protection devices in Vietnam also had a therapeutic effect on troubled minds, this is a reminder that the sound of stone can operate on different levels of functionality.

## Paul and Limpe Fuchs

Towards the latter part of the twentieth century a number of sculptors began to actively explore the sound of the stone they were working with. In Germany, Paul Fuchs, a musician and sculptor who made his own instruments, formed the band Anima in 1969 with his wife Limpe. Very much a band of their time, they travelled around with a tractor pulling a customised caravan which was both their home and the stage upon which they performed wherever they happened to arrive, playing to impromptu audiences made up of any unsuspecting pedestrians with time on their hands. Anima's music was not so much prog rock as a kind of indeterminate folk music combined with free improvisation and they were among the first bands in more recent times to take up the use of stone as part of their instrumentation. After their marriage ended Paul Fuchs carried on working as a sculptor, combining that with musical collaborations and performances which incorporated the use of his stone instruments. Limpe Fuchs used only marble when she was playing in Anima, but later began experimenting with different types of rock, finally settling on sepentinite which she was able to source from a quarry in the Bernina mountain range in Italy. Limpe Fuchs has continued to use lithophones in her largely improvised solo work.[19]

## Elmar Daucher

Another sculptor from around the same time who developed an interest in the sound of stone, it bringing a new dimension to his work, was Elmar Daucher. Born in Switzerland in 1932 but spending most of his life in Germany, Daucher had originally trained as a stonemason before studying sculpture in Stuttgart in the early 1950s, then worked as a sculptor, exhibiting widely in Germany, Austria and Japan. In 1974 Daucher first began to explore aural possibilities in his sculpture, influenced by the theories of musicologist and scientist Hans Kayser whose

---

[17] Ibid and personal communication with staff at the Henry Moore Foundation.
[18] Personal communication with Ann-Margreth Bohl, October 2024.
[19] Personal correspondence with Limpe Fuchs, October 2024.

*Figure 15.6. Elmar Daucher's Klangstein, the replacment for the sculpture accidentally destroyed in Lahr.*

research had pointed to a link between the principles of harmonious structure in nature with the fundamentals of harmonics.[20]

Elmar Daucher's favoured rock types were granite, basalt and marble and by making deep parallel cuts, creating a series of thin plates, he was able to produce a powerful resonance from the stones by striking them. Daucher then discovered, by chance, a way of drawing a quite different sound from stone. One day, walking through his outdoor studio, he wiped away some water which had gathered on one of his sculptures following a rain shower and the sculpture sang back to him. He had accidentally created a friction idiophone, a stone version of a glass harmonica, the same principle as running a wet finger around the rim of a wine glass. The sound he was able to produce from the stone was extraordinary: an ethereal wail, with greater depth and more mellow than that of glass. From then on this became his favoured method of playing his sound sculptures.

Daucher first exhibited one of his *Klangsteine* in 1980 in the city of Lahr at an international symposium of stone sculptors.[21] One of the themes for the symposium was collaboration and in Daucher's case this involved working with a group of composers and musicians to produce a number of concerts. At the end of the symposium the city of Lahr took ownership of one of Daucher's sound sculptures which, according to the city's culture website, "was shaped like a human silhouette, which looked like a stone harp due to deep, regular cuts".[22] Unfortunately the sculpture didn't survive for long, being "destroyed by a collision with a delivery vehicle".[23] It was later replaced by another of Daucher's sculptures (Figure 15.6), but this one, taking the form of a large cube about a metre in each direction, seems not to have been as generally loved as its predecessor, being described as "massive, heavy, and its musicality only accessible to those in the know".[24]

The following years brought more exhibitions of Elmar Daucher's sound sculptures, in towns and cities including Würzburg (1985), Ulm (1986) and Munich (1989). In the meantime his work had come to the notice of the composer and musician Stephan Micus who contacted Daucher and they met up for an exchange of ideas. Micus had already encountered musical stones on a trip to Korea in the early 1970s, seeing a set of *pyen kyang* (stone chimes) in a museum,

---

[20] Steven Halliday, MA thesis 2017.
[21] Internationale Steinbildhauer-Symposium, Lahr 1980.
[22] From City of Lahr website: https://kultur.lahr.de/
[23] Ibid.
[24] Ibid.

MUSIC STONES

*Figure 15.7. Stephan Micus playing one of Elmar Daucher's Klangsteine in Ulm Cathedral during the recording of his album The Music of Stones. Photograph © Jean Gallus.*

later making some for himself, firstly from slate then using marble and other types of stone. During the time Daucher was preparing for his exhibition in Ulm, a year or so after they'd met, he contacted Micus asking him if he would be interested to collaborate in a concert. The exhibition was to take place in Ulm's large cathedral and Daucher had been particularly taken by its rich acoustics. Unsuitable for intricate music with fast flurries of notes the architecture would provide a natural reverberation which would enhance the long slow tones of the stone sculptures, as well as Micus's minimalist compositions. Micus accepted and when he visited the cathedral was as impressed as Daucher at heard what it offered.

> "It has an amazing acoustic. If you clap your hands there will be sound for eight seconds. So it's very extreme - when the priests speak you can't understand a single word."[25]

---

[25] All About Jazz interview with Stephan Micus by John Kelman, January 2005.

Stephan Micus wrote compositions specially for the concert and over a period of months the two men visited the church trying out the material *in situ* and working at night (Figure 15.7). By the time of the concert they had decided to also record the music, which they did the following day, deciding that the recording must also take place in the cathedral.

> "That was very special; as you can imagine in this acoustic you have to create music especially for this space. If you just go there and play ordinary music it becomes one big soup." [26]

The recording was released three years later in 1989 on the ECM label, entitled *The Music of Stones*, with four musicians credited: Elmar Daucher, Günther Federer, Nobuko Micus and Stephan Micus. As well as Daucher's resonating stones it also features stone chimes made by Daucher, in the style of the ancient Chinese *pien ch'ing*.

## Klaus and Hannes Fessmann

Following the release of the album *The Music of Stones*, later the same year, Elmar Daucher died, at the age of fifty-seven. His work continued to be exhibited in galleries and this prompted others to explore the principle behind his sound sculptures. One such was musician and composer Klaus Fessmann, also living in the south of Germany. He had an academic background in music, having studied at the University of Stuttgart, where he then taught before later taking up a lecturing position at the Mozarteum University of Music in Salzburg.

In the late 1980s Fessmann had become interested in interdisciplinary performance work and began collaborating with a poet, using the environment of a cave for its atmosphere and acoustic properties and combining speech with music, including the sound of stones. As a result of some local media attention, Fessmann was contacted by a gallery owner currently displaying one of Elmar Daucher's sculptures. Unable to produce a sound from it he had sought the help of Fessmann who then visited the gallery and was awe-struck by what he saw and heard. He decided to develop the idea himself and in 1992 he and his son Hannes, then in his early teens, took a trip to the Swiss Alps in search of some suitable stone.

Klaus Fessmann began producing a series of instruments using the same method as Daucher, having deep cuts sawn into blocks of stone, and he became adept at this quite different way of playing, stroking not striking the stone. Producing music from stones in this way requires a very different approach to other instruments, the sound needing to be coaxed out, building slowly over a period of time, the result being music characterised by long notes made up of pure sine waves with no overtones. Fessmann formed a trio he called Klangstein along with drummer and percussionist Manfred Kniel and cellist Friedemann Dähn, creating music born out of these new instruments. Fessmann and Kniel played the sound stones and Dähn used his e-cello, which allowed him to inhabit a similar, ethereal sound world. The group achieved a degree of success, performing widely, but soon Fessmann began to have ambitions to do more with his sound stones. He proceeded to set up a centre, which he called Klangsteine, taking the name used by Elmar Daucher, and developed a series of activities there with the sound stones as the focus. As a continuation of his music educational background he opened an academy

---
[26] Ibid.

*Figure 15.8. Klangsteine by Hannes Fessmann.*

with courses teaching how to play the sound stones, and also developed a form of music therapy tailored to their use, drawing on the meditative aspect of playing the instrument, already signposted by the Stephan Micus ECM recording with Daucher.

The courses run by Klangsteine were programmed progressively, the completion of one qualifying a participant to go on to the next stage. The therapeutic aspect of Klangsteine was built into the educational model so that by the time a student had completed the final course they would be qualified to teach the playing of the instrument, practise sound stone therapy and teach others to do the same.

Klaus Fessmann's philosophical and musical beliefs had their roots in the East and in India in particular and his pronouncements regarding Klangesteine have an esoteric, spiritual ring to them without being specifically religious. To make music from stone, the very material of which the earth was formed is, for Fessmann, to connect with primeval forces and he attributes to the stones an almost mystical quality.

> "For me, the sound of stones is a previously unheard music. It is a music of the earth, the memory of this matter formed in sound, beyond all speculation or idealization. It is often described as music full of secrets."[27]

It was this thinking which seems to have led Klaus Fessmann to develop the idea of the sound stones playing a central role in a form of alternative, restorative therapy. By its nature this type of sound stone needs to be played slowly over an extended period of time to discover its potential and that process may well prove beneficial in a number of ways, but to what extent this followed the principles already tried and tested in the long-established practice of music therapy isn't clear. On the Klangsteine website and in his book[28] Fessmann makes claims for the proven effectiveness of his centre's sound stone therapy in addressing a range

---

[27] From Klangsteine website: https://klangsteine.com
[28] *KlangSteine*, Klaus Fessmann, Südwest Verlag 2008.

*Figure 15.9. Hannes Fessmann playing one of his Dolphin series of Klangsteine.*

of issues, related to physical and psychological health as well as social concerns such as violent behaviour, though more actual evidence of its efficacy would have been welcome.

Klaus Fessmann's son Hannes (Figure 15.8), having been there at the outset of the project, later became closely involved in its activities. Unlike his father he has no background in formal music education though he remembers being surrounded by music from an early age. Consequently, his approach to music-making has always been an intuitive one, drawn to it more for its expressive potential than to its theoretical aspects. In 2006 he began making the stone instruments for Klangesteine and through his work the designs for them continued to evolve. Initially the sound stones were cuboid, or box-like, with each plane having the possibility of producing different sounds, but Hannes Fessmann found these not to be particularly user-friendly with their sharp right-angled edges so he transformed the design, giving them a more curved shape, easier on the palm of the hand as it moved across the surface. Two distinctive styles emerged, one he called "the dolphin" (Figure 15.9), the other "the tulip".

Hannes Fessmann considers himself to be a sound artist, a term he regards as eschewing conventional, socially defined roles such as musician, composer or sculptor. The sound stones produced and played at Klangesteine certainly had their roots in sculpture and while definitions can be arbitrary, it's an open question as to whether these objects could be described as sculptures, or whether they have become musical instruments in their own right, whose visual appearance, like any other instrument, arise principally from musical requirements, with form following function. Hannes Fessmann seems clear that it is the sound of the instrument which is the most important aspect, and that although visual aesthetics might be a consideration, they are not the primary one. But he is of the view that we remain too hidebound by categorization, giving as an example the way in which Elmar Daucher's sound sculptures have now gone back to being exhibited purely as sculptures. On one occasion Fessmann went to a gallery to see one of them, which he was able to do, but he was not permitted to play it.[29] For Hannes Fessman definitions are unhelpful, seeing the activities he is involved with, which include building instruments, studying geology, composing music, staging performances and playing his sound stones, as being inseparable parts of a whole.

## Pinuccio Sciola

The sculptor Pinuccio Sciola had already secured his international reputation by the time he began to explore the potential of sound in his sculpture. Born in 1942 in Sardinia, he spent most of his life in the village of San Sperate in the south of the island, attending the local art school in Cagliari from the age of seventeen and going on to study sculpture in Florence, followed by some extensive foreign travel. Having undertaken further study in Salzburg, Madrid and Paris, he visited Central and South America, in particular Peru and Mexico, travelling there in 1973 as a result of a UNESCO invitation, leading to a collaboration with Mexican muralist David Alfar Siqueiros. Three years later he was chosen to exhibit at the 50th anniversary of the Venice Biennale which helped pave the way to further opportunities abroad, including a touring exhibition in Germany in 1987.

In 1990 Scuola took up a teaching appointment at the Academy of Sassari in Sardinia which continued for six years and it was during that period that he began making his sound sculptures. Like Elmar Daucher, he produced sound from stone principally through friction rather than in a percussive way, gently caressing the cut surfaces with the wetted palm of his hand and fingers. When he'd first come across Daucher's sculptures is uncertain, but it seems that Sciola

*Figure 15.10. Pinuccio Sciola in front of the installation created for Turandot, Teatro Lirico, Caligari. Courtesy of Sciola Foundation Archive. Photograph © Fabio Marras.*

---

[29] From interview with Hannes Fessmann by Steven Halliday.

# The Gift of Sound and Vision

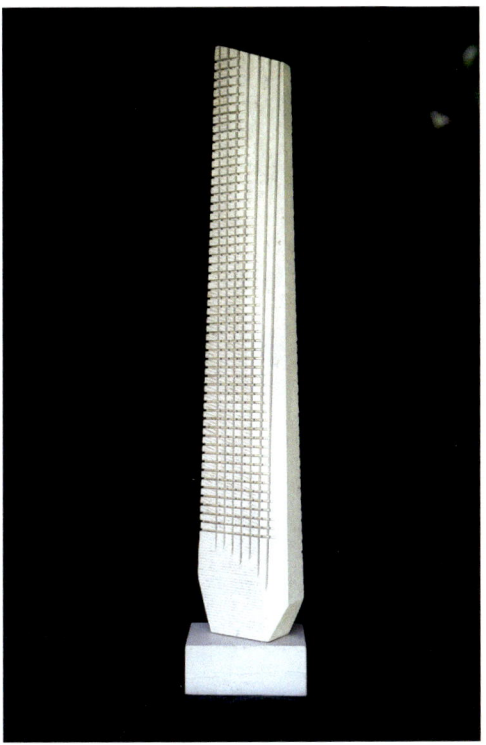

Figure 15.11. Pinuccio Sciola, Sound Harp Courtesy of Sciola Foundation Archive. Photograph © Ettore Cavalli.

and Daucher had been in contact at some point.[30] Daucher had died some years before Sciola began producing his sound sculptures but seeing Daucher's work may well have influenced his thinking in producing sound from stone using friction. Nevertheless, having worked with stone daily for around three decades Pinuccio Sciola had inevitably built up an understanding of the material, its qualities, its behaviour and the differences not only between the various types available to him but also between different sections of the same piece of rock. He was also fascinated by its history, frequently talking about the fundamental importance of stone, telling of how the Incas in Peru had called stone "the backbone of the world". Sciola liked this image "because we all know that all continents rest on stones" and he believed that stone, in some way, also carries an aural record of the earth's evolution.

"Every material has its own memory. Stone today - and this is not what I say, but what science says - is of crucial importance. I don't think I can stress enough how important stone is. Let's just think of a simple watch, all computerized technology works with stones. Silicon, quartz, they're all stones. Inside this material there is a memory of the universe. And it was indeed with these considerations that years ago I started wondering, if the stone has such a retentive potential, why shouldn't it also carry sound?"[31]

The first public performance of what Sciola called his Pietre Sonore was in 1996 at the Time in Jazz Festival in Berchidda, Sardinia, with Swiss drummer and percussionist Pierre Favre playing the stones alongside Sciola himself. Recently Favre recalled the performance and his impressions of Sciola:

"The sculptures arrived in a huge truck and the first thing they had to do was support the floor of the stage to prevent it from collapsing under the weight. Then they asked me to try playing on the sculptures. For this they gave me all kinds of big hammers all made from different materials, but I settled on a camping hammer, made of rubber, and I started to play gently, almost caressing the stone, not fast, just at a medium tempo. After a while I heard a dull sound, the stone was responding. I continued, still striking it gently and the sound began to build, growing louder and louder. And then I suddenly thought: this doesn't like being hit. It's like drums, they too like being caressed and not hit; just

---

[30] Personal correspondence with Andrea Granitzio, composer and Artistic Director, Sciola Foundation.
[31] From Angela Corrias's film *Pinuccio Sciola - Sounding Stones - The Memory of the Universe*.

*Figure 15.12. The Sound Garden of Pinuccio Sciola. Courtesy of Sciola Foundation Archive. Photograph © Ettore Cavalli.*

as we too don't like to be hit but caressed. Some of these sculptures were very fine to play. Using knitting needles for example I could make them vibrate and sometimes even sing, they could even sometimes produce harmonics. After the Berchidda experience, I had the opportunity to play several times on Pinuccio's sculptures."[32]

Later that year Pinuccio Sciola took his Pietre Sonore to Milan, where they were played at La Scala. A widespread interest in Sciola's sound sculptures ensued and a series of exhibitions and commissions followed over the following years, including a 2002 collaboration with architect Renzo Piano for the design of the Auditorium della Musica in Rome, with one of his basalt sound sculptures being placed in the internal garden. Two years later he was the subject of a large solo exhibition in Luxembourg entitled *Pierres Sonores* and in the years that followed Sciola worked continually, exhibiting in both his own country and abroad. In 2013 he was awarded one of Italy's highest honours, Commendatore dell'Ordine al merito della Repubblica Italiana.

The sounds Pinuccio Sciola was able to produce from his Pietro Sonore were remarkable, but while this became a central feature of his sculptures and a determining factor in their creation, on another level these work could be viewed in more conventionally sculptural terms, formally and conceptually. They varied considerably in size, from small pieces which could be lifted and carried, to large, towering sculptures requiring hoists or cranes and a team of assistants to move or transport. Sciola experimented with different types of rock, including granite, limestone and basalt, but it was basalt which seemed to have a special appeal for him, because of the sound it produced but also because of its history:

---

[32] Personal correspondence with Pierre Favre. Translation of his recollections. September 2024

*Figure 15.13. Pinuccio Sciola playing a sounding stone. Courtesy of Sciola Foundation Archive. Photograph © Riccardo Rigo.*

> "Limescale is a deposit. In its creation it is like a flowing stone and that also enables its special sound. The basalt is a wonderful element. Islands arise from the basalt. It is the origin of all lands."[33] (Figure 15.14)

Pinuccio Sciola was evasive when asked about the source of the ideas in his work, typically replying that if he answered such questions he would kill the magic that nature had created around the stones.[34] Yet he was prepared to talk about his work up to a point, in a way which showed he had an understanding of the natural history of the earth and its evolution into the form it now takes, but his declared scepticism about geologists perhaps indicates his rejection of what he saw as a reductionist view of the world in favour of a more pantheist belief.[35]

The Sardinian landscape features numerous stone edifices including *nuraghi*, stone towers dating back to the bronze age, and *domus de janas* or "fairy houses", also dating back to prehistory. There are also what are referred to as "giants' tombs" which have been thought to have therapeutic properties for those lying beneath them.[36] This tallies with some of the things Pinuccio Sciola spoke about in a short film about his work:

> "I believe that through my sculptures, especially those from the most recent period, there is a precise thread tracing the continuity in the life of the stones, right through to the final successful releasing of its sound. This, I believe, is one of the most important aspects, so that this stone can continue to tell its story. To talk about the civilizations who have used it, with the cosmic sounds that come out, and then to communicate

---

[33] From video by Beat D. Hebeisen *Pinuccio Sciola - Singing Stones - In Memoria*.
[34] Angela Corrias online article about Pinuccio Sciola.
[35] Ibid.
[36] Ibid.

*Figure 15.14. Pinuccio Sciola caressing one of his basalt sculptures. Courtesy of Sciola Foundation Archive. Photograph © Luca Pinna.*

with the stars, with the sun, with the moon....The stone is the structure which carries our planet, the world's spine, as the Incas said, today's stones are the memory of the universe....To enter into a stone and listen to its silence, I believe would be just as strong an emotion as listening to the sound of the stones...and the music of the silence inside the stone, inside the world, is that which accompanies us forever."[37]

His talk of releasing the sound of the stones is something he often came back to and it recalls the famous quote attributed to Michaelangelo Buonarroti about a sculpture already being complete within the block of marble before he started work and him just having to chisel away the superfluous material. In a similar way, Sciola sensed that the sounds were already lying dormant within the stone he was working on and that his job was merely to allow them out. In preparing the stones in order to release their sounds Sciola used different methods. In some, which he referred to as "harps", he cut a series of vertical, parallel cuts from the top down, forming thin plates only attached at the base, allowing them to vibrate and sound, rather like a free reed in an accordion. In others he would make cuts vertically and horizontally, creating a grid with the resultant squares of stone each having a different note when struck or rubbed. These he called his "keyboards". Sometimes Sciola or another player would use a smaller length of cut stone to scrape the top or edge of a sound stone, or at other times draw a bow across the stone to create long, sustained notes.

On some occasions Pinuccio Sciola would perform on his own with the stones, at small concerts or even in the street, but in later years, he took to playing alongside other musicians. There might be up to six on stage, each player having a particular role, employing different methods of playing in carefully planned performances, properly lit, and presented as a highly

---

[37] From film by Franco Fais: *Sciola: Oltre La Pietra (Beyond the rock)* Text taken from English subtitles.

atmospheric piece of theatre. Through close-miking or by using contact mics even the gentlest of sounds produced would become audible.

Pinuccio Sciola died in May 2016 at the age of seventy-four but remained active until shortly before that, attending an exhibition of his sound stones in Milan a month earlier and playing at a concert in Rome a couple of weeks later. Perhaps more than anybody, Sciola was able to create a synthesis in his sculpture between the visual, the haptic and the aural. There were many exhibitions and the sound aspect was always an acknowledged element, while in concerts the visual element, the sculptures, almost upstaged the presence of the performers. He collaborated with numerous musicians in these public performances including many with Elio Martusciello who remembers him fondly:

> "He was a lovely person - genuine, friendly and it was very good to spend time travelling and relaxing with him. The topics of conversation were many, Pinuccio being an inquisitive person with wide interests and also generous: I jealously treasure one of his beautiful stones that he gave me after noticing that it was one of my favourites, for the beauty of its shape and also for playing. Unsurprisingly, his great love was reserved for his stones. We have been many times to his wonderful stone garden in San Sperate (Figure 15.12) We picked and ate the fruits of his trees, while we gazed at his magnificent stone monoliths. He loved the idea that those enormous and very heavy stones were at the same time transparent, that through the cuts that passed through them it was possible to watch the sunset. He was fascinated too by the thought that such a hard and heavy material could produce the most shifting and unimaginable of forms, the form of sound and of music. This was a central part of his work, connecting the earth to the sky, the force of matter to spirituality. He often spoke of mother earth and her divine song. Pinuccio was truly a very spiritual person, but one who loved to get dirty and scratch his hands digging in stone, in the earth."[38]

## Andrea Granitzio

Composer Andrea Granitzio, born in Cagliari, Sardinia in 1974, had known of Pinuccio Sciola by reputation since he was a teenager but was not to meet him until 2011, by which time Granitzio had begun studying for a masters degree in composition at Birmingham Conservatoire in the UK. Following a chance meeting with Sciola, when Granitzio told the sculptor that he hoped to compose an orchestral piece incorporating his sounding stones, the two men became friends and went on to collaborate in a number of performances. Granitzio was drawn not just to the sound of Sciola's sculptures but also to the philosophy behind it, the way the artist thought about his work, including Sciola's belief that stones hold a sound memory from the long and continuing process of their evolution through time. Later Andrea Granitzio went on to study for a PhD at the Conservatoire in which he examined these ideas further, relating them to the writing of Pythagoras, who had proposed in his theory of Music of the Spheres:

> "....that the heavenly bodies must, like other large bodies moving at speed, produce a sound as they whirl through space; since the bodies move at different speeds they must produce different notes, but together these are harmonious."[39]

---

[38] Personal communication with Elio Martusciello.
[39] Granitzio, quoting from MC Howatson "Harmony of the Spheres" in *The Oxford Companion to Classical Literature Online*,

*Figure 15.15. Andrea Granitzio conducting the final concert by Pinuccio Sciola in San Pietro, Vincoli, Rome. Courtesy of Andrea Granitzio.*

> According to Granitzio, it was in this context that "Sciola liked to think that, during their journey through the universe, stones had absorbed its sound".[40]

Andrea Granitzio's research culminated in a series of compositions combining sounding stones with conventional instrumentation. This involved him exploring many different ways of producing sound from the Pietre Sonore, some learned from Sciola, others through his own experimentation and he also developed a notation system to be used with the stones.

The final collaboration between the sculptor and the composer was to be in April 2016, only two weeks before Pinuccio Sciola died. It featured the premiere of Granitzio's *Time Persistence* for sounding stones and string quartet (with double bass replacing the usual second violin) and took place in the church of San Pietro in Vincoli, Rome. (Figure 15.15). This is the location of Michaelangelo's sculpture of Moses and before the performance, in which he played his Pietre Sonore, Sciola addressed the audience.

> Sciola told the audience the story that when Michelangelo completed his statue of Moses he was so fascinated by its perfection that he asked the statue: 'Why don't you speak to me?' Frustrated by its silence, Michelangelo slammed down his hammer on Moses' knee. Sciola explained that Michelangelo carved the sculpture on a saccaroid

---

2013 p275
[40] Granitzio p14 24/131 (online thesis).

marble: a kind of material that, due to its texture, is very soft and easy to carve, but that does not allow vibration, or thus sound. With the aim of reconciling Michelangelo with the 'inner voice' of the stone, Sciola played his Sounding Stones in front of Moses and then we performed *Time Persistence*.[41]

The theme of *Time Persistence* reflected Sciola and Granitzio's engagement with the idea that "the presence of stones on Earth preceded the appearance of humans and will arguably last longer"[42] The piece starts and ends with the sound of stone, with the musical changes of key and time signatures on the strings intended to represent human evolution while "the sound of the stone always remains the same."[43]

Although he has not produced his own sound sculptures Andrea Granitzio has been drawn to the idea of "found sculpture" and around the same time as he was working with Pinuccio Sciola he became interested in sounding stones existing in nature and in particular stalactites and stalagmites, known collectively as speleothems. His research led to him sharing his ideas within the geological community, speaking at conferences and bringing together artistic and scientific ideas in a way that recalls Honoré Baudre's activities a century and a half earlier.

Stalactites, stalagmites and their smaller variant helictites, which in gravity-defying manner can extend horizontally, are calcium carbonate formations created from precipitation within caves. Formed over a relatively short time period compared to most geological changes, the nature of that process is particularly visible and was the inspiration for Andrea Granitzio's composition *Speleothemes*:

> The whole composition is informed by the idea of material in constant organic development: a metamorphosis that involves its constitutive components in a continual transformational process, such as occurs in natural phenomena.... *Speleothemes* consists of four movements. The first three represent, respectively, the formation of a 'Stalactite', a 'Stalagmite' and the 'Joint' between them. The fourth one, entitled 'Before', aims to emulate the chamber where speleothems grow.[44]

## Peter Randall-Page

British sculptor Peter Randall-Page has become internationally known over a period of more than forty years, working principally in stone. His work too is inspired by forms in the natural world and the geometry underlying them, but it is a flawed geometry, never quite perfect. Even in nature they are variations on a theme, and that concept, that phrase with its musical association, is one used by Randall-Page when talking about patterns in nature and about his work. He has given the title *Theme and Variation* to many of his sculptures, including a commission from the University of Birmingham for the façade of the Bramhall Music Building in 2014. This reflects the fact that throughout his career as a visual artist he has also been passionate about music.

---

[41] Ibid p41 51/131
[42] Ibid
[43] Ibid
[44] Ibid p50 61/131

*Figure 15.16. Peter Randall-Page's sound sculpture Bell. Courtesy of the artist.*

"Music's always been incredibly important to me, though I'm not by any means an accomplished musician and I do relate sound to shape. I listen to music a lot when I'm working. I love baroque music and I love jazz, it being an improvised form. I love improvisation and it's a very important part of my work as an artist, so the two things cross over in that way. I'm in a very small minority of contemporary sculptors who hit stone and the musicality of carving is something I've always been very much aware of."[45]

Another commission, this time for the University of Music in Karlsruhe, Germany was given the title *Harmonic Solids*, while some works reference particular musicians and songs: *In mind of Monk*, a tribute to Thelonious Monk and *Rocks in my bed*, from a Duke Ellington blues, being just two examples.

While he has long been aware of the musicality of carving, Peter Randall-Page has not chosen to follow the path of making sound sculptures but he has on occasion experimented with the idea. In 1997 he collaborated with percussionist Dame Evelyn Glennie in a project to make a sound sculpture which he entitled *Bell* (Figure 15.16) and the process was documented in a BBC/ Arts Council 30 minute film, part of a series entitled *Date with an Artist*. The film includes footage of Randall-Page selecting a suitable piece of rock, striking it to test its resonance.

Some years later Peter Randall-Page was involved in another collaboration relating to the sound of stone, culminating in a series of events staged at London's King's Place in 2007. This crossover music and visual arts project began with a trip to Lolui, an island situated in Lake

---

[45] Conversation with Peter Randall-Page, September 2024.

*Figure 15.17. Peter Randall-Page's sculpture Dartmoor End. Courtesy of the artist.*

Victoria between Uganda and Kenya, by composer Nigel Osborne, two Ugandan percussionists, members of the London Sinfonietta, two Ugandan sculptors and Peter Randall-Page. Lolui Islands has a number of formations of rock gongs which, judging by markings on them, were played musically in former times. All those involved tried their hand at playing the gongs as well as playing along with other instruments and by sampling the sound of the stone gongs Osborne was later able to compose an orchestral piece incorporating the stone sounds. Randall-Page produced a sculpture on the site using a split boulder, incising and colouring concentric circles on each exposed face, a metaphor for sound being released from the stone. There was, unsurprisingly, a manifest difference in musical approach between the two musical groups, one with a background in Ugandan traditional music, the other classically trained orchestral players. In a film made about the project[46] one of the London Sinfonietta players notes that, of the European visitors taking part, it was the sculptor, Randall-Page, rather than any of the orchestral musicians who was "going for it....doing all sorts of interesting experiments – scraping the rock with a stone to get this scratching effect and getting physically involved."[47] It's tempting to think that this may have been the outcome of years of intuitively striking pieces of stone in addition to having some experience of jazz improvisation.

Like other stone sculptors, Peter Randall-Page recognizes the part sound plays in the process of sculpting stone and it's a consideration right from the start:

---

[46] *Rock Art Rock Music* Distant Object Productions 2008.
[47] Ibid.

> "One way of telling if a stone has got a crack in it, even if you can't see it, is to lift it up with a crane or something and give it a good bash with a hammer; if it's got a dead thud it's probably got a crack in it, if it rings, it's fine."[48]

Sometimes, as in the case of German sculptor Elmar Daucher, a sculpture will produce sounds unexpectedly which can then give the work an extra dimension. This happened with a sculpture Peter Randall-Page produced to mark where a Devon footpath, Two Moors Way, crossed from Dartmoor to Exmoor. He used, as in his Lolui piece, a naturally split large boulder into each face of which he drilled a multitude of holes to create a phyllotaxis type of spiral pattern. At some point after the piece was finished he happened to run his hand across the surface and was surprised to hear it emit a surprising and distinctive sound.

The term "theme and variation", which Peter Randall-Page often comes back to in talking about his work, is of course a term usually used in relation to composed concert music, but he also recognizes the important part it can play in improvised music, including his particular interest, jazz: the melody of a song or tune is stated and that is then extemporised with a series of variations which may go anywhere, but not necessarily with a preconceived idea of the path they will take. Randall-Page often chooses to work in a similar way in his creative practice.

While acknowledging the rhythmic nature of stone-carving Peter Randall-Page doesn't go as far as seeing a direct musical connection when he is engaged in the process, but he does recall being told of an occasion when other stone-carvers did just that:

> "Many years ago, when I was in my early twenties and working on my first big commission I did, a piece I made out of Portland stone in Lewes in Sussex, I was helped by a retired mason. He was amazing and taught me an enormous amount. He was a great musician, a violinist and a poet and a very unusual and special character to have the honour of knowing. He was called Skylark Bunstone because after the second world war they were making so many gravestones they had 300+ masons working in an enormous shed and they would all hammer in time and they'd sing all day with the rhythm and they'd be topical songs – perhaps one of the young masons had a girlfriend and they'd make up a song to embarrass him, or it might be somebody's birthday, or it might be an anniversary of some sort, or it might be just a way of having some banter…I've never experienced that but I thought it sounded wonderful."[49] [50]

Both sculpture and architecture can, like music, be considered as time-based in the way we experience them. Unlike a painting whose totality can be seen in an instant, free-standing sculptures or buildings only fully reveal themselves as we move around or through them. Depending on the pace at which we are walking, or the spatial distances between different physical features, there will be a visual equivalent of a musical sense of rhythm evident in this unfolding, musical rhythm being merely a description of the manner or rate at which sounds are revealed in time.

---

[48] Conversation with Peter Randall-Page September 2024.
[49] Ibid.
[50] Lisa Kindersley has a different experience of collective stone-carving. For her, the sounds produced by others can become a distraction, interfering with her own rhythmic flow, particularly if one individual's sound becomes dominant. For the same reason she cannot have music playing in the background when she is carving, though others choose to.

# The Gift of Sound and Vision

Figure 15.18. Ann-Margreth Bohl, Sound in Stone 1. Courtesy of the artist.

Figure 15.19. Ann-Margreth Bohl, Sound in Stone 2. Courtesy of the artist.

## Ann-Margreth Bohl

German sculptor Ann-Margreth Bohl, while being very aware of the sounds involved in the stone-carving process, does not use the sound of stone in her sculptures but sound has played a crucial part in some of her installation pieces. Lüsenen, a 2019 installation in the magnificent Gloucester Cathedral, brought sound and stone together in a collaborative work with musicians, a composer, a sound designer and a sound engineer. While none of the sounds were produced directly from the stone of the medieval crypt where the installation was sited, what was heard was determined by the reverberating acoustics from the crypt's different chambers, each one producing its own unique quality of sound reflecting off the surfaces of the stone. Aspects of *Lüsenen* were time-based, in the way referred to earlier whereby a sculpture or a building is revealed as the viewer walks through or around it. But here this process happened aurally: visitors to the installation were encouraged to move closer or further away to experience how the sound naturally changed "creating an individual experience for everyone".[51]

Other works by Bohl are also time-based. In some she has created monumental stone sculptures which cast complex, shifting shadows as the natural light changes. "Like modern Stonehenges, they're precisely aligned with the sun as it moves across the sky."

Like Barbara Hepworth, even if she is not intentionally making sound sculptures the sound produced by the carving process is, for Ann-Margreth Bohl, intrinsic to it and cannot be ignored:

---

[51] Statement on website: https://annmargrethbohl.com

*Figure 15.20. Will Menter, Touchstone. Courtesy of the artist.*

"I have been teaching others to carve stone for many years now and you can imagine the variety of sounds that sing beyond the confines of the studio, depending on what a human hand works on. It might be the loud metal ping ping ping of the rhythm developing as big chunks of stone fly through the air, landing metres away from the workbench and landing with a dull thud on the floor. And that might be in contrast to a circular almost silent brushing, polishing sound as fine sandpaper removes the last blemishes on the surface of a sculpture and many other audible tooling sounds in between. In my experience stone carving is closely linked with sound and rhythm, and I sometimes tune my ears into just the sound, thinking of it as a song or a choral piece that is sung by the rock as it takes on a new form."[52]

That there might be a route taken from stone-carving and stone sculpture to an exploration of the sound of stone is understandable, even if it happens less often than might be expected. Less common is a move in the opposite direction, but there are examples. British musician Will Menter, now living in France, began playing contemporary jazz and free improvisation in the 1970s. Through exploring the sound potential of different materials from the natural world, he started making his own instruments, choosing outside spaces to perform with others. An interconnection developed in his work between music, sound, the objects he used and created and the natural environment. From being purely musical his work broadened out to become also visual and sculptural. Will Menter writes about his work in Chapter 16.

---

[52] Personal communication with Ann-Margreth Bohl, October 2024.

# Chapter Sixteen

# The new stone age

## Statements from contemporary practitioners

The final chapter of Music Stones brings the subject up to date, presenting a selection of different ways in which the sound of stone continues to be explored. After something of a hiatus, It seems that an increasing number of instrument-builders, composers and musicians are taking this path, many of whom probably identify with all three of those activities. I have invited practitioners from twelve countries to write about the way they have chosen to work with stone in a musical way. Their statements follow and I am grateful for their contributions.

### Jim Doble - USA

Shortly after I started professionally making instruments, I happened to notice a pile of old roofing slate I had stashed away. Hmmm...wonder what that sounds like...

*Figure 16.2. Jim Doble.*

*Figure 16.1. Jim Doble lithophone.*

It happened to be Monson Slate from Maine, arguably one of the finest slates available anywhere. The sound was incredible. I had previously just worked with wood and glass instruments. The slate had a similar tone quality to the glass, but somehow richer with more depth. I absolutely loved it! So, slate immediately became my favorite material to work with, mostly due to the tonal quality (I could easily and happily noodle around on a simple pentatonic instrument for hours, just sinking into the sound) and partly because I could cut and tune the slate without use of power tools, making the building of it that much more enjoyable. Lithophones were quickly added to my line of instruments.

It wasn't long until I started experimenting with other forms of stone, digging around in quarries, fields, stone suppliers, and beaches for anything that had a good ring to it. I started making haphazardly tuned instruments out of rough stone of various types; every nice sounding stone find that had an elongated shape was an incredible treasure! I was now making instruments for playgrounds and children's museums, so being able to use indestructible stone was essential.

Now I had to start tooling up a bit better to handle the larger stone: core drill, masonry saws and blades, stone grinders. A bit more dust and grit than working with slate, but so worth it!

Around the same time I started playing with rough stone, I discovered the discard pile of a local stone shop. Here were scrap pieces of beautiful, uniform, polished granite to be explored.

The vast majority of what I tried out was pretty thunky, but occasionally there would be some dense, super hard, black granite that had a beautiful ring to it. I eventually collected enough to start offering tuned instruments for sale. Again, I would finish making an instrument and be mesmerized playing it for an hour or so, not even realizing time had gone by. Stone has that kind of effect on me ( a very different way of getting stoned!)

I've now been making stone instruments, mostly lithophones, for about 40 years; but I'm not done with exploring. I still go around tapping likely rocks I find laying around. My current major goal is to make a stone gong, not the small chunks of rock that get hung up occasionally and called a gong, but a large suspended stone that has some of the sustain qualities of a metal gong and the textured depth of stone. So much to explore still....

*Figure 16.3. Jochen Fassbender lithophone.*

## Jochen Fassbender - Germany

A song is sleeping in all things...

It is well known that materials such as metal, wood or glass can produce sound. But you don't normally trust stones to do that. We are surrounded by stones every day. We have been using it as a material since time immemorial. But we only know its noisy side. We know what it sounds like when you walk on a gravel path and we also know that stones can rumble a lot, but we usually stay with that which we already know.

But when music emanates from stones, many people are strangely touched because the stone reveals itself to them in a completely new, unknown way. Each stone has its own, specific sound. A basalt from Iceland sounds different from an Italian freshwater limestone or a gabbro from India because it has different minerals and molecular structures.

Geologists have developed the ability to determine the age of rocks and how they were formed based on structures and colours. They identify small indentations as imprints of raindrops and can thus prove that it rained on earth tens of millions of years ago. So you can read the rocks like a diary of our planet.

When stones sound, they don't need such translators, because now they tell the story themselves. They don't throw around dates or chemical formulas. When it comes to stone, the forces that shaped it always resonate. The story of its origins – indeed the history of the earth – becomes audible. What the stones all have in common is that they were created over periods of time that are unimaginably long for us humans and tell of ancient pasts. The effect of the sound of stone on our soul corresponds to this. We gain an inner quietude. Time seems to slow down infinitely. We resonate with the forces of the earth.

*Figure 16.4. Jochen Fassbender.*

Chlorite schist is a metamorphic rock from the Swiss Alps. If you know how it came about you can easily understand why its sounds have such a healing character. It originally flowed to earth as red-hot lava during a volcanic eruption and then cooled to form basalt. Over millions of years it was then pushed back up to thirty kilometres below the earth's surface due to the formation of the Alps. There, under strong pressure and heat, it was transformed into this form of slate. As a result, the minerals are transformed into wafer-thin plates that lie close together in the same order. Because it is structured down to the smallest detail here and there, sound vibrations are transmitted undisturbed and can produce a long resonance. Lithophones made from this stone have a high therapeutic value and have been shown to be of great comfort for those with stress, for example with burn-out syndrome. Precisely because the stone has suffered the most severe crises, something inside it has been restored to order. The stone tells us what comes after stress, namely pure relaxation.

For over 30 years I have been researching a wide variety of sound phenomena, developing and building new types of sound objects. As I see it, at least four factors play an important role in sound production: the material, the shape, the movement that creates the sound and the space around it that resonates. There are many sound possibilities to discover, an infinite number.

The externally visible worlds have already largely been explored. In the past, Christopher Columbus and Alexander von Humboldt were able to discover distant continents. Today, all it takes is a few clicks on Google Maps to see which spot on which remote South Sea island there is a palm tree. But the inner worlds that are conveyed through sound are still hidden. Going on a search there can surely not be any less exciting. Because there you encounter the forces that hold the world together.

A song is sleeping in all things,
Which are dreaming on and on,
And the world starts to sing,
If you just hit on the magic word. (Joseph von Eichendorff)

*Figure 16.6. Páll Gudmundsson.*

## Páll Gudmundsson - Iceland

In the 1980s in Húsafell, I began to develop a lithophone from liparite stones found in the surrounding mountains. Liparite breaks up into thin flakes that have a clear tone when struck. I put a lot of effort into finding the right tones and like to dig deep for stones that split into a kind of sandwich. They often contain beautiful intervals. I then arrange the stones so they correspond to a chromatic scale and it becomes a kind of marimba.

I am also a visual artist and connect art with music by carving pictures into each tone slab. The pictures are then painted with colours which also derive from nearby stones.

I have seven lithophones, the largest spanning more than five octaves and numerous musicians have requested to use them, including percussionists Arthur Lippner and Frank Arnik and the band Sigur Rós. One of my lithophones was also used in the concert "Iceland – Ireland", led by Hilmar Örn Hilmarsson and the Irish musician Dónal Lunny.

I compose my own songs, taken from poems, on the lithophone and perform them at various musical events, often with chamber choirs. I have travelled widely with my lithophone,

*Figure 16.5. Páll Gudmundsson.*

including playing at the Barbican Hall in London, the Grand Hall in Paris and the Nordic House in the Faroe Islands, and have also has played at a number of smaller music festivals, including those in Hafnarborg and Reykholt, playing with Hilmar Erni Agnarsson.

Johann Sebastian Bach has been a great influence on my music and he holds a central place in the music I like to play on the lithophone. Among my favourite works to perform on it are Bach's Cello Suite in G major and also his Prelude in C major.

# The New Stone Age

*Figure 16.7. Jay Harrison's electromechanical lithophone.*

## Jay Harrison - UK

In 2015, as part of my dissertation for a BSc degree in Creative Music Technology at Staffordshire University, I constructed a semi-autonomous electromechanical lithophone. Throughout the first couple of years of my degree I had developed an interest in the disciplines of musique concrete, DIY electronics, and acousmatic music, as well as the work of pioneering composers such as Pierre Schaeffer, Karlheinz Stockhausen and John Cage. Prior to building the lithophone I had explored this interest, in part, by building a series of autonomous musical devices, including an electromechanical glockenspiel, an autonomous lap steel slide guitar, and a robotic plotter that would plot pictures generatively on a sheet in response to real time musical input.

Shortly before starting to make plans for my final dissertation project I happened to see the documentary Heima, which followed the post-rock band Sigur Rós on their 2006 tour of Iceland. In one scene the band is shown searching through a vast swathe of rocks that appear to have fallen from a hillside, occasionally stopping to tap individual stones and listen to the sound they made. The four band members are then seen in a cave with the rocks they found arranged on a frame before they tentatively begin playing a beautiful composition with their new instrument. This was the first time I had encountered a lithophone and I was spellbound.

Almost instantly the idea formed that I should try and construct a lithophone that was capable of autonomously "playing itself". As I researched the history of the lithophone I became increasingly fascinated by the idea of exploring the affordances of this most ancient of instruments if applied to the comparatively modern, and decidedly experimental, concepts of aleatoric composition, musical spatialisation and DIY electronics. I was particularly interested in how the construction of a robotic apparatus that could facilitate autonomous performance would open a wealth of musically spatialised performance opportunities.

Conventionally, a lithophone, like a xylophone, glockenspiel or marimba, has individual tone bars arranged on a frame in a chromatic keyboard formation, to be played using beaters. This means the lithophone is spatially limited, needing to be wholly in the reach of the player or players, with listeners perceiving the sound as emanating from a single point source, particularly if heard from a distance. In contrast, having a lithophone in which the only limitation on the position of individual notes would be the length of cable you could acquire, would bring about a wealth of new performative and compositional

Figure 16.8. Jay Harrison.

possibilities. The relationship between the positioning of the instrument(s), the listener(s), and the acoustic properties of the performance space could then take on a new importance.

So, I set about creating the electromechanical lithophone with those principles in mind. The result was a two octave chromatic lithophone equipped with an Arduino microcontroller with a series of rotary solenoids to enable fully autonomous performance. It was also possible for musicians to play the lithophone in real time using a midi keyboard. When fully spread out the individual notes covered a diameter of approximately 10 metres, allowing listeners to step inside the instrument and experience spatialised compositions that surrounded them.

The lithophone was constructed from North Wales green slate which was obtained from a slate company located close to the sites of the three Aberllefenni slate quarries: Foel Grochan, Hen Gloddfa, and Ceunant Ddu. Interestingly, despite the company's yard harbouring a vast collection of slate sourced from all over North Wales, the small collection of slate that I used for my lithophone was all I was able to find which possessed any discernible resonance.

After completing my dissertation, I went on to spend the following year exhibiting my electromechanical lithophone as an installation at various festivals, museums and galleries. My fondest memory from this time was probably the two weeks it spent at the National Slate Museum in Llanberis, where visitors were able to listen to and interact with the instrument in the cavernous beauty of the old quarry forge.

## Sylvain van Iniitu - Belgium

I'm not exactly sure how I first came across the *Stones* score by Christian Wolff, but it was probably around 2015. A year or two earlier, I had organized an improvisation workshop at the hospital where I worked, in Brussels, inviting Alan Courtis to lead it. This workshop primarily focused on using graphical scores or tools to inspire creativity and reduce the pressure on virtuosity, encouraging a more interpretative and less restrictive approach to performance.

Around that time I also read Alvin Lucier's book *Reflections*, exploring, as his work often does, the physical properties of sound and space, which resonated with my growing interest in open and visual scores. While exploring more such books from the same publisher, I discovered *Cues*, a book about Christian Wolff. In *Cues*, his piece *Stones* is mentioned and discussed, piquing my interest further. By then, I had also delved into Daniel Goode's *Frog Peak Rock Music Book* and in 2016 I obtained a copy of the score of *Stones*.

*Figure 16.9. Sylvain van Iniitu.*

After the hospital workshop ended, we relocated all the instruments and recording equipment to a barn in the countryside, where we began organizing regular improvisation sessions known as the E42.A8 sessions. In November 2016, we seized an opportunity to record some performances of *Stones* with a few friends. One notable session took place at a megalith in Brunehaut, a nearby village; a perfect way to connect with my own history, having grown up in that region. The bigger history spanning thousands of years, the new connections with music and friends and overseas connecting through scores. It was a particularly cold day and some young people passing by wondered what we were doing: you can hear them in the recording, asking us what exactly we were. Our "Camoufleur" moment. Our interest in stones wasn't just musical, it was also deeply connected to the geological surroundings: the studio for the E42.A8 sessions is situated in a semi-industrial zone, home to the largest open-pit stone mine in Europe.

As the 50th anniversary of the *Stones* score approached we thought our winter recording would be a fitting starting point for a compilation. I invited other musicians to contribute their versions, welcoming all variations: solo, duo, group, hi-fi, or lo-fi. That's how we got contributors as diverse as Brecht Ameel, Alan Courtis, Gregory Büttner and Goh Lee Kwang to participate. Wolff's score, with just a few lines, offers plenty of room for improvisation, interpretation, and even misinterpretation. The compilation, made available on Bandcamp, exceeded our expectations in showcasing this potential. The diverse contributions demonstrated how the inherent properties of stones - density, texture, size - can influence sound in a myriad of ways. And then, of course, back to my hospital roots, there is the place of interpretation at play.

Later, I proposed holding a concert for the 50th anniversary of the score at the mining site, thinking it would be a perfect homage to both the musical and geological significance of stones. The idea was declined. Headz aint ready.

*Figure 16.10. Sylvain van Iniitu; Brunehaut megalith.*

# The New Stone Age

*Figure 16.11. Terje Isungset's musical stones.*

## Terje Isungset - Norway

I first started using stone as part of my developing interest in what I call natural instruments. This goes back to the late eighties or early nineties when I was a regular drummer playing Gretsch and Sonor drum kits, but beginning to feel I didn't have anything new to contribute to music that wasn't already being done. There were so many good drummers around that I wanted to search for something else and this led me to reject all the accepted rules of music, and only work with expression and body balance, trying to become part of the instrument.

I started to tune my drums differently, thinking more about the tone, the different sound qualities I was finding. This was when I was first getting into free improvisation, also working with the trio Utla, along with Karl Seglem and Håkon Høgemo, and I wanted to expand the variety of sounds I was using. Too many people wanted their drum kit to sound like Steve Gadd or Tony Williams or someone else. I wanted to get away from those references. I began to make things from wood and I got some bells from my parents' barn - we used to have sheep there. I was seeking out things in Norwegian nature at a time when everyone else seemed to be searching for music or instruments from other continents. So using stone came out of this

*Figure 16.12. Terje Isungset. Photograph © Knut Bry.*

and I remember one of the first occasions I used them was at a concert I did with Karl inside a mountain in Sogn, in the west of Norway.

I like working with natural sound, and in doing that I trust nature and I also believe in art by accident. I don't want to construct instruments, I just want to find them, or maybe the instruments find me. I remember one occasion when I had flown back to Norway after playing in England and a piece of granite I'd taken with me had broken in transit. A couple of weeks later I went on holiday with my family up in the mountains, close to the Jotunheimen glacier. We had been walking, but after a while my youngest daughter didn't want to walk any further, so we stopped to make some food. That year there was very little snow and we could see more of the stones there and my daughter began playing with them. Suddenly we heard a loud "ping" coming from one of the stones. So I took it back home with me and I was able to replace the broken one. The stone had found me!

Now, once again I am again focusing very much on stones. I've done a couple of recordings recently based on natural instruments and stones in particular, exploring the contrast between stone and electronic sound. As part of that I've started to work with slates. I don't tune them, but they all have their own natural tuning and I like to use that. The current plan is to go to Otta, in Gudbrandsdal, where they have a lot of slate and we're going to produce a slate symphony for a festival.

These days I use stone in most of the concerts I give and I'm still learning more about the different ways it can be played, depending on how it is hit and what is used to strike it, but I never try to change its natural sound. Recently I have started a deeper investigation into the qualities of the natural materials I particularly favour using - stones, wood and ice. As part of this project I'm recording with guitarist Eivind Aarset and trumpeter Arve Henriksen and I'll be playing a range of drums and percussion, but there will be a focus on stone. I collect stones all the time now and have many of them. Each stone has its own sound.

# Music Stones

*Figure 16.13. Will Menter. Lithovortex.*

## Will Menter - France

Stony moments

1986 Mount Snowdon, North Wales

The first stones I used for musical purposes came from an enormous hole in the ground, the Llanberis quarry, right next to Mount Snowdon. I was given a block of slate, quite irregular in form, about 30cm long, 10cm wide and 8cm thick. It weighed less than 10kg and was a pinkish shade of grey, which I later found out was called heather red. I asked the quarryman who gave it to me to split it into thin sheets around 5mm thick. Each one was a slightly different thickness and by chance, when I tested their sounds, the seven pieces played a harmonious scale which outlined a C ninth chord. Starting from D in the middle of the bass clef, the scale rose through E, G, Bb, C, D and E. I made a plywood stand to support the slates and mounted plastic resonating tubes beneath them to bring out the warmth of their fundamental tone. I named my new instrument a llechiphone, from the Welsh word for slate.

# THE NEW STONE AGE

*Figure 16.14. Will Menter. To hear the world in a grain of stone.*

All the other slates from this enormous hole in the ground had been used to roof the factories of the early industrial revolution in the north of England and for thousands of houses, some of it being shipped as far away as Chile.

1989 Rain Songs

Back at home near Bristol, I took several llechiphones into the garden to photograph them under a tree. It started to rain and I noticed what a beautiful sound the big drips filtered by the tree made when they hit the slate.

1990 Can Y Graig - Slate Voices

By now I had made an ensemble of about ten llechiphones and I wanted to make a concert that honoured the history of the slate industry and resonated strongly by being performed in the quarries themselves and I looked at slate as a subject for a series of songs. I worked with poet Gwyn Thomas and singer Sianed Jones to realise this project.

1998 Sound sculptures

After moving to live in Burgundy, France, I continued to source my slate from North Wales but also from the Tarn and the Pyrenees. My objects became sculptures that had their own characters and were no longer directed at being played by musicians to interpret pieces of music. Many explored the sounds of slates scraping against each other, either horizontal close to the ground or hanging vertically on wires.

I also collected many small slate pieces from a beach in North Wales that had been rounded by the action of the sea. Their sound was still bright and I drilled a small hole in them, attached a string and then dragged them across stone or concrete floors, making an instrument that also expressed the texture of a place.

2017 and later

Always trying to go deeper into the sound of stone as elemental matter I made installations with heavy rounded river stones found in the Durance. Stones with a history of descending from the mountain, pushed by water and ice, a long way from the industrial history of my slates. I also made 5 metre tall pendulum structures that used some of these river stones juxtaposed with slate. This I called *Inhabitation*.

Most recently I have been using flat stones from the Massif Central. These are stones that are also used for roofing. They are harder and thicker than slate but some of them have a bell-like musical resonance. The local name for them is Lauzes. With them I have made a sculptural structure that the public can enter, two at a time, so that the sounds of the colliding stones vibrate as close as 3 or 4 centimetres from their ears. This one I have called *Hear a World in the Grain of Stone*, echoing William Blake from over 200 years ago.

2024

Now, looking back, I redefine my life-path. Starting from contemporary jazz, moving through sound sculpture I have often not known what to call myself. The best fit at the moment seems to be "Orchestrator of Matter".

*Figure 16.15. Ruskin Rocks. Project led by Bobbie Miller.*

## Bobbie Millar - UK

My interest in musical stones began after a conversation with landscape painter David Walker Barker in 2001, during the merger of Bretton Hall College with the University of Leeds. He wanted to meet geologists to learn more about the land he was painting. My role in the university was to help staff from different disciplines to meet in order to stimulate novel interdisciplinary projects. My own background was in arts education, particularly dance and music. We assembled a group of geologists and artists to explore the changing landscape from their different viewpoints and decided to create opportunities for artists and scientists to work together in local quarries. In 2003 Yorkshire Quarry Arts was formed.

Murray Mitchell, a retired palaeontologist, introduced us to the huge Keswick musical stones, Joseph Richardson's 'Rock, Bell and Steel Band'. Murray was involved with the first project to help find quarries in the Yorkshire Dales which were both accessible, interesting geologically and artistically and had potential for ringing stone. Over the years we visited a range of quarried landscapes, providing fantastic opportunities for engaging artists, scientists, musicians and engineers with the quarrying communities and to communicate to the public what amazing inspiring and educative places they were. These projects were funded mainly through competitive schemes (such as DEFRA'S Aggregates Levy Sustainability Fund and Arts Council England) plus huge in-kind support from the aggregates industry.

From 2003 to 2024 we worked with many schools, museums, communities and quarry companies, focusing particularly on the ringing properties of different types of rocks. Why did some rocks ring well whereas others did not? How could you spot ringing rocks in quarries and the neighbouring hillsides? How could you make a piece of rock sound better? We started making instruments from found or discarded rocks and then from boulders which could be sawn into regular bars to create perfect pitch.

Our most ambitious project was the development of both a four octave chromatic lithophone, which we called the Brantwood Musical Stones, and a hybrid interactive lithophone, the iRock. They were designed by Dr Kia Ng with the geological input being led by Professor Bruce Yardley, both from the University of Leeds, and the two instruments were created for the Ruskin Rocks project, involving a large number of schools in the Lake District and musicians interested in stone instruments. The Brantwood Musical Stones and the iRock were launched in 2010 at Brantwood, once John Ruskin's home on the edge of Coniston Water, by Dame Evelyn Glennie, who was also involved in the design. The Brantwood Musical Stones, which incorporated four different rock types from the region were on display at Brantwood for ten years and in September 2024 were relocated to the Yamaha Music School in Northumberland. The iRock instrument, created out of fourteen different rocks with a visual display to show the geology and technology of the ringing bars, remains at Brantwood.

*Figure 16.16. Bobbie Miller. Photograph of Bobbie Millar by CS Millar.*

In time Quarry Arts continued as an independent company to engage with new communities and organisations to create musical instruments from stones quarried in the Lake District, Yorkshire Dales and Lancashire. The first of these was the 2014 two octave chromatic Kirkby Blue Slate instrument in Clitheroe Castle Museum. The most fun were probably the 2018 Pentatonic Picnic Benches created from 4 different types of rock for primary schools in the Yorkshire Dales. Another lithophone, the 2019 Horton limestone set at Horton-in-Ribblehead station on the Settle-Carlisle Line, has had a huge amount of positive written feedback from hundreds of surprised walkers and travellers. A magical-sounding instrument, built using limestone from Stainton Quarry, was specially tuned for Tom Lydon's *Lithophone Concerto* for the Yorkshire Dales National Park Authority and Grassington Festival in 2015. Particularly useful are the Portable Pentatonic Sets for use in schools, with one having been specially created for Cliffe Castle Museum in 2022. Quarry Arts also brought to life the 1905 Phillipson Musical Stones at Cliffe Castle Museum for the public to play.

# THE NEW STONE AGE

*Figure 16.17. Tony di Napoli. Photograph: from the Fête de la préhistoire, Musée de l'Homme. © MNHN J.C.Domenech.*

## Tony di Napoli - France

I studied sculpture at the Academy of Fine Arts St Luc in Liège, Belgium from 1989 to 1991 and stone soon became my favourite material. After I left there, in parallel with my visual art work, I became interested in the sound characteristics of stone. At first my creations were mainly sound stone sculptures of various shapes and thicknesses, suspended stones and engraved stones. Later their design and production evolved to them becoming musical instruments in their own right, music approached through the medium of acoustic physics.

In 2002, with a grant from the SPES Belgium foundation and the support of musicologist Professor Tran Van Khê, I spent eight months in Vietnam studying prehistoric Vietnamese lithophones. In Ho Chi Minh City, I was trained by musicologist The Viên in the art of tuning stones. This opened up new horizons for me, sound became another aspect of sculpture, to be perceived not only with the ears but also with the body.

In 2004 I travelled to Italy, Switzerland, France and Vietnam to meet visual artists and musicians working with sounding stones and three years later, In 2007, in collaboration with art historian Florence Fréson, I organised the event " Un rêve de pierre» as part of Luxembourg's Cultural Capital of Europe programme, featuring exhibitions, concerts and conferences on sounding stone, in various locations including the Museum Schloss Fellenberg, in Merzig, Germany, Neumünster Abbey in Luxembourg and the Museum of Modern and Contemporary Art in Liège, Belgium.

I often perform in concerts with my lithophones, solo or with other musicians and dancers, in various countries including France, Italy, Switzerland, Belgium, Luxembourg, Holland, Germany, Denmark, Poland and Vietnam. Sound installations of mine which incorporate lithophones can be found in the Klankenbos space at Musica Impulscentrum voor Muziek Neerpelt, Belgium, the MAMAC, Liège and the Ferme du Vinatier in Lyon, France.

The stone I use to make my lithophones is a limestone from Belgium, a sedimentary rock dating from the Lower Carboniferous period and composed of 99% calcite.

My current instrumental set, called the lithophone TDN, is made up of several oblong stone blades of varying dimensions from 20 cm to 110 cm long and 15 cm wide; discs from 55 cm to 100 cm in diameter and half-discs measuring 100 cm in diameter. All these stones are 2 cm thick and are placed on wooden resonance boxes. Depending on the project, they are tuned in equal temperament or in micro-intervals, quarter, ninth, up to sixteenths of a tone. They are set in vibration by percussion using mallets or by the friction of superballs. Since 2010 I have also been developing audio-visual work in which sounding stones are set in vibration using an electronic device.

### Nguyen Minh Ngiệp - Vietnam

In 2002, when I was in my early twenties I heard some people in my neighbourhood talking about the discovery, in the area he was from, of a set of stone instruments dating back around two thousand years. I decided that it would give me great pleasure if I could build such an instrument, so I invited a few interested people to help me collect some suitable rocks. Sometimes we searched long in the hot sun with no luck but I was not discouraged and when I did find good rocks it made me feel very happy. To strike a stone bar and hear it resonating is an indescribable feeling. It's not a normal sound, it seems to go straight to the heart.

I spent ten years looking for rocks around the mountain area of Tuy An, in the southern, coastal region of Vietnam and since that time I have built more than twenty instruments. I make them to modern tuning, the same as a piano or a keyboard, though there was one set which I didn't tune at all. They each have between twelve and twenty bars, all with different tonal qualities. To begin with I tuned my lithophones purely by ear, but later I bought a tuner, when I heard there were such things, but it still takes a full month to build each set. To perform publicly with these instruments takes even more time, preparing the music, teaching the musicians and recording a backing track, though sometimes when we play we have all the musicians playing live.

Some years ago I opened a heritage centre in the Tuy An district where I display different domestic artefacts, which I call the Ancient Soul Centre. I have my lithophones there and visitors can hear them being played. I have also worked with young people, showing them how to play the instrument and perform well known Vietnamese songs. In April 2024 my instruments made an appearance at the Festival of Bands in Phú Yên Province. There in the bustling town square, when people heard the the deep resonance of the stones it seemed to touch their hearts. Tuy Hòa's ocean waves are abundant, the sea breeze is strong and the sound of stone instruments adds to the flavour of our home place, weaving magical, unique melodies, like the voices of ancestors echoing back to us.

Many people, from Vietnam and abroad, have visited the Ancient Soul Centre, but it's not easy to keep such a place going from a commercial point of view. I have to find different ways of making a living through selling drinks, snacks and souvenirs to visitors, but that doesn't bring in much income, especially outside the tourist season. But my stone instruments are the most important things to me and I hope to get more support from the authorities, other experts and also from the media in my efforts to promote their heritage. The Central South provinces of Khán Hòa, Phú Yên, Binh Thuan and Ninh Thuan, plus the Central Highlands provinces of Lam Dong and Dak Lak, are considered the home of stone instruments, offering opportunities for further development. In recent years more attention has been paid in the tourism sector to the significance of stone instruments in these regions and my hope is to help spread this interest further, sharing with others my love and admiration for the ancient, enchanting sound of stone instruments, perhaps opening a museum. By bringing together musicians, bands, dancers and craft-workers, and offering training to participate in cultural and artistic programmes including the importance of stone instruments, we can show pride in our ancestors and attract tourists from afar.

## Music Stones

*Figure 16.18. Nguyen Minh Ngiệp. Photograph Thuy Van Nguyen*

*Figure 16.19. Pietro Pirelli*

## Pietro Pirelli - Italy

Il Suono Liberato

I have been playing the stones since 2003 and since then I have never stopped exploring their sound universe; composing musical pieces for these sculptures, putting them in dialogue with instruments and voices. I alternate inharmonious sounds with defined pitches, so I have material to articulate a musical narrative, a timbral/harmonic counterpoint with the other musicians.

I have a rich sound material at my disposal. Using an internal microphone I never cease to be amazed at the tonal range which can be produced from this hard material. There are light rustles, high-pitched hisses, metallic noises, harsh sound flows and other muffled sounds. Using the bow I enter the cuts of Pinuccio Sciola's stones and discover the flute sounds for Biber's *Passacaglia*, and in the large basalt sculptures I find deep bass tones. Without the electric sensors I would not be able to produce those low sustained sounds, barely audible and heard more with the abdomen than with the ear; entering into feedback with the subwoofer they resonate even more. These low sounds are produced with curved stones weighing several hundred kilos. I sustain these sounds with a double bass bow and also by pulling many metres of packing tape as I walk backwards through the audience.

MUSIC STONES

*Figure 16. 20 Pietro Pirelli*

I have never recorded a CD with this material as I can't imagine the sound of the stones separated from the presence of the performer, from the poetic quality of seeing them being played and from their sheer beauty. I called this musical journey of mine "suono liberato"; not only because the amplification has the effect of freeing the inaudible, but because to make the stones sing you have to know how to treat them. They lie heavy on the ground and we have to allow them to levitate.

The stone is only partly percussion: it is also a chorus of sound bands generated by sliding stone against stone or even by sliding one's bare hands over the chessboard of keys of Pinuccio Sciola's limestone sculptures; from deep grooves dug out with a diamond blade I draw very sharp clusters of sound. I called one of these sound sculptures *Ligeti*. Without going into detail about how I find a fine sound I will simply say that just as we recognize people by their voice, so every stone carries with it its geological identity. Basalt, for example, reminds us of its ancestral volcanic history and the variations in its density remind us how many air molecules remained trapped in the solidifying lava. By playing the stones that I collect in the river and sculpt them appropriately, the flow of water returns. The white marble of Trani Cathedral has a luminous sound. The voice of the white stones of Aphrodite's beach in Cyprus is extraordinary: one beating against the other produces a powerful sound capable of being projected for hundreds of metres.

I began playing stone a few months after meeting Pinuccio Sciola, the great sculptor of sound stone. As a trained percussionist, I have always made sounds from different objects, but without this encounter I would never have imagined that this hard stone could sing so sweetly.

He is the one who taught me to caress the stones. We became friends and collaborated for a long time. Over time I also built my own stone tools and later I collaborated with Giancarlo Sangregorio, a very elderly sculptor who, before leaving us, wanted to try to include the sonic dimension in his artistic creation. We sculpted soapstone from the Italian-Swiss mountains - and what a sound!

I have played the Sound Stones, mine and Sciola's, in so many different contexts: concerts, ballet, theatre, live installations and also accompanying films including a screening of the film *La Roue* by Abel Gance. So many possibilities for wonderful research, which I continue to cultivate.

*Figure 16.21. Sound of Stone 1 Matevž Bajde and Franci Krevh*

## Sound of Stone 1

### Franci Krevh and Matevž Bajde - Slovenia

**Sound of Stone** is a music and sculpting project made in cooperation between the Slovene Percussion Project (Franci Krevh & Matevž Bajde) and sculptress Alenka Vidrgar.

Stone is not just an aesthetic or visual element, nor just an origin of sound; it is a synergy of the visual and the sonic because the project links sculpting and music and opens up new ways in visual art and music. The sculptress and the percussionists explored together and spent a lot of time in stone quarries and studio, tracing the sound of stone. The results are thrilling. **Sound of Stone** is an innovative project reflecting the complementary nature of the arts of music and sculpting. It is also interactive: the sculptures are equipped with mallets, allowing visitors to create their own music and to hear the stone.

The sound of the stone is really very special for us (classical) percussionists. Let us describe the sound of the lithophone: the initial stroke is like a xylophone, but the sound sustains more like a vibraphone.

To popularize the sound of stone, we organized three international festivals (2020, 2021, 2022), where we brought the sound of stone to a wider audience.

The **Sound of Stone** project is alive, which means that new stone sculptures and new compositions are created, based on needs.

We are primarily interested in presenting stone at concert venues, which is why four compositions were created in active collaboration with renowned Slovenian composers:

Pavel Mihelčič: *Green Field* and *Red Soil*

Tilen Slakan: *Awakening* (for trumpeter and two percussionists playing stones)

Blaž Rojko: *Stones – I'm calling you* (for vocals and 2 percussionists on stones)

Bojana Šaljič Podešva: *The Power of Stone* (sound story for children, narrator and two percussionists on stones and other instruments)

## Music Stones

### Sound of Stone 2

### Alenka Vidrgar - Slovenia

In 2016, musicians Franci Krevh and Matevž Bajde and I searched for Slovenian stones for the production of fine sound stone sculptures and instruments. Only in the quarry in Lipica were

*Figure 16.22. Sound of Stone 2 Sound stone bench by Alenka Vidrgar*

we able to find stone with such an excellent sound quality as the Lipica Unito there. We were really impressed and fascinated by the sound of our Slovenian stone.

I ordered the stone and then produced all the necessary concert sound sculptures. Particularly special are two large stone bells, in which I emphasized the sound of stone with a waviness on the surface of the of the shaped stone – affecting both the purity and the length of the sound.

The sound sculpture we call *Star Wars* is unique in that it is cut to the limits of the load-bearing capacity of the stone and its low tones are a distinctive feature. *The Meditation Tower*, sounding as if it comes from deep space or from the depths of the sea, immediately won me over. I really could not stop caressing it with circular motions over its finely sculpted surface. In my opinion you could call it "pure meditation between hand movement and the sound that arises".

Each individual piece was unique and what was required at that time. Gaining an understanding of the stone we had found helped me, as the sculptor, to make the first series of sounding pieces successful. Of course I was also using my ample and rich sculpting experience to really help me produce what proved to be a very successful first series of "our singing stones".

I realized that its sound quality is hidden in the fine sedimentary layers of our stone and I've thought there are similarities to using wood, in which the rings and growth of a tree are

*Figure 16.23. Alenka Vidrgar*

important for the sound. To order a stone, it is essential to see the stone at the quarry, to check its sound quality by striking the block of stone. Defects can be hidden within the block: poorly compressed layers, impurities, holes, etc. The sound quality of the stone is hidden and I check it while it's still in the caverns, where it is cut from the core of the stone wall hundreds of meters deep below the surface of the earth. The way the marine layers have twisted or wrinkled over a thousand years of being deposited affect the resulting sedimentary stone block. Loading directions are the law of cutting.

Slovenia does not have volcanic rocks, but we do have large enough uniform blocks of stone to make my big sounding sculptures. I made the first public stone sounding sculpture for the memorial to the fallen and missing in World War I. With one strike, the stone bell sounds, and with the sound we remember and pay tribute to the fallen.

The second sounding monument was erected on the occasion of the thirtieth anniversary of Slovenia's independence. It strikes with three large differently tuned stone bells. For the park in the Karst, I also made the *Sounding Stone Bench*, where you sit on the wood and play the stone (pictured). The Museum of Natura Karst stores most of the first works. They are on display and you can try out the sounds. Let the sound of stone fascinate many more.

# The new stone age

*Figure 16.24. Jesse Stewart Photograph © Nate Storring*

### Jesse Stewart - Canada

I learned about the musical properties of stone by accident. In 1998, I happened to come across a stack of marble slabs in a used building-supply store. The pieces were three-feet long, two-and-a-half inches wide, and three-eighths of an inch thick. Although I couldn't think of any use for the marble at the time, I thought it might come in handy someday, so I purchased the lot for fifteen dollars.

Carrying the marble to my car, I inadvertently dropped and broke one piece. I noticed that the two stone fragments I was left with yielded different pitches when struck. This made me wonder if these strips of marble could be cut and tuned to different pitches. It turned out they could: over the next three months, I cut and tuned ninety-seven marble bars using an electric hand-drill and several carbide-coated rotating disks.

I began by making two octaves tuned to the Western chromatic scale between 293.7 Hz (a "D" by Western standards) and 1174.8 Hz (a D two octaves above). Having a substantial amount of marble left over, I decided to move into the realm of microtones, subdividing the chromatic intervals into quarter-tones, thereby yielding a total of forty-nine bars. Still left with some marble, I subdivided the pitches again into eighth-tones for a total of 97 bars. This eighth-tone grid allows me to approximate any pitch within the range of the instrument to a maximum deviation of 12.5 cents. A tuning discrepancy of 12.5 cents would not be acceptable in many musical contexts or on many instruments, but the spectral complexity of stone bars of uniform thickness makes it tolerable (to my ears at least).

Ninety-seven pieces of marble proved to be too cumbersome for transportation or performance. So, I generally select a subset of pitches to approximate different tuning systems. This has meant that any sort of fixed mounting device for the stone bars would be impractical. I found that small foam supports positioned at the nodal points of each bar (which are located at 0.224 times the length of each bar) allow the bars to vibrate relatively freely. This system allows me to set up the instrument quickly on virtually any flat surface and affords a variety of spatial configurations. I rarely set the stone bars up in the usual fashion of lowest to highest from left to right. Rather, I generally set them up in a *tonnetz* or tone lattice, which enables me to explore different harmonic configurations through composition and improvisation.

In the decades since I made that first stone instrument, I have made several other lithophones out of a variety of stone types including granite, schist, slate, and even ice (which, oddly enough, meets most mineralogical definitions of stone). I have found that stone drill core samples are an inexpensive and relatively plentiful source of sonorous stones that have the added benefit of allowing for a variety of playing techniques and timbres (in addition to striking them, they can be scraped or rolled). Many of these stone instruments consist of sets of found stones and, by extension, found tuning systems. But, on occasion, I still get out my hand drill and carbide discs to tune stones to particular pitches.

Figure 16.25. Stone Alphabet. Photograph © Matthias Brodbeck

## The Stone Alphabet - Switzerland

Matthias Brodbeck and Dominik Dolega

In 1991, during the National Research Exhibition "Heureka", Professor Walter M. Meier from ETH Zurich proposed creating music from stones through mechanical impact. This idea inspired a team at ETH to explore resonant stones. They discovered the ideal stone: sturdy, finely structured, and resonating with clarity. Their research led to the creation of a unique instrument, which became a focal point of curiosity at the "Heureka" exhibition.

The sounds produced by these stones ranged from crystal-clear chimes to deep, lingering bass tones, fuelling the Lithophone Project's exploration. The focus then shifted from analyzing the

*Figure 16.26. The Stone Alphabet Matthias Brodbeck and Dominik Dolega*

acoustic properties of different stones to integrating them into modern music and developing innovative prototypes. This resulted in a range of instruments that embodied both creativity and scientific precision.

In response to a desire amongst musicians to explore the sonic potential of stone, the first "Litonart" instrument was created in 1999 in collaboration with Swiss percussionist Felix Perret. Built using marimba-like construction principles, it allowed direct interaction with the stone. The instrument, even in its prototype stage, was notable for its range, tuning, accessibility, and versatility.

In 2014, inspired by Felix Perret's vision, we formed "The Stone Trio" to explore the ancient and mysterious sounds of resonant stones. The vast array of instruments, coupled with the primal power of the stones, captivated us from the start. Each stone reacts uniquely to different playing techniques and materials, revealing a rich tapestry of possibilities and inviting deeper listening. This fascination with the world's oldest instruments is what we seek to share with the world.

In addition to performing, we initiated symposiums to create a network of musicians, instrument makers, and composers focused on stone sound music. In 2018, "The Stone Trio" expanded to include composer Mathias Steinauer as a keyboardist, evolving into the quartet "The Stone Alphabet". Since then, we have performed in the following line-up:

Dominik Dolega: Lithophone & Percussion
Mathias Steinauer: Keyboards
Felix Perret: Lithophone & Percussion
Matthias Brodbeck: Lithophone & Percussion

Through our music, we aim to transport listeners into a unique sonic universe where silence is as powerful as sound. Our compositions weave together intricate soundscapes, inviting audiences to experience a lyrical tapestry of sonic marvels. What distinguishes "The Stone Alphabet" are our unconventional instruments. We blend familiar sounds with the ethereal beauty of stone using instruments like the Orgalitho, Fender Rhodes, lithophones, stone gongs, and more. Our "alphabet" includes quarter-tone clavinets, stone tables, stone bells, handheld stones, gongs, drums, MIDI keyboards, and many other sound generators. Alongside Professor Meier's lithophones, we primarily use stone sound instruments crafted by Swiss instrument maker Beat Weyeneth. Our projects and concerts often feature artists from various genres such as classical music, free improvisation, jazz, dance, and performance art, creating unique connections and experiences.

Personal Statements:

Dominik Dolega: *Since my first encounter with the 5-octave lithophone in 2007, I was captivated by its timbre and overtone play. The range of sounds it could produce was far richer than on a marimba or vibraphone. Over time, I expanded the stone instrument collection, bringing the stones to life. Collaborating with various artists and exploring new sound combinations allowed me to discover previously unknown sonic realms.*

Matthias Brodbeck: *First coming across resonant stones in 2014, I began to experiment with combining stones with other percussion instruments like gongs and drums and have continued to do so. Today, I primarily use serpentinite stone slabs on a bass drum, using the drum as a resonating body. The vibrations and blends of sound, from subtle textures to powerful tones, move me deeply in every performance and drive me to explore new soundscapes and techniques.*

*Figure 16.27. Christian Wolff Photograph © Kelly Burgess*

## Christian Wolff - USA

My own involvement with stones has been making the prose instruction piece *Stones* (1968). The result of a morning at a beach which had more stones than sand. Having not much to do I found myself trying out the sounds various stones made when struck together. I also remembered Cornelius Cardew's use of stones in Paragraph I of his *The Great Learning*, a title that referred to a text by Confucius. Cornelius knew that ancient Chinese classical music used tuned stones.

Since then I sometimes call for the use of found stones by percussion players (e.g. *Percussionist*, 2000).

In general, I don't think of stones as instruments (say, with fixed pitches) but as sound sources.

*Figure 16.28. Rockenspiel by Gayle Young*

## Gayle Young - Canada

Listening to Stones

Typical summer pastimes for our family include skipping stones at a beach and decorating sand sculptures. In this setting, stones are reliable playthings but not exactly toys. During a summer afternoon on a Newfoundland beach I tested some water-washed blue and pink slate stones for audible resonance, and they responded.

Imagine that a stone may be similar to a xylophone bar, where each bar is attached to a frame at approximately one quarter of its length. This part of any vibrating material is called a node, a stable zone where resonance is not reduced. As I held each stone at that spot, between thumb and finger, I tapped it with another stone. It would vibrate if it wasn't cracked and if its crystalline structure allowed it to resonate.

For me this was a turning point. I hadn't considered playing stones before that day, though the verb 'play' applies to both music and sand castles, and I was accustomed to playing *with* stones.

I assembled groups of resonant stones in rows on nearby picnic tables, the stones resting on sticks at their nodes: my first lithophone. (To create a similar instrument, identify the two 'nodes' of each stone, then create a support structure that allows you to hear the pitch within the sound.)

In the summer of 2017 I presented a group of indoor lithophones at the Bonavista Biennale, placing rows of stones on tables in the exhibition space that also housed my sound installation, *Cross-waves*, featuring the sounds of stones rolling back-and-forth in the waves along nearby shorelines. I invited visitors at the exhibition to play the lithophones with the sound installation, and during outdoor workshops I showed participants how to test different ways of supporting stones, try different options, and discover ways of holding a stone to allow it to vibrate.

*Figure 16.29. Gayle Young*

Soon after the Biennale I incorporated stones into my concerts, playing the stones as they lay on the strings of my instruments, yielding sounds of strings combined with stones. In a duo with composer James Harley, who specializes in live electroacoustic processing through multi-channel diffusion, I play the stones with fingers, bells, and hex bolts, among other objects. Heads of hex bolts are rolled over the stones, resulting in fast rhythmic sounds. Harley responds by spacialising the sound, expanding the resonance, and shaping the sound through electronic treatment, as the stones rock on the strings. Our album, *Lithophonica*, on Farpoint Recordings demonstrates our explorations.

# Bibliography

## Books

Aliffe, A. 2007. Rolling Out The Stones. Unpublished.

Barnes, J. 2006. Joseph Richardson (1790-1855) & Sons and the Famous Musical Stones of Skiddaw, in Foot, E. and P. Howell (eds) *Keswick Characters Vol 1*: 32-40. Carlisle: Bookcase.

Bingham, R. 1995. *Kendal - A social history.* Kendal: Cicerone Press.

Blades, J., E. Glennie and N. Percy. 2021. *Percussion instruments and their history.* London: Kahn & Averill.

Buzzarté, M. and T. Bickley (eds) 2012. *Anthology of essays on Deep Listening.* Kingston (NY): Deep Listening Publications.

Blom, E. 1975. *Everyman's Dictionary of Music.* London, Melbourne and Toronto: J M Dent & Company.

Cage, J. 1978. *Silence.* London: Marion Boyars

Cardew, C. 1974. *Stockhausen Serves Imperialism.* London: Latimer.

Carse, A. 1951. *The life of Jullien.* Cambridge: Heffer.

Cohen, D and B. Greenwood. 1981. *The Buskers, A history of street entertainment.* Newton Abbot: David & Charles.

Cooper, E. 1973. *A History of Swaledale.* Clapham (Yorkshire): Dalesman

Crosthwaite, P. (Friendly Traveller). 2018. *The Ensign of Peace.* London: Forgotten Books

Davies, J.Q. and E. Lockhart Ellen (eds). 2016. *Sound Knowledge: Music and Science in London 1789-1851.* Chicago and London: The University of Chicago Press.

Elkin, R. 1955. *The Old Concert Rooms of London.* London: Edward Arnold.

Fessmann, K. 2008. *KlangSteine.* Munich: Südwest Verlag/Random House.

Fagg, M.C. 1997. *Rock Music* Oxford: Pitt Rivers Museum.

Goode, D. (ed.) 1995. *The Frog Peak Rock Music Book.* Lebanon (NH): Frog Peak Music.

Gell, W. 2000. *A tour in the lakes 1797.* Otley: Smith Settle.

Glover, David. 2014. *The quarries of Lakeland.* Carlisle: Bookcase.

Griffiths, P. 1994. *Modern Music.* London: Thames and Hudson.

Hamilton, W.R., A.R. Wooley and A.C. BISHOP. *Minerals, Rocks and Fossils* London: Hamlyn1992.

Hankinson, A. 1988. *The Regatta Men.* Kendal: Cicerone Press.

Hepworth, B. 1970. *A Pictorial Autobiography.* Bath: Adams & Dart.

Keay, J. 1991. *The Honourable Company A history of the English East India Company.* London: Harper Collins.

Liess, A. 1966. *Carl Orff His life and his music.* London: Calder and Boyars.

Mills, J.W. 1985. *The Technique of Sculpture.* London: Batsford.

Nicholson, N. 1955. *The Lakers: The first tourists.* London: Robert Hale.

Nyman, M. 1999. *Experimental Music, Cage and Beyond.* Cambridge: Cambridge University Press.

Pearsall, R. 1973. *Victorian Popular Music.* Newton Abbot: David and Charles.

Pegg, B. 1976. *Folk - A portrait of English Traditional Music, Musicians and Customs.* London: Wildwood House.

Phillips, J.H. 2021. *The Rock, Bell and Steel Band, The story of Joseph Richardson and his musical stones.* John H. Phillips

Phillips, J.H. 2023. *The Richardsons of Applethwaite.* John H. Phillips

Sachs, C. 2006. *The History of Musical Instruments.* New York: Dover Publications.

Saville-Smith, K.J. 2018. *Provincial Society and Empire: The Cumbrian Counties and the East Indies, 1680-1829.* Martlesham: The Boydell Press.
Stuckenschmidt, H.H. 1969. *Twentieth Century Music.* London : Weidenfeld & Nicolson
Sutcliffe Smith, J. 1930. *The Music of the Yorkshire Dales.* Leeds: Richard Jackson.
Scott, D.B. 2008. *Sounds of the Metropolis.* Oxford: Oxford University Press.
Tilbury, J. 2008. *Cornelius Cardew (1936-1981) : a life unfinished.* Matching Tye (Essex): Copula.
Till, M. 2021. The Best Original Rock Band  A history of the Till Family Rock Band and their extraordinary rise to fame. Unpublished.
Toop, D. 2004. *Haunted Weather.* London: Serpent's Tail.
Wilson, D. 2007. Peter Crosthwaite (1735-1808), in Foot, E. and P. Howell (eds)    *Keswick Characters, volume 2*: 19-34 Carlisle: Bookcase.

## Articles and papers

Adcock, M. 2017. The Ancient Stone Instruments of Vietnam. *Time & Mind, The Journal of Archaeology, Consciousness and Culture* 10: 23-37
Ashton, D. 2006  On Constantin Brancusi.  *Raritan: A Quarterly Review 25:* 34
Brears, P. 1992. Commercial Museums of Eighteenth-Century Cumbria. *Journal of the history of collections.* 4:107–126
Fagg, B.E.B. 1956. The Discovery of Multiple Rock Gongs in Nigeria. *Man* 56  2: 16-18
Lynch, K. 2015. Patriotism and the picturesque on the shores of Lake Windermere c1797-1803. *Garden History 43  2  237-255 footnote 80*
Montagu, J. 2004. How old is music? *The Galpin Society Journal* 57:171-182

## Online references

The author's website devoted to the subject of lithophones documents their use in different parts of the world and contains information and photographs, plus links to audio and video recordings. https://lithophones.com
Adcock, M. 2023 Illustrated article with audio and video links. *The lost lithophones of Vietnam.* Accessed 4th April 2025 https://www.rootsworld.com/feature/lithophones-23.shtml
Adcock, M. 2017 *The ancient stone instruments of Vietnam*  Accessed 6th April 2025  https://www.tandfonline.com/doi/full/10.1080/1751696X.2016.1264112
Blackburn, P. 1995.  Article: *Voices of Vietnam.* Accessed 20th March 2023. https://www.rootsworld.com/rw/feature/vietnam2.html
Bohl, A-M.  Artist's website.  Accessed 6th October, 2024. https://annmargrethbohl.com
Brett, G.   Article on Peter Crosthwaite.  Accessed  4th November 2018.  https://www.beneaththebeaconinterpretation.com/peter-crosthwaite-read-more
British Newspaper Archive. Accessed 23rd April 2025. https://britishnewspaperarchive.co.uk
Corrias, A.  Article: *The mysterious world of Sardinian artist Pino Sciola.* Accessed 14th January 2025. https://www.sardinianplaces.co.uk/blog/the-mysterious-world-of-sardinian-artist-pino-sciola
Garcia-Roca, C. Article about Antonio Roca y Várez. Accessed 23rd October 2024.  https://garcia-roca.blogspot.com/2009/02/el-litofon-de-don-antoni-roca-varez.htm
Fraga, J.P. Article  on Antonio Roca y Várez by editor of Diario Menorca. Accessed  21st October 2024.    https://www.menorca.info/opinion/firmas-del-dia/2017/11/22/1337120/roca-varez-litofono-illa-colom.html

Geocurator (online archive Geological Curators Group newsletters). Correspondence about Richardson Rock Band. Accessed 14th May 2025. https://www.geocurator.org/images/resources/geocurator/vol2/geocurator_2_5.pdf  https://www.geocurator.org/images/resources/geocurator/vol2/geocurator_2_7.pdf

Granitzio, A. PhD dissertation, Birmingham City University: *Stone and Water in Sound: A Composition Portfolio Informed by the Natural Growth Process of Stalactites and Stalagmites.* Accessed 20th January 2025. https://www.open-access.bcu.ac.uk/6890/

Halliday, S. 2017 MA dissertation, University of Huddersfield: *Klangsteine. Exploring the sound stones of Hannes Fessmann.* Accessed 10th January 2025. https://stevenmhalliday.wixsite.com/stevenmhalliday

Kelman, J. 2005. Interview with Stephan Micus. Accessed 16th April 2025. https://www.allaboutjazz.com/musicians/stephan-micus

Klangsteine website. https://klangsteine.com  Accessed 16th February 2025.

Lahr Kultur. Local government website, with section on Elmar Daucher's sculpture. Accessed 24th April 2025. https://kultur.lahr.de/klangstein-4-198-von-daucher.137927.htm

Madden, Blake. Article: *Inside the Great Stalacpipe Organ: The World's Largest Musical Instrument.* Accessed 20th August 2024. https://sonicscoop.com/inside-great-stalacpipe-organ-worlds-largest-instrument/

Newspapers.com  USA newspaper archive. https://newspapers.com

Phillips, J.H. Website devoted to the Rock, Bell, and Steel Band. Accessed November 3rd 2023. https://richardsonrockband.com

Queen Victoria's journals. Containing diary entry for Rock, Bell, and Steel Band's appearance at Buckingham Palace. Accessed 19th February 2024. http://www.queenvictoriasjournals.org/home.do

Randall-Page, Peter. Artist's website. Accessed 16th May 2025. https://www.peterrandall-page.com/

Skjaerved, P.S. Article and information about Ivy Priaulx Rainier. Accessed 6th September 2024. https://www.peter-sheppard-skaerved.com/2009/11/priaulx-rainier/

Soden, O. Article: *Priaulx Rainier: Fearless and pioneering composer.* Accessed 6th September 2024. https://engelsbergideas.com/portraits/priaulx-rainier-fearless-and-pioneering-composer/

Stephens, G. Article: *The life and times of William Irwin 1822-1889*  https://www.mustrad.org.uk/articles/irwin.htm  Accessed 24th April 2025.

SWAAG (Swaledale and Arkengarthdale Archaeology Group) website, with various references to Keld musician Neddy Dick. https://swaag.org/  Accessed 6th May 2025.

Till, M. Website about the Till Family Rock Band. Accessed 17th April 2025.  www.michaeltill.com

Vaughan Williams Memorial Library. Edwin Irwin's correspondence with Anne Gilchrist. Accessed 3rd March 2025. https://www.vwml.org/search?q=Anne%20Gilchrist%20Irwin&is=1

Zbigowski, L.M. Article: *Music, Dance and Meaning in the Early Nineteenth Century.* Accessed 3rd July 2024. https://zbikowski.uchicago.edu/pdfs/Zbikowski_Music_dance_meaning_2012.pdf

# Index

A
Abraham family  110–116
Anderson, Mary  126
Anima  196
antediluvian piano  96, 99, 100
Antigonae  158, 160
Applethwaite  23, 41, 65, 147
Ardentes, Indre  96
Ashton, Dore  192, 193, 194
Australia  134
*A Variety of Rocks*  189
Aztec Lilliputians  135

B
Bach, Johann Sebastian  82, 95, 195, 222
Bajde, Matevž  242-244
Barnes, Jamie  x, 148
basalt  xiii, xiv, 149, 197, 204, 205, 206, 218, 219, 239, 240
Baudre, Honoré  96–109, 117, 129, 177, 209
Baugniet, Charles  57, 58
Bayonne, NJ  80, 86, 87, 91, 92, 93
Becker-Ehmck, Klaus  158–161, 166
Beethoven, Ludwig van  30, 43, 195
Belgium  xvii, 102, 225, 235, 236
Blades, James  54, 55, 58, 115, 159, 194, 216, 236
Blyth  6
Bohl, Ann-Margreth  196, 213, 214
Boucher de Perthes, Jacque  98, 99
Boulder, CO  162, 163, 211, 212
Bowe, William  34-36, 50, 110
Bozza, Carl  132, 138, 142, 143
Bozza Troupe  132, 138, 142, 143
Brancusi, Constantin  192, 193
Brantwood  16, 76, 77, 78, 148, 234
Brodbeck, Matthias  249-251
Brothers Wills  137, 138
Brown, D. Adna  90, 95, 184
Bryars, Gavin  181
Buckingham Palace  56, 57, 58, 135
Budworth, Joseph  12
Bunstone, Skylark  212

Byers, Norman  147, 148

C
Cage, John  106, 177, 183, 184, 191, 223
Canada  64, 81, 88, 95, 103, 104, 107, 108, 248, 254
Cardew, Cornelius  177–185, 253
Cardew, Michael  182
Castle, Roy  18, 75, 116, 234
Chamberlain, William  116
Chant, Michael  180, 182
Chautauqua  81, 84, 85, 91, 92
Chautauqua Institute  81, 84
Cheltenham  48, 49, 179, 180, 181
China  4, 53, 167
chlorite schist  219
circus  132, 133, 135, 136, 138, 140
Clarke, Reverend F.E.  79, 81
Coates, Albert  144, 145
Coleridge, Samuel Taylor  7, 12, 13
Condominas, Georges  166
Confucianism  178, 181
Confucius  179, 181, 182, 183, 253
Coniston  16, 76, 77, 78, 79, 148, 234
Costa, Sir Michael  46, 47, 56
Crichton, Ronald  181
Crombie, Lennox  120, 121
Crosthwaite family  1–23, 26, 28, 36, 38, 39, 40, 41, 50, 62, 76, 80, 112, 113, 146, 162
Crosthwaite Museum  1, 9, 11, 12, 13, 14, 15, 16, 17, 20, 26, 40, 62, 76
Crystal Palace  64, 72, 73, 76
Cumbria  7, 17, 29, 34, 49, 61, 65, 76, 87, 100, 147, 148
Cumpson, Helen  148, 149

D
Daucher, Elmar  196-199, 200, 201, 202, 203, 212
Davey, William  145-147
Davies, John  30, 32, 50, 64
Davis, Alexander  195
Derwentwater  7, 8, 148

Dick, Neddy 117–127, 164
Dieu Bang 173, 174
di Napoli, Tony x, 235
Doble, Jim 215, 216
Dolega, Dominik 249-251
Dvorak, Antonin 95, 151

E
East India Company 2, 3, 4, 5, 10
Edison, Thomas 84, 85, 86, 93
Elgar, Edward 95
Elterwater 37, 38, 39, 40
*The Ensign of Peace* 6, 14
experimental music xvii, 106, 177, 180, 181, 185, 187, 189

F
Fagg, Bernard xiii, 182
Fanque, Pablo 133, 134
Fassbender, Jochen 218–219
Favre, Pierre x, 203, 204
Fessmann, Hannes and Klaus 199–202
Fisher, Hannah 6, 16, 21, 26, 34, 38, 39, 62, 112
flint xvi, 96, 97, 98, 100, 101, 102, 103, 104, 106, 108, 109, 129
Fluxus 177
Forestié, Édouard 99, 101, 102
Forest, Louis 108
Four Jees xvii, 136
France 96, 103, 107, 108, 117, 138, 214, 230, 231, 235, 236
Fréchette, Louis 107
*Frog Peak Music* 187–189
Fuchs, Limpe 196
Fuchs, Paul 196

G
gamelan 5, 161, 163, 164, 166
Gatiérrez, Ignacio 128
Gell, William 11, 12
geological piano 96, 97, 98, 99, 101, 102, 103, 104, 107, 108
Germany 159, 196, 199, 202, 210, 218, 236
Gibson, Jon 187-188
Gilchrist, Anne 39, 40

glass 16, 50, 64, 82, 84, 138, 174, 189, 197, 216, 218
Glennie, Dame Evelyn 210, 234
Goode, Daniel 187, 225
Gould, Julia 58-61
Gounod, Charles 82
Grainger, Percy 54
granite 140, 148, 174, 197, 204, 216, 217, 228, 248
Granitzio, Andrea 203, 207–209
Gray, Thomas 7
*The Great Digest* 179–181
*The Great Learning* xii, 178, 179-183, 253
Great Stalacpipe Organ 152–158
Greenip, William 21, 38, 62
Greenup, Dorothy 39, 40
Greta 1, 16, 39, 87, 91
Gudmundsson, Páll x, 221-222
Gunung Padang xiii

H
Handel, George Frederick 30, 42, 45, 46, 54, 56, 70, 75, 95, 140, 195
Hanoi 167, 169, 170, 172, 174
Harmonic Solids 210
Harrison brothers 36, 110
Harrison, Jay 223–224
Hartford, CT 149, 150, 151, 152
Henderson family 65, 66, 70, 113, 114
Hepworth, Barbara 193–195, 213
Hilmarsson, Hilmar Örn 221
Ho Chi Minh City 169, 171, 173, 174, 235
hornfels xii, 1, 17, 18, 22, 24, 37, 38, 52, 100, 147
Hutton Museum 26
Hutton, Thomas 13, 14, 17, 26

I
Iceland xvii, 218, 221, 223
igneous xiv, 1
India 2–6, 7, 9, 10, 14, 200, 218
Iniitu, Sylvain van 225–226
Ireland 30, 50, 51, 64, 65, 100, 135, 221
Irwin, Edwin 34, 39, 40
Irwin, William 34, 39-40
Isungset, Terje xii, 227–228
Italy xvii, 46, 110, 192, 196, 204, 235, 236, 239

# Index

**J**
Java xiii, 5
Jee Brothers 136
Jullien, Louis 42-44, 49, 56, 58, 135

**K**
Kandinsky, Wassily 192
Kayser, Hans 196
Keld 117–127
Kendal 17-18, 37, 38
Kendal Museum x, 37, 38
Keswick xiv, xvi, 1-10, 14, 17, 20-26, 28, 30, 32, 33, 34-37, 39, 50, 61, 65, 66-72, 74, 76, 78, 79, 81, 87, 96, 110-116, 117, 120,125, 133, 136,145, 147, 148, 162, 233, 256, 257
Keswick Museum xii, xvi, 1, 2, 3, 4, 8, 10, 11, 13, 14, 15, 16, 20, 24, 37, 40, 55, 145, 146, 147, 148
Khánh Son 168, 169
Kindersley, Lida 190-191, 195, 212
Kinh people 167, 170
Klangstein 197, 199
Klangsteine Fessmann 199-201
Kniel, Manfred 199
Knowles, Alison 189
Korea 197
Krevh, Franci x, 242-244

**L**
Lahr 197
La Plante, Skip 189
limelight 110, 113, 114
limestone xv, 17, 18, 19, 37, 123, 181, 194, 204, 218, 234, 236, 240
*Lithophone Concerto* 234
London xii, 6, 14, 17, 25, 31, 32, 33, 34, 37, 41, 42, 43, 44, 45, 46, 47, 48, 49, 50, 51, 52, 56, 58, 62, 63, 64, 65, 72, 75, 76, 82, 96, 98, 100, 102, 103, 110, 133, 135, 137, 138, 140, 141, 144, 146, 181, 183, 194, 210, 211, 222
Lost Angel Stone Ensemble 164
Lucier, Alvin 225
Lunny, Donal 221
Luray Caverns, VA x, xvii, 152-157
Lydon, Tom 234

**M**
Maidstone 51
Manchester 27, 31, 32, 33, 138
Mann, William 180
marble xiii, xiv, 106, 181, 196, 197, 198, 206, 209, 240, 248
Martusciello, Elio 207
Meier, Walter M. 249, 251
Menorca xvi, 127, 129, 130
Menter, Will x, 214, 230-232
metamorphic xiv, 1, 219
Micus, Stephan 197-199, 200
Millar, Bobbie 233-234
Miller, Lewis 84
Miller, Mina 84
M'nông Rlăm people 169, 174
Moigno, Abbé 98
Moore, Henry 95, 195, 196
Mozart, Wolfgang Amadeus 48, 101, 130
Mulford, Wendy 184
*The Music of Stones* 198-199
music hall xvii, 50, 51, 89, 94, 132, 136-140

**N**
Naples 129, 130
Napoli, Tony di 235
Nasmyth, James 31, 32, 33
Ndut Lien Krak 166, 167, 168
Nelson, Arthur xvii, 132-136
New Haven, CT 141
New York 76, 80, 81, 82, 87, 88, 89, 91, 92, 93, 104, 105, 106, 107, 132, 133, 135, 140, 141, 142, 145, 148, 177, 184
Nguyen, Minh Nghiep x, 173, 174, 176, 237, 238
Nha Trang 169
Northampton 52
Norway xii, xvii, 185, 227, 228
Nyman, Michael 179, 184, 185

**O**
Oliveros, Pauline 185–187
Orff, Carl 158–161, 166
Osborne, Nigel 211
Ottawa 107

## P

Paris  57, 62, 98, 105, 138, 140, 141, 142, 166, 167, 193, 202, 222
Parsons, Michael  xii, 181–184
Pavanellas  138–142
Perret, Felix  250-251
Phan Tri Dung  173-174
Phillips, John H.  33, 46, 47, 50, 53, 57, 58, 59, 60, 62, 63, 66, 67, 147
phonograph  84, 85, 86, 93
Piano, Renzo  204
Pirelli, Pietro  239–240
Pocklington, Joseph  8
Pohnpei  xiii
Pollock, Jackson  192
Pound, Ezra  179
promenade concerts  42–44
Prometheus Bound  160
Purcell, Henry  45
pyen kyang  197

## R

Raglai people  168-170
Rainier, Priaulx  194-195
Randall-Page, Peter  x, 209-212
Reilly, Tommy  xiii
Rhythms of the Stones  194
Richardson family  xii, xvi, 20–33, 42–67, 69, 70, 144, 146, 147, 148, 191, 233
Roca, Carles-Garcia  x, xvi, 117, 127, 128, 129, 130, 131
Roca y Várez, Antonio  xvi, 117, 127-131
Rock, Bell and Steel Band  xii, 20, 56-66, 70, 114, 146, 147, 233
rock harmonicon  17, 20-33, 34-38, 44-67, 68-95, 110-116, 132-136, 142, 145-148, 161, 189, 191
Rome  192, 204, 207, 208
Rossini, Gioachino  30, 48, 59, 95, 101, 128
Royal Institution, London  100
Royal Polytechnic Institution, London  96, 102
Rukin, Laurie  125
Ruskin, John  xvi, 14, 16, 76-79, 112, 148, 233
Ruskin Museum  78, 79, 148

## S

Sangregorio, Giancarlo  241
San Sperate  202, 207
Sardinia  202, 203, 207
Satie, Erik  192
Schaeffer, Pierre  223
Schaeffner, André  166
Schoenberg, Arnold  187, 192
Sciola, Pinuccio  xvii, 202–209, 239–241
Scotland  30, 35, 61, 75, 79, 110, 140
Scott, "Wee" Jimmy  116
Scratch Orchestra  181, 182-183
sedimentary  xiv, 236, 246
Selman, Joshua  189
serpentinite  251
Shenandoah Caverns, VA  149, 152
Sigur Rós  221, 223
Siqueiros, David Alfar  202
Skempton, Howard  181–184
Skiddaw  xvi, 1, 10, 18, 22, 29, 34, 37, 65, 68, 69, 71, 72, 73, 78, 80, 93, 96, 110, 112, 114, 133, 146, 147, 148
Skiddaw Rock Band  68, 71, 72, 73, 93, 96, 110, 112, 114
slate  xiv, 18, 34, 37, 38, 39, 40, 146, 164, 189, 190, 198, 215, 216, 219, 224, 229, 230, 231, 232, 234, 248, 254
Slovenia  xvii, 242, 244, 246
Smart, Sir George  45, 46, 64, 174
Somerville, MA  81
Souster, Tim  181
Southey, Robert  7, 13
speleothems  209
stalactite  149, 152, 154, 155, 209
stalagmite  209
Steinauer, Mathias  250-251
steinspiel  158, 160-161, 166
Stewart, Jesse  247-248
Stockhausen, Karlheinz  xvii, 177, 223
Stone Alphabet  249-251
Stravinsky, Igor  159, 193
Studio 49  158, 160-161
Sumatra  xiii, 5
Surat  3, 5
Switzerland  xvii, 84, 110, 196, 235, 236, 249

T
talempong batu xiii
Tangye, William 65, 66, 114
Thailand 5, 167
Tilbury, John 179, 181
Till family 68– 95, 96, 110–113, 144–145, 151
Todhunter, William 17–20, 37
Toga xiii
Toop, David xii
Troupe Fielitz 142
Troxell, Edward 149–152
Tuy Hòa 173, 174, 237

U
USA xvii, 60, 61, 64, 76, 79, 80, 81, 82, 83, 93, 103, 104, 112, 132, 141, 148, 153, 154, 155, 162, 177, 187, 215, 253

V
Verdi, Giuseppe 59, 95, 128
Victoria 56, 57, 64, 146
Vidrgar, Alenka 242-246
Vienna 62, 63, 64
Vietnam xiii, xv, xvii, 6, 144, 166-176, 196, 235-237
Vietnamese Institute of Musicology, Hanoi 167, 172

W
Wales 51, 53, 54, 62, 75, 110, 140, 224, 230-232
Ward, Cornelius 55
Wasinger, Tom 162-164
West, Thomas 8
Weyeneth, Beat 251
Whitehaven 19, 25, 26, 27, 28, 31, 34, 50, 56, 61, 71
Willis, Isaac 32, 33, 44, 46, 47, 48, 51, 61
Wilson, Enid J. 13, 115, 116, 140, 141
Wolff, Christian xvii, 184, 185, 187, 225, 252-253
Wordsworth, John 10
Wordsworth, William 7, 13

X
xylophone xv, 2, 45, 84, 95, 100, 136, 150, 160, 161, 171, 174, 224, 243, 254

Y
Yorkshire Quarry Arts 233
Young, Gayle 254–255